KNOWLEDGE 2.0

Staying Afloat in the Information Age

Mark Chisnell

Mum and Dad, my first source of knowledge

Copyright © 2024 Mark Chisnell

All rights reserved

First published by Rhyme and Reason Books in 2024

ISBN: 9798865103813

Cover design by Andrew Mays: www.maysdesign.co.uk

Mark Chisnell asserts the moral right to be identified as the author of this work in accordance with the Copyright, Designs and Patents Act 1988.

Please do not copy, distribute, reproduce, transmit, store or otherwise make this publication available in whole or in part, in any form, or by any means including electronic, digital, photocopying or recording without first receiving written permission from the publisher.

CONTENTS

Title Page
Dedication
Copyright
Introduction 1
Part One – Narrative 10
Chapter 1 11
Chapter 2 21
Part Two – Confidence 37
Chapter 3 38
Chapter 4 58
Chapter 5 76
Part Three – Prediction 89
Chapter 6 90
Chapter 7 108
Chapter 8 130
Part Four – Science 138
Chapter 9 139
Chapter 10 151
Chapter 11 165
Part Five – Chance 179
Chapter 12 180
Chapter 13 194
Part Six – Problem Solving 205

Chapter 14	206
Chapter 15	216
Part Seven – Coping with Covid	222
Chapter 16	223
Further Reading	234
Appendix	238
Endnotes	248
Acknowledgement	267
About The Author	269
Praise For Author	271
Books By This Author	275

INTRODUCTION

The concept of this book is simple: a user's guide to living in a world of Knowledge 2.0. This is not a world where knowledge is fixed and forever, with its foundations on a solid rock of unchangeable truth. This is a world where knowledge floats on a sea of uncertainty and doubt, where it changes over time and with every evolution it (hopefully) comes a little closer to what's really happening in the world.

Let's be clear that this is not a philosophy book selling skepticism. I'm making a practical proposal that we can be more successful if we understand the world of Knowledge 2.0. Think about the kinds of knowledge you need, the important questions that you want answered. For instance, is this a good time to be buying a house or moving? Or will interest rates and/or property prices fall, making it more affordable in a year's time? There is no definitive, final answer to that question, and whatever answer you settle on will change as more evidence, and more events accumulate.

It's the same with many health questions. Is there such a thing as gluten or dairy intolerance? Or is it all a marketing fabrication to sell over-priced gluten-free cakes, bread and pastries? Should we take statins to help with our heart health? Does a diet of all protein and no carbohydrate work? This book is about understanding the knowledge that sits behind the answers to these questions; where it comes from and why there is uncertainty in the answers, and why the answer evolves over time.

It doesn't help that we – as human beings – have trouble discerning truth from untruth, and fact from fiction. There is a powerful personal component to what we carry around with us in our heads and call knowledge. We process and generate information with a set of unique experiences and biases, and we all have traits that can predispose us to error.

This is the third element of a Knowledge 2.0 world; all knowledge comes with a set of personal biases. In this book, this notion will sit alongside the ideas that there is limited certainty to be found in our knowledge about the world, and that this knowledge will change over time. A better understanding of all this means we will be able to decide how much weight we can put on any given piece of information.

In one sense, there is nothing new about this, it's always been hard to be sure about what you know, whether it's at work, in business, politics or healthcare. Reliable knowledge has always been the key to success, but 'facts' can be wrong because of a lack of comprehension or understanding or, worse, because they are distorted by laziness or incompetence. 'Truths' are sometimes twisted or hidden for financial gain, or to evade the consequences of mistakes or failures. It was always thus . . . nothing has changed.

What is new is the environment in which all this exists. There has been a transformation in the scale of knowledge production. We have industrialised the process of data collection and manipulation, generating vast quantities of new information. Scientific research is big business, with professional success judged by an individual's publishing output. These incentives created a global academic publishing market worth US$28 billion in 2019.[1]

The mechanisms for the transmission of information have also been supercharged by the coming of the internet and 24/7 global news coverage. Our access to knowledge is extraordinary, much of it available through a phone that rarely leaves our side. The problem is no longer access to knowledge; it's sifting it for the good stuff. There is plenty of information, but how much of it is useful?

So, there is more information out there. We have more access to it. We are getting it quicker than ever before and must process it faster. We can't be sure what we can rely on, what we do know is changing and we are wired to make mistakes. It should be no surprise that the opportunity this environment creates for deception and manipulation has led to a perfect storm of misinformation. If this wasn't bad enough, the artificial intelligence (AI) algorithms of social media have learnt to show us the information most likely to get an emotional rather than a rational reaction, because that's what maximises 'engagement' and profit.

One apparently reasonable response to all this would be skepticism; but being more sceptical of everything we read and hear only leads us into an unnecessary abyss of permanent uncertainty. We have a great deal of reliable knowledge. Look at the world: how could we possibly have built satellites and space stations, restored sight, replaced hearts and manufactured pandemic-ending vaccines if we know nothing and can't rely on anything? There's plenty of evidence that someone, somewhere knows a hell of a lot. We need to be able to tap into that reliable knowledge – but we must learn to do it ourselves. There are too many people with too much to gain by spreading misinformation; we must take responsibility for our own understanding of the world.

There are two aspects to getting better at judging the quality of the information around us. The first is to understand where it comes from and why it exists. The second is to understand how it works on our error-prone minds. We need to understand the ways in which a lack of comprehension, bias, deception and outright lies have influenced the information that we are being asked to accept as knowledge, *and* the ways in which our own biases and experiences will affect our processing of it. This deeper understanding of these two aspects of knowledge will significantly improve our ability to pick the good stuff from the rubbish: to know that we *know* and to have the confidence that we *know* it and can reliably act on it.

I'm going to focus on six types of knowledge that I think are vital to staying afloat in the 21st century:

> ***Narrative*** – a story is the single most powerful form of knowledge and that alone makes it both incredibly useful and incredibly dangerous. We'll examine narrative to understand why stories are so powerful, and how we can use them for our benefit, rather than being used by them to work to someone else's agenda.

Confidence – knowing the limits of our knowledge is central to using that knowledge in safe and effective ways. So, it's vital to understand our own confidence, what drives it and what can lead it astray. If we lack that self-knowledge, then we will still make bad decisions even when we understand the rest of the problem or situation.

Prediction – if we had perfect knowledge of the future, we'd be very wealthy and very safe. Unfortunately, we don't, but more accurate predictions and the confidence to trust them can only benefit us all. This can only come by understanding how predictions are made, and the extent to which we can rely on them.

Science – science is ubiquitous in modern life. A clear understanding of where scientific knowledge comes from, how it's produced, used and trusted is essential to safely navigating the world that science has built.

Chance – randomness controls a frightening amount of our lives, much more than many of us understand. This is the most important aspect of chance, but it's also vital to know how luck works, what's lucky and what's not, and to learn to respond to random interventions in our lives in the right way.

Problem solving — understanding the knowledge we do have is critical to living a happy and successful life, but we shouldn't ignore the knowledge we don't have. Finding solutions, innovating and problem solving are all important parts of modern life and this section will examine ways to improve all these things.

This review of knowledge is a personal take on the subject, but it started out as something different. The transition began in the autumn of 2019, when I went to see the British comedian

Ben Elton on his comeback tour, a return to live stand-up comedy after a 15-year break. I've always been a fan of Elton's acerbic and sometimes bitter satire and the new show was on familiar territory. What was less familiar was the serious turn that he took at the end, when he recounted an experience trialling his new material at a small club in the north-east of England. Apparently, a mild joke about Brexit had pushed an audience member off the deep end, and the man had been abusive to the point where it had ended the show.

The depth of the man's emotion, his anger and virulent hatred of an opposing viewpoint, would have been familiar to anyone engaging in political debate on the internet. Elton explained that he doesn't have any social media presence and coming face to face with this in real life had been a shock. The incident had crystallised things for him; his conclusion was that debate had ended, that the public space where this and other controversial issues could be discussed was narrowing to the point of non-existence, and that reason itself was now under attack. By the time I got home, the title and tone of the book that I was working on had changed. It had started out as a book about good strategies for achieving goals, taken from some hard lessons learned at sea. Now I wanted to talk about reason, about knowledge and where to find it.

By the following morning – with the cold, hard light of a late autumn day creeping in through the windows – I realised that what I was planning was ludicrously overambitious. Even if I managed to write it, who was going to read it? I had no credentials, no expertise on knowledge, nothing that would give anyone a reason to pick it up, never mind read it. My work on the book stalled.

A few months later, the coronavirus pandemic crashed around us and everything changed again. Firstly, it quickly became clear that all the topics I had in mind for the book had real relevance in how we dealt – both as individuals and as a society – with the challenge of Covid-19. Then, as the pandemic wound on, work dried up, wound down or just ended abruptly, and I found I had more time on my hands. And finally, I'd begun to realise that the personal perspective was the point.

This was never going to be a book about finding absolute truth. It could never be an instruction manual for chipping away at an amorphous mass of contradictory information until a set of forever-true axioms was revealed beneath, like a statue. Now *that* book – that would take some writing, and while I'd love to read it, I'm definitely not qualified to write it.

All knowledge is personal. The internal store of beliefs that we hold to be true will only ever approximate what's really out there in the world around us. This is a book about understanding that, and how best to navigate the world within that limitation. How to use it to make good decisions for ourselves and our families about everything from jobs to healthcare and personal finance.

We embark on a journey towards an understanding of the world when we're born, and we continue on it, hopefully, for our whole lives. The experiences we have along the way will shape how we ultimately understand the world, and the things that we hold to be true. If you are going to write a book about making that process more effective, then individual experiences are going to be core to the text. I owe it to you at this early stage of the book's journey to provide some idea of who I am and where I will draw those experiences from.

I have, and always have had, a bias towards rationalism and science, and a curiosity about truth. I swapped a single honours physics degree for joint honours with philosophy a couple of weeks after arriving at Nottingham University. I ended up writing a thesis on scientific 'truth' and that's really where my fascination with knowledge began. Out in the real world, this fascination became a lot less abstract and a great deal more practical.

I've spent thirty years working across diverse areas and topics. I've written five novels and eleven other non-fiction and technical books garnering over 600 reviews (averaging 4*s) at Amazon's US and UK websites. I've sold a movie option to one of those novels (it was never made). I've won an award for one of my non-fiction books. I've written on technology, travel and sport for *Esquire, The Guardian* and the *Daily Telegraph* amongst others. I've developed technical solutions to complex problems in marine electronics. I've hosted a broadcast event that won the Royal Television Society's Best Live Event award. I've won three sailing world championships. And I've sailed or worked with seven teams in yacht racing's America's Cup.

While I was writing this book, I also worked for the British team for the 2021 America's Cup as the coordinator for technology partnerships, and then as Rules Adviser to the British team for the 2024 America's Cup. The latter is a partnership between four-time Olympic gold medallist Ben Ainslie's sailing team, and the Mercedes F1 team. And no, I never managed to bump into Lewis Hamilton outside the simulator.

It wasn't my fate to find spectacular, life-changing success in any of these endeavours; my destiny – driven partly by curiosity and a low boredom threshold – was to keep moving on to the next problem, the next adventure, the next challenge. But each of those brought with it a new package of information that had to be processed, assessed and acted on. I have been a customer and consumer of every imaginable type of knowledge. I've stayed afloat in a multitude of roles by learning what information to rely on, and what not to trust.

I've used sailboat racing as the primary arena of experience because, of all the areas in which I've worked, that is the one which has demanded the greatest amount of information, the swiftest acquisition of knowledge and its most efficient and accurate processing. Competing in sailing's elite events – the Olympics, the America's Cup or professional ocean racing – requires high-level knowledge across many disciplines. It demands knowledge of science, engineering, data analytics, computer science, simulation and modelling, deal making, finance, human resources, management, marketing and communications – and that's before anyone gets in a boat.

Once on the water, the tactical and strategic decisions

made in sailboat races are determined by just a handful of things: present and future wind speed and direction, and the boat's position relative to the course markers and opponents. Perfect knowledge of these things reduces race strategy to a geometry problem. Since perfect knowledge is impossible, good decision making is about knowing what you know, and how much certainty there is that you know it. In this way, sailboat racing is a perfect microcosm of how we must process and deal with limited knowledge in life.

And finally, there is an existential danger in the sport that exists in few others – if you mess it up badly enough in a boat, coming last in the race is the least of your problems. And so, while I've drawn from lots of places for ideas and explanations, it is the stories of the sea that form the core of the book. A story is the most powerful way to learn anything – as we will see in the section on narrative – and I hope that these stories will keep the core ideas alive long after the more analytical points have faded.

I doubt that you would have found your way this far if we didn't agree that for the 300 years since the beginning of the Enlightenment knowledge has inexorably dragged mankind forward. Gains in knowledge have pushed billions of people from poverty into a life of comfort and security that would have been unimaginable to their grandparents, never mind their great grandparents.[2] All this will be lost if the knowledge we hold to be true depends too heavily on political or tribal affiliation, or on the media channels and websites that we choose. A culture where 'alternative facts' is anything but an oxymoron is a culture that will die. I want to show you how to hold the line, how to sift knowledge from nonsense at a time when both knowledge and reason seem to be sliding slowly under the waves of a storm of irrationality. We cannot let them sink without trace. We all need a better understanding of the new world of knowledge to keep us afloat in the Information Age. I hope this book helps you on the way to that understanding.

PART ONE – NARRATIVE

Don't be seduced by a good story

Storytelling is the most powerful way to put ideas into the world.

ROBERT MCKEE, 'WRITE THE TRUTH'

CHAPTER 1

The Flare Gun

Ancient Ways

A story is one of the oldest ways of communicating knowledge; there are stories that have survived for hundreds, even thousands of years. And it's quite possible that even before the advent of language – never mind books – stories were passed on using mime or signs; ancient ways of telling others where the hunting was good, or the berries would make you sick.

It's perhaps because it's so old – and we have become so attuned to it – that the narrative form has become one of the most powerful ways of communicating knowledge. We learn many things through stories, but sometimes these are the wrong things. Narrative can be potent when it's abused. To help us understand just how powerful it can be I'm going to start with a couple of stories. They are the same kind of story; they relate a human experience, and they are both about events in the same ocean race, one that took place over forty years ago.

Summer Storm

Thursday, 9 August 1979 – baking hot air was rising from the grain fields of the Great Plains of North America, while across Canada cold air flowed south from the pole. As the two met the hotter air lifted over the cooler and started to churn. It happens all the time – perhaps there's a thunderstorm. But on this occasion, the anti-clockwise rotation of the air built and gathered strength, the signature formation of a northern hemisphere low-pressure system, or depression.

The nascent storm moved east, dropping the atmospheric pressure, along with four centimetres of rain over the city of

Minneapolis, whipping waves and whitecaps across the Great Lakes. On the Friday, it flexed its muscles and claimed its first victim – killing a woman in New York's Central Park, as roofs were blown off houses and trees knocked down across New England. Weather forecasters tracked the low out into the Atlantic, where it rode the westerly jet stream towards the Bay of Biscay – a name synonymous with bad weather, but not usually in August.

The summer storm then made a late swerve to the north, pushed that way by two other weather systems. Sucking up energy, it accelerated towards the Western Approaches of the British Isles – and there it collided with an unsuspecting fleet of 303 yachts, sailing in a race across the Irish Sea. In the space of twenty-four hours, twenty-four crews abandoned boats battered by 60-knot[3] winds and 40-foot breaking waves. The Fastnet Race in 1979 was the greatest tragedy in modern sailboat racing history, with 15 lives lost amongst those that were competing.[4]

Griffin

In 1979, Stuart Quarrie was a young instructor at England's National Sailing Centre in Cowes, and the Fastnet Race was the climax of the summer's racing. Living where he did, and doing the job he did, it was inevitable that when the start gun went, Quarrie would be amongst the 2,500 or so sailors on the 608-mile course. He was racing with two other instructors from the school, one of whom – the skipper, Neil Graham – would, like Quarrie, go on to a successful professional sailing career. They had four students with them aboard the OOD34 *Griffin*, a new racing boat designed by an American, Doug Peterson, and built in the UK by Jeremy Rogers.

The course of the Fastnet race headed west from Cowes, along the south coast of England to Land's End. There it turned north-west towards the Fastnet Rock off the southern tip of Ireland, which the fleet was required to go around before returning to Plymouth, via the Scilly Isles. It was the section of the course to and from the Fastnet Rock that was the most exposed, and this is exactly where the storm's unexpected turn to the north caught the fleet.

The forecast fresh gale of 34 to 40 knots turned out to be much, much more, with winds claimed at anything up to 70 knots. There's a big difference between the two. The Beaufort Scale was originally devised to assess wind speed at sea, but also describes the equivalent conditions we might expect to see ashore. This is helpful in trying to understand the experience. A force eight gale of 34 to 40 knots will break twigs from branches – but a 60-knot, force eleven storm will uproot the whole damn tree.

At sea, that same storm produces what are described as 'exceptionally high waves'. How big is that? Well, big enough that 'small- and medium-sized ships might be for a long time lost to view behind the waves'.[5] That means waves up to 50 feet high in a sea completely covered with long white patches of foam, where wave crests are blown into froth. And that's the dispassionate, scientific description of the Beaufort Scale, devoid of hyperbole.

The unsuspecting *Griffin* was trapped in this maelstrom along with most of the rest of the fleet, and when she was caught by one of those waves big enough to hide a medium-sized ship, Stuart Quarrie was at the helm. As the wave crashed over the boat, it plucked him off the wheel. If he'd had time to think about it, he would have anticipated the shocking jerk around his rib cage as his safety harness came up tight. But the hook that should have secured him to the boat straightened (like others that night) and he was swept off the deck. When he surfaced, choking out mouthfuls of water, there was every reason to believe that the boat would be gone.

It wasn't: Stuart Quarrie was luckier than most, a lot luckier. *Griffin* had been turned over in the same wave that had taken him overboard. The boat was now upside down and dead in the water – just metres away. With her lights buried underwater, the only reason he could see the boat in the black night was because the gravity switch had turned on the emergency light on a buoy designed to be thrown to someone overboard. And the only reason it was bright enough to see underwater was because the crew had installed a brand new, high-powered bulb in the device right before the start of the race.

Quarrie started to swim with all the effort and none of the technique of a man five metres from winning an Olympic freestyle gold. The boat was settling in the water, but it became unstable upside down and another big wave roared in and rolled it back upright. At this point, Quarrie struggled back on board, where Neil Graham was exhorting everyone to bail the water out. Barely a breath later, he changed his mind and yelled the instructions to abandon ship. Water had filled the cabin; the deck was just centimetres above the sea. The crew left *Griffin* for the life raft and had drifted no more than 20 feet away when the yacht sank.

The life raft turned out to be a place of temporary sanctuary. It was less than an hour before it was tipped over by another wave. The force of the roll ripped the canopy away and although the seven men got it back upright, they were now sitting in a giant life ring, completely exposed to the seas, to the wind, rain and cold. With one of their number dressed in just a T-shirt and jeans – he had been changing when the boat had gone over – the situation was grim.

Stuart Quarrie's luck held: their flares were spotted by a French yacht, the *Lorelei*, a 36-footer owned and skippered by Alain Catherineau. Getting the men of the *Griffin* off the raft in those conditions was anything but simple, and it took several attempts to get the *Lorelei* alongside. But Alain Catherineau calmly went about the work and an hour later the last man was hauled off the raft, his hypothermic fingers prised away from the handholds. After two hours in the water in a T-shirt, he was fortunate that the *Griffin*'s story avoided the tragic ending of so many others.

There is an odd postscript – two years later, the Cowes police phoned Quarrie to say that they had his credit card wallet. Strange – he wasn't aware that he'd lost it. No, the police explained, this one had come up in the nets of a trawler, still in the compartment aboard *Griffin* where Quarrie had placed it at the start of the 1979 Fastnet. The chances of that wallet finding its way home are even slimmer than the luck that allowed Stuart Quarrie to survive that night in the Irish Sea. His nightmares went on for five years. When I last talked to him about it, he still had the wallet, and he still maintained contact with Alain Catherineau – Yachtsman of the Year in 1979.

While there was plenty of courage and skill on display in this tale, the main thing I took away from it was that Quarrie was lucky. Lucky that the boat rolled over in the same wave that took him overboard. If it hadn't his chances of being found in the water were close to zero. He was lucky that the man-overboard beacon allowed him to see the boat. They were all lucky that Catherineau found them in the life raft before it disintegrated, and lucky that he had the skill and nerve to pull off the rescue in horrific conditions.

Luck: it's important in all our lives. It's not often that it's as important to us as it was to Stuart Quarrie and his crewmates on that night in the Western Approaches, but it really does matter. Hold on to that thought; we're going to come back to it after the next story – and again in much more detail in Part 5.

Golden Apple Of The Sun

The star of the second story is Harold Cudmore, an Irishman with a marvellous line of blarney and an almost frighteningly stereotypical twinkle in his eye. He was a top small-boat sailor in the late sixties and early seventies who successfully switched to racing much bigger boats for their wealthy owners. He carved a stellar career across several decades, and at the height of his powers he would claim he could walk into a pub or bar and come out with the money to build and campaign a boat.

In 1979, he was hired to call the tactics on a 44-foot-long yacht owned by Irish Fine Gael politician Hugh Coveney, a boat called *Golden Apple of the Sun*. The designer, Ron Holland, had also chosen to sail on *Golden Apple*, and they had brought on board Rodney Pattisson, who – until Ben Ainslie came along – was Britain's most successful Olympic sailor, with two golds and a silver. The yacht had painted on her stern the last stanza of the William Butler Yeats poem, 'The Song of the Wandering Aengus'. This was the source of her name: *Golden Apple*, and it was sailed by the golden boys – the yacht was, as Harold later put it, 'one of the glamour boats of the year'.

They were contesting what was then one of the sport's leading events, the currently defunct Admiral's Cup. This was the unofficial world championship of offshore racing for many years. Three boat teams from the world's sailing nations met in the Solent for a biannual series of races through and around Cowes Week, culminating in the Fastnet. In 1979, the Irish were having a good year – at the start of the final race they were leading eighteen other teams. And early on the morning of 14 August, with the storm reaching its peak, *Golden Apple of the Sun* was the first of the Admiral's Cup yachts around the Fastnet Rock.

The boat turned for the next mark on the course in a world of monstrous waves and howling spray and, when the wind shifted far enough aft, the crew hoisted the spinnaker. The spinnaker is a big, extra sail that's only used when a boat is sailing at particular angles to the wind (when the wind is blowing from behind rather than from the front). It's powerful and can be unpredictable, particularly when it's windy – in those conditions it was a bit like sticking an F1 engine in a family hatchback and letting it rip in the middle of London. All the power and none of the control.

Now, given the carnage that was going on further back down the fleet, this might seem like bravery verging on recklessness, but Cudmore took some precautions: he had a man strapped to the mast armed with a flare gun. The instructions were simple. If the driver started to lose control, shoot the flare through the spinnaker. The plan was that the flare would destroy the sail and allow the driver to regain control of the boat and avoid a destructive crash, or broach as the technical term would have it. What nerve, what bravado – men and women were abandoning yachts all over the Western Approaches, yet here was the piratical Cudmore, hurtling through this awesome storm with the spinnaker set and only a flare gun to separate death from glory. In this story, it wasn't luck which mattered in that storm, it was courage and skill.

Transmissible

When that vicious storm subsequently made a landfall, lifting over the highlands of Britain's west coast and dumping another deluge, it was the final straw in a sodden summer that cut short our family camping and sailing holiday on the shores of Lake Coniston. The faithful if short entries in my Motor Boat and Yachting Diary 1979 show absolutely no recognition of the disaster unfolding a few hundred miles away. It's much more concerned with the fact that we were going home early, and with subsequent preparations for a local race event.

I don't know whether this was an omission, or because news, even bad news, was much easier to avoid in those days. But our sailing community was pretty insular – huddled as it was around a muddy-coloured stretch of water just inland from the bleak North Sea fishing port of Lowestoft. I wouldn't knowingly meet anyone who had been in that 1979 Fastnet Race until another seven years had passed. And so, the stories of tragedy, triumph, bravery and failure largely passed me by – but I did hear one story that was told around the sailing club by my dinghy-sailing friends. And it was one of the two that I have just told you – the question is, which one? If you guessed that it was the story about the buccaneering Cudmore, then you would be absolutely right.

I first met Harold Cudmore seven years after that Fastnet

Race (as I'll come on to in Part 4) and I saw quite a lot of him for a few years. I sailed with him in a later Fastnet Race in 1989, which was the tenth anniversary of that dreadful storm. I was the navigator aboard a boat called *Jamarella* – part of a winning British Admiral's Cup team that was managed by Harold. Even then, even after going around the Fastnet Rock with him on another pitch-black night in 35 knots of breeze, I never got around to asking him to tell me the 'flare gun' story – which is strange. Who wouldn't want to hear it from the horse's mouth? I guess I was young though, and Harold was a very big personality in our sport – but a year or so ago, I thought it was finally time to change that.

On the afternoon of 13 August, *Golden Apple* was locked in a battle with a 50-foot boat called *Blizzard* at the front of the Admiral's Cup fleet. 'There was a long oily swell and very little wind,' Harold recalled. 'We realised there was bad weather coming. We were having a blinder, leading the Admiral's Cup at the time. The weather was obviously going to come in from the west, so we held out to the west and it came in that evening . . . Just before that period we had the last supper, because we realised we weren't going to eat again. So, we headed into nightfall . . . we were going to have a beating. The glass [barometer] was falling something like three millibars an hour.'

Golden Apple led the fleet at the Fastnet Rock and turned back to the south-east for the 150-nautical-mile journey back to the Bishop Rock, just off the Scilly Islands. 'We got around the rock, and it was fifty-two knots [of wind speed] across the deck; I remember looking at the dials as we rounded,' Harold continued. 'We were over-canvassed [too much sail up], we had two reefs in the main . . . We speared off and fairly shortly afterwards when it began to really kick in we dropped the mainsail [the biggest sail attached behind the mast] . . . Later we dropped the jib [smaller sail that goes in front of the mast] and replaced it with the storm jib [even smaller sail] . . . It [the wind] was west and then round to north-west. We ended up running back to the Scillies.' They were sailing with the wind behind them and this would have been the time that they could have used a spinnaker.

'It was a pretty wild night, no doubt about it. We were nerveless. I would be terrified if I was out there today, knowing what I know,' went on Cudmore. 'We survived the night, driving pretty hard, and then come morning it began to ease up and the sea began to build some length into it and so it was less threatening... We put the main back up, and I remember saying to the guys, "We're down to thirty-five knots; we should put the spinnaker up." It was the only time – you know what I'm like in a boat – the only time I had a strike. "We will not!" So, we settled for a jib, number two jib. The guys were up on deck to do that when the rudder broke.' It was the end of their Fastnet Race. There had been no spinnaker, no flare gun. 'The only thing of note that came from that was the note we left on the chart table saying, "Gone for lunch,"' added Cudmore. The yacht was later safely recovered, but they were done – the race, the Admiral's Cup, all gone, along with my favourite sailing story. Or so it seemed at first, but was the tale really dead?

The question I started to ask myself was: Had the story about Harold Cudmore lost its value because it wasn't true? Both of these stories purported to be the same thing: true stories relating a real experience. There was knowledge woven into each story – they weren't purely entertaining fictions, they related human experience in a way that encouraged us to take something away from both of them. In the story about Stuart Quarrie and *Griffin* it was that luck mattered. In the second story about Harold Cudmore and the flare gun it was that skill and courage mattered. What was interesting was that the story which travelled furthest and fastest and stuck in the head of an impressionable teenager was the one that didn't have a shred of truth to it.

It's no real surprise that there appears to be no connection between the truth of a story and its success. A study done at the Massachusetts Institute of Technology established that falsehood travels six times as fast as truth on the internet.[6]

Nevertheless, it's worth asking why these stories are so successful when they appear to be *trying to teach us something from the experience of others*, but they aren't telling us the truth. A simple explanation would be that the most entertaining stories are the ones that get passed on, regardless of whether or not they are true.

The absence of truth does not mean an absence of useful information though: the knowledge just isn't being communicated in the obvious way. I think this is something that we can easily forget – especially when we are faced with the amount of information that has arrived with 24-hour news channels, social media and streaming services. We need a greater ability to see through the surface layer of a story, past its apparent truth or falsehood, to see the real information it contains and how that information is working on us.

Staying Afloat

- *The knowledge held within a story may not be the simple truth or the facts that it states.*

CHAPTER 2

The Power of Story

Patterns And Stories

The very first stories, the oldest stories – the ones that have been passed down to us through untold generations – started with an innate need to find patterns. This is a critical part of survival. We need pattern recognition to be able to recognise our parents, find food and learn language – and that's just for starters. Even a humble rabbit won't last long unless it learns that a shadow of a particular shape means *hawk, run!*

We have theories about how humans and animals recognise patterns, and now we have ways of making machines recognise patterns (this is an area of huge research interest because it's fundamental to the development of artificial intelligence), but there is an enormous amount we don't know. We can theorise that, unlike other animals, humans didn't stop at finding and recognising useful patterns.

Humans have a greater capacity for pattern recognition, and it must have helped us develop language. It pushed us to ascribe causes and develop explanations for the patterns. In time, these explanations naturally became more complex; they developed a life of their own; they became stories. These were the kinds of stories that we are looking at – the ones that pass on tales of human experience which we can learn from, which may help us survive all that the world throws at us.

The best stories, from the best storytellers, gathered a special momentum. They started to be retold by others and slowly some of these ancient, early stories acquired a very special status as myths. They still have power even today, a power that leaches over into all the stories that we hear, read or see.

The Monomyth

The on-going power of ancient stories has been revealed through the work of mythologists like Joseph Campbell. Campbell recognised, as others had done before him, that there were repeating patterns in the stories told across different cultures. This should not surprise us; there are fundamental patterns to the human experience that repeat wherever you are and whoever you are. Similar stories should bubble to the surface in one form or another in every culture.

What Campbell did – in his 1949 book *The Hero with a Thousand Faces* – was to pull out a single thread of story that he claimed bound together myths from many different cultures separated by both time and place. Campbell called this story the monomyth; a story so basic to our consciousness that it appeared everywhere. Campbell's work has its critics[7] but the impact of his ideas can't be denied. It was the idea of the monomyth that Hollywood script analyst Christopher Vogler then developed in his work, and eventually his book, *The Writer's Journey*.

Vogler created a mythic structure for writers that he called the Hero's Journey. The basic form of this story has become one of the major go-to plot outlines for modern Hollywood. The outline is a story that will sound familiar to anyone. It's rooted deep in our past in the tales of heroes told around campfires and is now reflected back at us everywhere from the latest offerings on the streaming services to the many screens of the multiplex. George Lucas is just one director that has acknowledged a debt owed – by his *Star Wars* movies – to the monomyth.[8]

The monomyth finds a hero-to-be living an ordinary life, until they are called into action to right a wrong. At first, they refuse the call, then they commit, often at the bidding or persuasion of an older mentor. They pass across a threshold, travelling to a new world of drama and action, with many challenges and temptations but also with guides and allies. Despite the forces set against them, they win a remarkable victory and return both a changed person, and a person who is now able to change things for the better back home, for themselves and for others. I remember the first time I saw this explained, and the almost visceral impact of the recognition – it's *Star Wars*, *Batman Begins*, *The Matrix*, *Harry Potter* . . . This story or elements of it underlie a great deal of what we now watch, read or see – it is so familiar because it is everywhere.

Myths didn't develop across thousands of years and thousands of different cultures to help wannabe screenwriters and novelists out of a hole that they have written themselves into – although it's been very useful to me in that respect; instead, myth serves a much richer and deeper purpose. Myths aren't true in the sense that the facts are accurate, and they are rarely presented as truth (at least in modern times). However, they contain truths that guide us in the best way to live our lives, how we should deal with challenge and adversity, how we should deal with our friends, family and enemies and the qualities we will need to help us succeed. This is why the same patterns and archetypes appear in stories across many different cultures because they all need similar qualities in their populations to overcome competition from other groups.

Vogler believes that the Hero's Journey contains within its forms the basic life lessons passed down to us by our ancestors. 'I came to believe that the Hero's Journey is nothing less than a handbook for life,' Vogler wrote in his preface to the second edition of *The Writer's Journey*.

It's an idea that can be traced back through the work of Campbell and the folklorists and mythologists that came before him. In Vogler's words, myths, 'are not abstract theories or the quaint beliefs of ancient peoples, but practical models for understanding how to live'.[9] The message is that thousands of generations of our ancestors have relied on stories as a handbook for life.

If, as seems likely, stories are the way that we have always communicated our deepest truths, then it's still the way we expect to hear them. This is why stories hold such power over us; why we have such strong expectations and why we are so disappointed when they let us down.

Staying Afloat

- ☐ Our nature and nurture have evolved so we have a strong response to the narrative form. Stories have power.

Myth Becomes News

When I told Harold Cudmore the story about his extraordinary exploits with the flare gun that I related in the previous chapter, his reaction was immediate. 'That's an old story that dates a generation before my time. I heard the story back when I was a kid. It's an apocryphal story,' he said, before explaining, 'I think the story related back to after the Second World War when you could buy these Very pistols, and the word was . . . that if you were caught with a sail up in heavy conditions and the halyard jams . . . what do you do? You fire a Very pistol into the sail – seamanship in the 1950s!'

In fact, the story goes back even further than that. I've heard a version about the clippers, the fastest ships in the age of sail. When they were running before a storm, hard-driving captains were said to have chained a man to the main mast with an axe. The instructions were that should the helmsman lose control at the wheel, the ropes holding the sails up were to be cut. If anything, this story is more plausible than the one about Harold Cudmore and his boat *Golden Apple*. If there was one thing that boats like *Golden Apple* (a particular style of yacht built to be fast under a popular racing rule of the time) didn't need with the spinnaker up, it was extra weight at the front of the boat. It was guaranteed to make the boat more difficult to steer. No one in their right mind would position a man at the mast. And what if the flare did hit the sodden spinnaker? Would it do much more than punch a hole through it, leaving you with what you had anyway – a mess of flogging nylon?

In contrast, the clipper ships had what were called square-rigged sails, and when running before a storm they absolutely could not afford to lose control. The masts were not supported strongly enough for the ship to point into the wind with sail up in a gale. All the rigging was set to hold the masts up with the wind coming from the side or the back – not directly from the front of the boat. If you lost control sailing with the wind behind in a big sea, the ship would turn up to face into the wind and the entire rig would come crashing down around your ears. It would likely be the end for all on board – the wreckage dragging the ship under before it could be cut away.

So, where did the flare-gun story come from? John Rousmaniere's book, *Fastnet, Force 10* is probably the most authoritative account of the 1979 Fastnet storm (outside of the official inquiries). He tells of the need for the survivors to talk it down, to convince themselves and each other that the storm was not that much worse than others they had experienced. My suspicion is that the entire sailing community was involved in this process and that the story about Cudmore became part of it – finding a time-honoured myth and recasting it to feel more comfortable with the ferocious challenge of that storm.

There's no doubt about the appeal of the flare-gun story, particularly to a starry-eyed teenage boy. This is a story of heroic bravado; it rams home how courage and skill can get you through anything, even while all about you are failing and falling. In contrast, the lesson from the story about Stuart Quarrie and *Griffin* is that luck matters. Unfortunately, while that's a truth, it's a truth no one really wants to hear. At least, no one considering going back out to sea. No one caught in a storm like that, or going somewhere where they might be struck by a storm like that, wants to believe that the outcome could come down to luck.

The purpose of the story about the flare gun was not to teach us caution by truth-telling about that terrifying storm. It wasn't warning people about how dangerous and rough the sea could become – it was the converse; it was about getting people to feel more comfortable about going back out there in the next race. The message was that the storm really wasn't so bad . . . if you were talented and brave enough. That's just not true, so the message was carried by an older story, with all the weight of our storytelling traditions. A message that people wanted to hear, but not one that held any truth.

We can recognise in the story about Harold Cudmore one of the most important traits of myths – it's a lesson about survival, in this case how the bold will endure. This puts it in the same category as many urban myths, modern adaptations of the mythic form that seek to do much the same work. One of the most important purposes of these stories, just as with older myths and legends, is the message, the educational content. It might be a warning, there might be a moral within the tale or, like the flare-gun story, there might be a call to action – whatever it is, society will have a use for the message. And that – apart from an intrinsic entertainment value (no one knowingly retells a dull story) – will be why it transmits onward into the culture, like a virus.

Myths and legends could only propagate orally, but now, urban myth can travel via all the mechanisms of our modern, connected society; be that email, social media or even the mainstream media. This is because the form of these stories – based as they are on ancient mythic forms that run so deeply through us – are a powerful way to get a message across. Before we take any story seriously – before we let it move from a moment or two's light entertainment to something that may influence the way we think and behave – we should examine whether or not it's true, but also what lies beneath its surface. What's the story really saying, what information is it trying to impart? What bias or expectation does it play to, and what behaviour is it trying to encourage?

Staying Afloat

☐ *The real information in a story may lie beneath the surface – search for it or risk being fooled by the story.*

Narrative fallacy

I've told you a story about the history of story, how it developed through the ages to carry our most important cultural messages about how to understand the world and live our lives. I've made the point that these messages often lie beneath a false surface. We should look out for that and try to see what motivated the story's telling and retelling, to learn the real knowledge that any tale is trying to pass on. We've seen that stories are powerful, and they will push on existing biases to manipulate people – be those political, religious, technical or personal biases. This is a well-established idea in psychology.

Nassim Nicholas Taleb, the author of *The Black Swan*, coined a cool name for this problem, the 'narrative fallacy', so we'll start with him.[10] Taleb's suggestion was that, surrounded as we are with a world of almost infinite complexity, we look for patterns and rules because they simplify, they allow us to fit the world into our very finite minds. This builds on the idea that story developed from pattern recognition. Next comes the adoption of rules to describe them and then the application of an explanatory story that allows us to simplify a complex world into one we can hope to understand. We want to see patterns, but sometimes we will see them where there are none, we will ascribe causal connections where there are none, and as a result we will come up with some very bad explanations for things that affect us deeply.

Taleb proposed 'narrative fallacy' as a term to explain our need to connect events in such a way that it created an explanation, but as he said: 'Where this propensity can go wrong is when it increases our impression of understanding.' There are many ways in which a narrative explanation can increase our impression of understanding but leave us with completely the wrong idea. A lot of these are what's called cognitive biases. This is an idea that has been gaining traction in the public space for a while and is the substance of the content of many popular books and podcasts.[11] If you haven't come across it before, then briefly, the concept originated with two Israeli psychologists, Daniel Kahneman and Amos Tversky. A cognitive bias is a hard-wired predisposition to think in a particular way, and a number of them show how we find the wrong patterns, ascribe the wrong causes and develop bad explanations for events.

In his excellent book, Thinking, Fast and Slow, Kahneman – after acknowledging Taleb as the originator of the notion of narrative fallacy – agrees.[12] He goes on to point out that consistent themes crop up in our explanatory stories, they:

- Simplify events
- Rely on concrete rather than abstract explanations
- Put more weight on our ability, stupidity and intent than on randomness or chance – seen strongly in the flare-gun story
- Focus on things that did happen, rather than things that did not

It neatly sums up many of the issues with stories. I've already mentioned that we will examine how we tend to overlook the role of luck in events (at least in comparison to human agency) in more detail in Part 5. In Parts 3 and 4 we will see at work the need for simple, concrete explanations rather than abstract, complex ones – although I'm going to introduce those ideas in a moment both here and in the sections on *Plausibility trumps probability* and *The limits of words*.

The last point is an example of what Kahneman and Tversky called 'What You See is All There Is' or WYSIATI.[13] This rule explains that people don't naturally go looking for more information, they take what they see, what they already know and treat it as though it was all the available information. There is no natural human bias to want to go out and find more information to corroborate or falsify a story. We are very good at fitting a story to the available facts, and the fewer facts there are the easier it is to fit a story around them. And once we've got our story, we believe it, and it takes an awful lot to shake that belief.

Sport is a particularly rich place to see this at work,

generating endless fake narratives because a whole bunch of people get paid – commentators and pundits – to come up with stories to explain team or individual performances. It adds to the entertainment and gives us the sense of increased understanding, a feeling that is largely an illusion. A great deal of essential information is kept hidden from those watching sport by the teams and athletes who are participating. And so, journalists and commentators have little choice but to fit stories to a limited number of facts.

I've spent time within professional sailing teams, watching the gaping discrepancies between the actual events and the stories that journalists tried to fit to them. I've also worked as a commentator at many major sports events, so I understand the pressure to find a narrative, to make some sort of sense of it for the spectators. The thing that has changed in the last couple of decades is the greater availability of performance data from the field of play from all the major sports. This has provided the opportunity for stories with greater insight, based on facts about what happened on the pitch rather than, for instance, an off-the-record briefing from a disgruntled employee or dodgy stories about locker-room tantrums and training-pitch dust-ups explaining Saturday's four-nil drubbing.

In 2005 I spent some time with the Italian Luna Rossa America's Cup in Valencia. They had a zero-tolerance attitude to illness, so the day I walked into the base looking a little peaky it was quickly established that I had a temperature of 39 °C. I got told to go straight home and stay there until it had subsided and stayed down for at least 24 hours. I was lucky that the Tour de France was in full swing, so I sat and watched as Lance Armstrong and his Discovery Channel team wrote history with his seventh victory. The commentator made much of Armstrong's cadence, the speed at which he pedalled, which he had steadily increased over the years that he had been riding. This – apparently – explained his phenomenal performance . . . I think we all know now that this wasn't the reason that he 'won' those seven Tours.[14]

The facts about Armstrong's cadence (its increase over time, and the high rate compared to many other professional cyclists) were true, but the narrative that had attached to it was not. Truth is deeper than a simple correlation with the facts. This is obviously necessarily true of myths, legends and novels where we expect the 'truth' of the story to lie somewhere other than in verifiable facts about the events that have been narrated. The problems start when these types of stories shift across to social media and perhaps even end up as news stories. Our expectations change with that shift and they shouldn't – it's a mistake to expect the truth and the verifiable facts to be the same.

Business and stock-market commentary has the same need to generate over-arching narratives as sport does. We should be just as wary of them. Most of us will have seen those 'The market fell today because . . .' stories – and sometimes they may contain a kernel of useful information. But the truth is that on the average, nothing-much-going-on kind of day, the market was moved by a great number of different factors and events that, in the aggregate, pushed it in the direction that it actually went. No one event or action was responsible for the movement, but that's not an interesting narrative so you don't hear it.

The weird thing is that while those stories about market movements may not be true in any strict sense, they may be the very thing that's driving the market onward. They become a kind of self-fulfilling prophecy. Yale economist and Nobel Laureate Robert Shiller believes that narrative may actually be the most powerful force in the big economic events that impact all of our lives, a case he made in his book, *Narrative Economics: How Stories Go Viral and Drive Major Economic Events* – on the face of it, it's an extraordinary idea, but the power of stories should be no surprise to us at this point.

Staying Afloat

- ☐ **Be wary of neat explanations based on little evidence; we** *may not understand as much as we think we do.*

Plausibility Trumps Probability

There are many, many ways that we can be fooled by a good story, and one of them is a real blind spot that Kahneman and Tversky called the 'conjunctive fallacy'. This is a great example of our innate preference for a simple concrete narrative, rather than using more abstract ideas – like basic logic. We will see a lot more of this kind of thinking in Part 3.

The classic formulation of the conjunctive fallacy is a story (what else?) about a bank teller called Linda, but I'm going to give you another one from Kahneman's book that returns to the sports theme. He explained how the participants in this particular study were asked to list four possible outcomes of the next Wimbledon tournament from most to least likely.[15] The study was done when Swedish player Björn Borg was world number one, and famed for his unflappable temperament.

The interest in the study centred on two of the four choices; that Borg would either lose the first set, or lose the first set but still win the match. The second cannot be more likely than the first – because for the second to occur (Borg losing the first set and winning the match), the first must also occur (Borg losing the first set). A statement about a single event is always more likely than a statement about that same single event *and* a further event. And yet, as Kahneman explained, 72 per cent of the respondents thought it was more likely that Borg would lose the first set and win the match, than just lose the first set.

This is presumably because of the narrative that surrounded Borg at the height of his career; his ability and legendary cool temperament. He was an automaton, a robot, the Ice-Borg. The Björn Borg of this narrative would never let a little thing like losing the first set unsettle him; *of course* he would go on to win the match! And there you have it, plausibility trumps probability to lead us to completely the wrong conclusion. This is an excellent example of an appealing narrative overwhelming a more abstract concept – logically consistency.

Staying Afloat

☐   *One of the easiest ways to be fooled by a story is to rely on it when there could be other, more useful information available in logic or maths.*

The Limits Of Words

We've just seen how we can be completely fooled by a toxic mix: an absence of logic and an over-reliance on a narrative. I've said that I will address the role that logic and maths play in our search for knowledge in more detail in Part 3, but I want to make one more point here because it's all about the power of story and the weakness of abstract explanation in our culture.

There is a fundamental contradiction that underlies all modern life: *while our primary desire is to explain with words and stories, many of our best and deepest explanations are mathematical.*

We have no words for some aspects of the reality that science is revealing in some of its theories and formulae. The conflict and contradiction are creating a kind of cultural cognitive dissonance as we try to grapple with two things that just won't mesh. We're not about to shake off the deep-rooted cultural idea that words and stories are our handbook for life, and this makes it really hard for us to grasp some of our best scientific explanations which are only expressible as data and formulae.

What do I mean by that? Well, our understanding of the world has leapt forward in the last five centuries with the development of two things. The first was science, which has given us a way of testing the causal links that we love to make in our narratives. By allowing us to rigorously test our ideas about what event or action might be the cause of what outcome, we've been able to significantly cut down the number of bad explanations. So, the use of leeches to bleed sick people is no longer a mainstream medical treatment.

The second thing is the new mathematics that has been invented along the way, maths that has enabled us to describe and explain more of the patterns that we could see and investigate. This mathematical capacity combined with a scientific approach has led to knowledge and understanding. In turn, this has allowed us to create a much more complex world; one with sensors, instruments, computers and data sets. And then we need even more mathematics to understand and explain it.

These explanations have far outstripped the ability of language to keep up – our fundamental understanding of the underlying mechanisms of the universe can now only be expressed in mathematics. This has led to a deepening of the fault lines and flaws in the narrative tradition. And while it has enabled some people – those that 'get' the maths – to move forward our understanding, it has slowly edged out those that don't. Many of those excluded from the new understanding are still seeking and finding non-existent patterns, causes and explanations, because the best explanations are often expressed in a way (statistics and formulae) that many people will never grasp.

It's sometimes possible to cross the divide with precise language, careful explanation and well-constructed metaphors, but sometimes it's not and never will be, and we can trace this back to a particular moment. A moment when the narrative tradition failed us, when words became incapable of capturing the nature of something fundamental to human experience – light. It started a couple of centuries ago, with a debate about whether light travelled as a wave, as energy moving through a substance (air, water), or whether it travelled as a particle. The latter theory was championed by no less than Isaac Newton; however, the matter appeared to be settled in favour of waves by an experiment pioneered by Thomas Young in 1801.

Young's experiment allowed light to pass through two side-by-side slits in a thin, vertical and otherwise opaque material (like thin metal sheet), and then fall on to a surface beyond. If light were particles, then we would expect to see light falling on to the surface in the same pattern as the slit in the plate. What we see is very different, a pattern of light and shade that we call a diffraction pattern. It is identical to the pattern we would see if we allowed ocean waves to pass through the same pair of slits (like two small gaps in a harbour wall) and then travel onwards. This seemed irrefutable evidence that light was a wave.

And so it went for another hundred years, until a German physicist by the name of Max Planck found a way to explain another experimental result by using an equation where the energy (E) of an electromagnetic wave (like light) is dependent on a constant (h, now called the Planck constant) multiplied by the frequency (v) of the wave, so E = hv. The idea was completely counterintuitive to the idea of light as a wave, since it implied that the energy in light was travelling as discrete quantities, or packets – their size determined as a multiple of the Planck constant. Whereas waves transmit energy in a smooth continuum – a day at the beach will demonstrate that waves come in a limitless range of sizes.

It was Albert Einstein in 1905 that took Planck's idea forward to explain a phenomenon that had just been discovered – the photoelectric effect, which is when electrically charged particles are ejected by a material that's being hit by an electromagnetic radiation, like light. The explanation relied on treating light not just as a packet of energy, but as a discrete particle. Einstein's paper led to one of – perhaps to *the* most fundamental concepts of quantum mechanics, the idea that these particles also exhibit wave-like properties. This is called wave–particle duality and it's at the heart of the mystery of contemporary particle physics.

The theory that light has the properties of a particle *and* the properties of a wave is seriously counter-intuitive. It's impossible to describe in words what that actually looks like, and this duality is at the heart of the inability of words to explain the world as we now understand it. This is in stark contrast to the analogies to billiard balls that were used to explain earlier particle theories.

It was this moment, in 1905, when the world became a place that we could only truly grasp through the symbols of mathematics. It became a world lost to language, a world in which stories and narratives became an inadequate mechanism for transmitting our best explanations to future generations. Our deeply rooted and highly evolved narrative techniques for passing on knowledge are failing us; not least because they are incapable of describing our knowledge of the deepest levels of reality.

Staying Afloat

☐ ***Our desire is to explain with words and stories, but many of our best explanations are mathematical.***

When we shape words into stories, we can create powerful weapons for both good and bad. They can lead us to make some terrible mistakes. A story feels like knowledge, and it may contain useful knowledge, but exactly what that knowledge is may not be obvious at first sight. So, don't just accept the obvious narrative. The purpose of the story will inevitably be more nuanced, more complex and more difficult to understand. When it matters to you, it's always worth taking the time to look at the detail to figure out what's really going on. This is the central idea I want to take forward into the rest of the book.

Next up, we're going to see what happened when the power of stories – like the one about Harold Cudmore and his flare gun – combined over many years with our innate blindness to risk. The result was that many people made serious and almost fatal errors. I was one of them, but one of the lucky ones.

Part 1: Staying Afloat Summary

☐ ***The knowledge held within a story may not be the simple***

truth or the facts that it states.
- *Our nature and nurture have evolved for us to have a strong response to the narrative form. Stories have power.*
- *The real information in a story may lie beneath the surface – search for it, or risk being fooled by the story.*
- *Be wary of neat explanations based on little evidence; we may not understand as much as we think we do.*
- *One of the easiest ways to be fooled by a story is to rely on it when there could be other, more useful information available in logic or maths.*
- *Our desire is to explain with words and stories, but many of our best explanations are mathematical.*

PART TWO – CONFIDENCE

No one's judgement is perfect, so be prepared

Risk comes from not knowing what you're doing.

WARREN BUFFETT, OMAHA WORLD-HERALD

CHAPTER 3

Man Overboard

A Dangerous Simplification

The story of Harold Cudmore's epic ride through a terrifying Fastnet storm – with a man strapped to the mast with a flare gun – was a long way from the truth. The real stories of people like Stuart Quarrie, and even Cudmore's own account of the race, show how the truth was much more complex than the urban myth's simple story of nerveless talent.

The flare-gun story was a dangerous simplification. In reshaping the experience in this way, the story made the storm less frightening. This can help those who were involved deal with the experience afterwards by taking the edge off the terror – but it can also be dangerous if it encourages people to go back out there without fully understanding what they might be taking on, lacking the knowledge they require to be properly prepared. And that's what happened.

Time passed. The sailing community told each other these stories of skill and courage. We forgot the truth about the 1979 Fastnet and it fed a natural complacency. It was only a matter of time before another storm hit one of the big ocean races and when it did, I was there – the Sydney–Hobart Yacht Race in 1993.

The Sydney–Hobart had been the idea of a British Royal Navy captain, John Illingworth, who found himself stationed in Sydney at the end of the Second World War. It was going to be a cruise, but Illingworth suggested that they race, and so the Sydney–Hobart was born. It's always struck me as indicative of the times that they chose to turn right out of Sydney and head towards the South Indian Ocean (an area often called the Southern Ocean), when they could have turned left and headed for the tropics . . . I guess after six years of war, the thought of cruising past balmy, palm-fringed beaches into ever warmer climes and waters just wasn't exciting enough.

The Sydney–Hobart has never lacked excitement[16] and the power of stories and heroic accounts of old races can compound a bigger problem: our inability to assess risk. And by 'assess' I don't mean anything complex – we'll come on to that in Part 3. No, this is just about missing the risk; being unaware or not acknowledging that the risk existed and doing nothing to mitigate it. The main tip for staying afloat from Part 2 is to understand our extraordinary capacity for missing or ignoring the things that are going to try to hurt us.

So, here's a story about the 1993 race to Hobart in which luck, the awareness of risk and the level of preparedness for it all weave together to determine the outcome. Randomness is going to keep popping up since it's diametrically opposed to knowledge – we can't know everything because chance is woven through the very fabric of life. And that means we can't control everything either – shit happens, as it did in this story. We can't stop it, but we can prepare for it. To do that we need a level of self-knowledge, both of our abilities and the abilities of those around us.

Mayday

'Mayday, mayday!'

It was just before midnight on Monday, 27 December 1993, and it wasn't the first time I'd heard the words crackle through the radio static that day. It's not something anyone really gets used to, not in those conditions. The last time I had been on deck the wind speed had read 55 knots – almost 60 mph. The anemometer, the wind instrument at the top of the mast, had given up on us not long afterwards. No one on board the 50-foot-long racing yacht *Ragamuffin* thought that it had eased any since then, although most of us were now down below and not really in a position to make a judgement. We weren't risking people on deck for non-essential tasks.

We had a couple of guys strapped into position, one on the wheel, the other working on the sails, both trying to keep the boat the right way up. Everyone else was hunkered down, waiting for their turn, something to break, the boat to roll, a wave to swamp us. Theoretically we were still racing towards Hobart, one of 104 boats that had started from Sydney on Boxing Day in the 49th edition of Australia's iconic ocean race. In reality we were just trying to keep it afloat, protect the boat and each other from the onslaught until the weather moderated, at which point I think most of us hoped to start racing again. Frankly, I would have been happy if I could just go home.

I had braced myself into the corner of a bunk next to the navigation station – a somewhat grand term for a small table with a rack of electronic equipment screwed into the bulkhead (or wall) behind it. The bunk was a lightweight carbon-fibre frame with a canvas covering, suspended from the ceiling by a block and tackle. Every time the boat got airborne off the top of one of the endless sequence of monstrous, backless waves, the bunk went light underneath me. The boat would land, stagger and roll, the highly loaded carbon fibre releasing energy from its bonds with a series of loud cracks and bangs.

It would have been safer on the floor, lying on one of the sails that were piled everywhere, but all the spots near the navigation station – at the foot of the companionway ladder that led on deck – were taken. Everything was wet including me, soaked through a layer of supposedly waterproof foul-weather gear. And I was cold. A cold that went deep inside. I could barely control my shaking, and it didn't help that I was chronically seasick.

I hadn't given a whole lot of thought to the fate of the other 103 boats that were still, presumably, trying to make their way to Hobart or to a safe port somewhere; as I said, we weren't really racing any longer. I think the last time I had thought about the opposition in a competitive sense had been earlier that evening. We had sailed into the eye of the storm. The noise and motion had suddenly and without warning almost completely disappeared. The boat had lurched upright and the sails started to slat, cracking as they filled first on one side, then on the other: the boat rolling to the motion of the huge swells. I had scrambled up on deck to take a look. There was no wind at all. Not a breath. The waves were still there, but smoother; the angry white faces tortured and flecked by the 50-knot breeze were gone, replaced by a clean blue-grey wall that reached in from the darkness to rise and fall under us.

'Let's think about the main,' said a voice. 'We can't just sit here; the others will still be pushing hard.' The others. The competition. We were still racing them, wherever they were, whatever they were doing out there in the black, black night. We had changed to the smallest sails we had just before sunset, because it's not the kind of job anyone wants to do in a near-hurricane, 30-foot waves and the dark. So now we had a tiny fraction of the sail area that we would normally carry in zero breeze. The suggestion was to go back to the full-size sails. It completely ignored the risk.

'No,' I muttered, 'it's going to come right back in a few minutes, and you don't want to be trying to change sails again when it does.' There were voices in support. Once I'd drawn attention to the risk, everyone could see that it wasn't worth taking. The small sails stayed up. We spent the time securing everything instead. We rolled and slatted for a seemingly endless ten minutes before the sidewall of the storm swept back over us and sucked the boat back into the maelstrom. I didn't hear anyone mention the competition and the race to Hobart after that. The fleet was still out there though, as the constant barrage of emergency radio traffic reminded us. And now, here was another mayday.

Risk Aware

Ragamuffin was owned by a local legend by the name of Syd Fischer. It was being sailed by another local legend, Peter Gilmour, who had been the starting helmsman for the

Australian boat that raced for the America's Cup in 1987. It also boasted a high-profile crew that included an old sailing friend, Neal McDonald. He would go on to skipper his own entry to a second place in the Whitbread (although by then the sponsor had changed and it was called the Volvo Ocean Race). *Ragamuffin* had a stellar crew, and we had a crack at winning in the right weather pattern. So, when they asked if I could do the Hobart, I said yes. I had reservations, I knew I was prone to seasickness, but it would have been hard to say no to the offer.

Like much of the fleet, *Ragamuffin* was far from an ideal boat for the journey to Hobart. It was a lightweight 50-footer that was optimised for racing close to shore in much calmer conditions than we could expect to see in the Bass Strait. At its widest point the Strait is just over 200 miles wide, separating mainland Australia (the state of Victoria) and an island to its south (the state of Tasmania, where the race finishes). Tasmania was created by rising sea levels flooding a land bridge that is believed to have been dry as recently as around 10,000 years ago. So, the Bass Strait is shallow, very shallow – 50 to 70 metres kind of shallow. This contrasts with the four- to five-kilometre-deep ocean that lies to the west, where the wind and waves are coming from.

When waves hit shallow water, they are slowed by the friction with the bottom, the distance between the peaks of the waves shortens, they grow taller and when the depth of water drops under 1.3 times their height, they break. That's all very well when a three-foot swell hits a sandy bottom and produces a nice, shoulder-high peeler. It's a rather different matter when the 100-foot monster waves that stroll round the bottom of the planet start to heap up and break. This is why the Bass Strait is notorious for bad weather; it comes up from Antarctica and the Southern Ocean to be squeezed and intensified as it goes through the Strait.

It will be no surprise, then, that a lot of the risk assessment for the race revolves around the commitment to try to cross the Strait. The Sydney–Hobart is a little bit longer than the Fastnet at 628 nautical miles. It always starts in the afternoon on Boxing Day, 26 December. So, the first night is spent sailing down the coast of New South Wales. The quickest and slowest boats may have a different timetable, but most of the fleet will get to the latitude of the town of Eden some time on the second day, 27 December. Eden sits at the northern tip of Twofold Bay, on the border of New South Wales and Victoria. This is where the protective coastline runs out, and any boat that carries on south beyond that point is moving into Bass Strait. Eden is the moment of truth, it's the last chance to pull the plug when the weather is bad – it's going to get a lot worse if you carry on.

The basic facts of the weather combined with the race's history all mean that there is an atmosphere surrounding the days leading up to the start of the Hobart. It's partly the timing. It begins on Boxing Day, so all the final preparations are undertaken in parallel with those for Christmas. The fact that the competitors will spend the biggest day of the festival with their families before heading out to sea adds an extra edge to it all. Everyone becomes mildly obsessed with the weather forecast – are we going to get a proper kicking this time? In 1993, the answer for me at least, was always, unequivocally . . . yes.

Risk Unaware

The Aussies call it a southerly change and it's very descriptive. The wind does just that – switches round into the south, often driven by the arrival of a cold front and an associated storm system sweeping up from the Southern Ocean and the Bass Strait. The shift from a north-easterly summer sea breeze to a southerly changes everything for anyone sailing to Hobart, and dealing with this change effectively is critical.

A northerly wind has come via the tropics, or at the very least the sub-tropics. It means sailing with the wind; so, the boat is flat, surfing waves at high speeds with the big sail up at the front, the spinnaker. The new southerly wind will be cold, and it will blow hard. It means the boat must sail against the wind, so it's pushed over on its side, held upright by the weight in the keel beneath the hull, and with the crew jammed into place on the outside edge of the deck. And it means bashing into the waves, not riding with them.

Now, sometimes these are just regular weather systems and regular southerly changes, and while the transition does nothing for the quality of life on board, they are not actually life-threatening. It always seemed likely that the 1993 Hobart wasn't going to be one of those. It was going to be worse: bigger, badder, windier, colder. The only question I had in mind as we gathered on board before the start – full of Christmas turkey – was how bad.

It all started innocuously enough. We exited Sydney Heads with the spinnaker up and for the first eight hours or so we poured it on with the wind behind us. It couldn't last and it didn't. The southerly change hit us that first evening, the spinnaker came down, the smaller sail for going into the wind went up, and the foul-weather gear went on. This was where I made my first mistake. The start had been in a broiling hot summer afternoon, and so I'd been wearing cotton shorts and a T-shirt. I'd intended to take off the cotton, replace it with a thin layer of thermal clothing designed to wick away moisture, then add another thicker layer of thermal fleece and the foul-weather top and trousers.

In the rush to change sails and get everyone back in position, the cotton stayed on underneath the fleece and foul-weather gear. It soon got wet and, unlike the thermal fleece material, it stayed wet, draining heat and energy. This was all to come though, as we bashed on into the darkness of the first night, and it slowly but steadily got windier. It was made worse by a two-knot current, water flowing south down the coast and pushing into the wind; wind against current always creates a rougher sea.

By 3 p.m. we were due east of Eden; at the same line of latitude as the eventual line honours winner, the 47-foot-long

Ninety Seven. It's offshore from Eden that the wind and waves coming through the Bass Strait meet the rough water thrown up by the southerly current coming down the east coast ... We were not far from the Bass Strait, and we all knew it was only going to get worse. It had already been blowing from the south-west for a couple of days down there and the waves were running strong. However, at that moment, with the right sails up, the boat was still controllable and safe. We had done the change to smaller 'storm' sails in plenty of time before it got dark and were hunkered down to get through it.

It was after sunset, once we had got further into the Bass Strait, that things got ugly. By now, although we didn't know the detail at the time, the weather system was strengthening beyond serious into properly dangerous – and significantly worse than the forecast. This was almost thirty years ago, and there was very little of the modern technology that we now take for granted. There were no mobile or satellite phones, for instance. GPS was a very new technology, and while we had it aboard *Ragamuffin*, not everyone did. The computer models that forecast the weather were much less sophisticated, not least because the computers running them were a lot less powerful. And even if the forecast had seen what was coming earlier, the only way to communicate it to a sailboat offshore was using a High Frequency (HF) Single Sideband (SSB). While this was an established technology that's still in use today, these were big heavy radios not normally carried by many of the yachts. They were temporarily installed for the race and – let's be honest – that job wasn't always done well.

The weather bureau reported afterwards that the storm topped out with a centre at just 986 hectopascals, the wind strength in the maximum gusts reaching that of a low-category hurricane at 70 knots. The yacht *Ninety Seven* subsequently reported seeing 75 knots at the top of their mast late on the 27th. Remember how the Beaufort Scale was designed to allow sailors to judge and report wind conditions without benefit of instruments, but also describes the effects ashore? A Storm Force 10 on the Beaufort Scale means winds between 48 and 55 knots, which is 'Seldom experienced inland; trees uprooted; considerable structural damage.' Beaufort Force 11, a violent storm, means winds of 56–63 knots which ashore is 'Very rarely experienced; accompanied by widespread damage.' And Force 12, which is equivalent to the lowest category of hurricane with winds of more than 64 knots? The Beaufort Scale is elegant in its simplicity about the impact ashore: 'Devastation.'

And then there were the maydays. The feeling of horror as that night unfolded has never gone away. The first time the radio really lit up had been after the keel[17] dropped off the yacht *Clwyd*. The skipper Craig Escott reported that there was a big bang, and then the boat started filling up with water. It was soon obvious that they had to abandon. They sent a distress signal on the radio, got into the life raft and fired off their flares. There was no reason to panic; there were boats around.

The crew were picked up by a yacht called *Nynja Go*, who had responded to the flares. The *Clwyd* was the first yacht to sink in the 49th Sydney–Hobart Race. In fact, she was the first yacht to sink in any Sydney–Hobart Race, but she wasn't the last. A boat called *Adjuster* was next; swamped by a wave, she also started to go under. The crew were eventually rescued by the yacht *Kingurra*. Then *Swuzzlebubble VIII* was rolled over and badly damaged. And so it went on; the calls came in one after the other, in pretty quick succession.

There's a well-established process in place for handling vessels in distress and the Australian emergency service dedicated to it that day was the Sea Safety Centre in Canberra. It's their job to launch helicopters and lifeboats, and coordinate support from merchant shipping. And they did all of that. In the case of the Hobart Race, the Cruising Yacht Club of Australia – the club that runs the race – also ran a radio support centre.

The CYC coordinated a regular schedule for the fleet to report their positions using a relay ship called the *Young Endeavour*. In normal times these positions were plotted to show the progress of the fleet at the club and passed on to the media to enable them to report on the race. The club's radio team were also trying to coordinate any boats that were close enough to help each of the distress calls – the result was a lot of radio traffic. There was little we could do for any of the distress calls as we were a long way south of the main action, so mostly we just listened with an increasing sense of helplessness. It was that one just before midnight on Monday 27th that was the worst though, and that's because the two words that came after the mayday were the grimmest two words you can hear on a sailboat. Or maybe any boat. Man overboard.

Shit Happens

It was 11.42 p.m. on Monday night, 27 December, when John Quinn was swept off his 35-footer, *MEM*. The crew hit a button that recorded the yacht's position, which was transmitted with the mayday, and the search started. They had just stepped out from the shelter of the mainland and were exposed to the full force of the storm in the Bass Strait. The water temperature was about 18 °C. This was on Quinn's side; the predicted time to exhaustion and unconsciousness is between two and seven hours at that temperature, with the outside survival time at 40 hours. It was the only thing he had going for him. A man overboard is absolutely the worst-case scenario, a man or woman alone in those monster seas on a pitch-black night . . . no one thought he had a chance. There were stories at the time that the CYC started writing his obituary after four hours, and that, in retrospect, seems generous to me.

At around 5 a.m. on Tuesday morning the oil tanker *Ampol Sarel* arrived at the search zone, after being redirected by the Sea Safety Centre. The captain, Bernie Holmes, took the decision to start at the original point where Quinn had gone off the boat, then shut down the engines and let the huge ship drift downwind. He turned on all the lights so she would coast silently through the search area lit up like a Christmas tree. It was an inspired strategy. Soon after, an Australian, Brent Shaw, an able seaman aboard the tanker, heard John Quinn's cries. 'I was on the wing of the bridge, port-side lookout, wearing my raincoat and rain hat, when I thought I heard a scream,' he told reporters afterwards. 'With all the wind and rain, I wasn't quite sure, so I took off my rain hat and then I positively heard the scream. I directed my searchlight towards the area – and there he was, waving and screaming.'[18] Quinn was about 20 metres away from the 100,000-tonne tanker.

> 'The scary part was we spotted him and then he drifted out of the searchlight, and then he was in the dark again. I thought I had lost him, and I thought I might have been the last person to actually see the man. It was just pure, pure luck. I heard him and I spotted him and that's when I yelled out. I just screamed out to him to make sure he heard me. I just kept yelling to get the attention of the bridge and the attention of John in the water.'

The *Ampol Sarel* radioed to the other searching boats that they had seen Quinn, and one of the boats that heard the message was a boat called *Atara*. They'd already had their own share of adventure that night. One of the crew was a 21-year-old called Tom Braidwood, who would go on to sail with America's Cup teams, race around the world three times and complete a solo race across the Atlantic in a 6.5-metre boat called a Mini Transat.

'You know as you do as a young fellow, watching the wind go up, and you're going, "Crap, I've never seen sixty knots before . . ." and then the wind is still going up. And I remember, the most I ever saw on the dial was like seventy-two . . . It got to that stage where you couldn't see the waves in the troughs . . . the white foam was filling all the troughs up . . . you didn't really see all the waves, you just saw white foam. And the only way we knew . . . you'd hear the wave coming like a train and you'd be like, "Fuck, here we go..."'[19]

Eventually one of those waves had rumbled in and hit the sails of *Atara* with such force that it snapped the mast. 'We spent a fair bit of time cutting that away. But while it was getting cut away, it was smashing into the side of the boat . . . and another wave came, and Peter Messenger got pinned underneath the mast on the leeward [downwind] side. And we're trying to lift the mast to get it off him, but we couldn't because the mast is attached still and lying around the hull. And then another big wave came; you heard it rumble and rumble and rumble. And it popped the rig up and we got Messo out. It took off half the rudder and punched it into the side of the boat before we got it cut cleanly away.'

Atara was now in serious trouble. They started pulling the bunks off the side of the boat and using them to try to shore up the structure because it was caving in under the wave motion. It was at this moment that they heard about John Quinn, and diverted towards the search area, still struggling to keep their own boat afloat. 'We got to the area and we're all just on deck with torches down each side of the boat. And we're just motoring around and next thing you know, we saw him, and it was like . . . talk about the luckiest guy on earth, well, unlucky falling in . . . but . . .'

It was far from over, though; they still had to get him out of the water. 'The problem was, and this is an interesting part of the psychology of stuff, because as soon as we got him, he gave up. So, he was like, "I'm rescued. I'm done."' They struggled to get him out of the water, lost him once and had to do a couple of passes to get back to him. By then, said Braidwood, 'He was pretty tapped out. He wasn't a very fit fellow, John Quinn, and we got him around to the back [of the boat] and we still could not get him on board.

'He was drifting on and off the boat and it's hard to keep him there. I had a harness on, so I turned around to the guys and said, "I'm going to go get him." I had my harness tied to a rope as well. I dove in, and swam out to him. And as soon as I got him, it was like, "Uuuuhhhh," you know, like complete collapse.'

Somehow Braidwood got him back to the boat. 'The theory was that the only way we'll get him is somebody under him and above him. So I got underneath and I'm . . . We're trying to get the wave matching with the lift and everything and eventually we got him on board, dragged him down below and he was hypothermic, because all he had on was thermals and a dinghy vest, like a little life jacket, a bit padded. That's the thing that saved his life, you know, because he didn't have a jacket, a wet weather jacket, or anything. He just had his wet weather pants, that dinghy thing and thermals.'

I first heard this story in Sydney, not long after that Hobart. It took me nearly thirty years to get around to tracking down John Quinn and asking him what he was doing in the water in hurricane-level conditions with no life jacket on. Meanwhile, I had framed my own narrative about Quinn as some Johnny-come-lately, wet behind the ears, brand-new to ocean racing and blind to good seamanship. It should come as no surprise that this was completely wrong. John Quinn was no naive newbie to sailing, the Hobart or the risks.

Quinn was brought up in Sydney and had spent his childhood in and around the water. 'It was mainly sailing,' he told me. 'As a kid, I used to do a lot of swimming and I did – like most Sydney kids – I did a fair bit of surfing, did a little bit of snorkelling and scuba diving, but it was mainly sailing.'[20] He messed around in canoes and dinghies and eventually progressed to a VJ, the iconic Australian junior boat. In the early 1950s, when Quinn was seven, his father had bought *Rani*, the winner of the first ever Sydney–Hobart. It was upgraded to a 9-meter-long Fife design and when Quinn left school at 17, he gave up the VJ and started sailing with his father.

What followed was a steady progression into ocean racing. 'I did my first Hobart Race at the age of twenty-one so I started actually ocean racing probably about the age of eighteen, nineteen.' By the time he was in his late twenties he was part owner of a 33-foot-long boat, his first ocean-racing yacht. Over the next two decades it was upgraded a couple of times, before Quinn bought *MEM*, a 35-foot-long type of boat called a J/35. 'I would have picked her up just at the beginning of the season,' he explained. 'We're racing under the IMS [International Measurement System] rule and they were very competitive at that particular time; a number of them had done very well in various races. But they're pretty light and pretty beamy.' Even more than *Ragamuffin*, the J/35 was designed with a focus on racing close to the coast, rather than longer-distance offshore races like the Hobart.

Quinn was a Hobart veteran though, and (unlike me) the forecast for the 1993 race hadn't particularly concerned him, despite the design characteristics of his boat. 'When we saw the race [weather] briefing it was a little bit fuzzy. It could have been tough, it couldn't have been tough, they were a bit uncertain.' The crew's biggest concern the morning of the start was whether to use a new mainsail. It represented an expenditure that was an unnecessary risk if conditions were particularly bad. 'We were tossing up whether to use it or not to use it, and we came to the decision to use it. As it turned out the thing [the storm] was a lot worse than what we thought it was going to be . . .'

It turned out to be a lot worse than anyone thought it would be – no one was expecting winds of more than 70 knots. When these conditions started to unfold *MEM* was east of Twofold Bay and Eden. Decision time. They weren't far north of the Bass Strait when they took the first bad wave over the side. 'It was at that stage that I decided that maybe we ought to get into the tri-sail [a much smaller sail that replaces the mainsail for storm conditions] which we didn't do, and we would have been better off in a tri-sail – but we didn't do that, we ended up going under a storm jib.'

They continued, even as the conditions continued to deteriorate. 'It was basically impossible to steer the boat from the side-rail [edge of the boat], so I was actually sitting in the bottom of the cockpit [the lowest part of the deck] . . . And a wave came up abeam of us. We'd basically been heading pretty much into the waves but there was a wave that came from an odd direction; it was a big wave. Picked us up, threw us straight over on her side . . . We had three down below, fortunately. All of us on deck, I think bar one, went over the side. I just got washed straight out of the cockpit. And when my weight hit the harness it busted. It was a harness inside the jacket that had been well cared for . . . it just must've split the webbing or whatever happened, but anyway, I ended up in the water.

'I had on a Musto flotation vest. They produced these vests which were actually more for warmth, but they actually gave you a little bit of flotation. So, I should say that I had that on, I also had on a normal [foul-weather] jacket, but the jacket was weighing me down, so I got rid of it. And I had sea boots on which I got rid of.' And, as Tom Braidwood had observed, he was not wearing a life jacket. John Quinn explained why. 'We had normal life jackets . . . You remember how bulky those bloody things were, you can't get around the boat on them . . . They're terrible bloody things.'

The life jackets that were onboard *MEM* were of a type that typically relied on closed-cell polyethylene foam for buoyancy. They were big and could be awkward to wear: they made it difficult to move around the boat. So, Quinn had decided not to wear it – although if ever there was a time to be wearing a life jacket, this was it. 'We were relying on our safety harnesses really . . . You don't expect to end up in the water if you're using a safety harness, not when you're clipped on.'

John Quinn had chosen the harness as his personal safety gear, and now the harness had failed him, just as Stuart Quarrie's had done 14 years earlier in the Fastnet Race. But unlike Quarrie, who had got back to his boat, Quinn was left in the water alone. 'We're talking about seas of on average eight metres and they're breaking, so the chances of seeing one individual off a yacht in that sort of condition in the middle of the night – and it was in the middle of the night – are sweet bugger all.'

John Quinn was not intimidated though. 'I guess when you live in Sydney and you spend so much time swimming as a kid, it's not something that . . . There was no, certainly in those days, no natural fear about the water. And there was a fair bit of buoyancy in this thing; you only had to do a very gentle sort of thing to keep yourself reasonably high. I guess if you didn't do that, you would have gone down to about your head.'

He tried a couple of survival techniques he'd picked up, including sealing the foul-weather jacket and filling it with air to provide buoyancy, which 'is a load of bullshit, there's no way that that will actually work in real life.' He also tried pulling into a foetal position to protect himself as the waves hit him. 'That was one of the worst ideas they ever came up with because you get one of these waves that picks you up and it chucks you around . . . you get a bloody roller coming up and it just picks you up and it just throws you. I mean, it'll throw a four-ton yacht . . . I tried that first, decided that was a really bad idea. No, you don't want to go there.'

The problem was the breaking waves. Anyone who's been paddling at the beach knows that the dangerous part of the wave is the breaking white water. A lot of what's involved in learning to surf is learning not to get swept up by this white water and dumped back on the beach. The trick is to go under, to 'duck-dive' below the breaking crest of the wave.

'What I ended up doing was what we always used to do when the waves came at us when we were surfing: I just dived under it. And I wasn't having to do that all the time; I guess you'd get one of these waves, and you could hear them coming, you could hear these things coming and probably get one every ten minutes or something like that. So, I used to dive underneath it and the flotation vest wasn't so buoyant that it stopped me doing that, so I was able to get through them. So, basically, that's what I did. I was looking around for lights all the time, of course. Doing a fair bit of praying, remembering all the fine things at home, and wondering what the bloody hell I'm doing there, that sort of stuff.'

This technique would have been impossible in one of the life jackets that Quinn had left aboard *MEM* because its buoyancy would have kept him on the surface. 'Very buoyant. I would've hated to have been out there with one of those things on . . .' he pointed out. The much less buoyant flotation vest that Quinn was wearing left him better able to handle the breaking waves – so long as he was strong enough to keep himself afloat with its limited support . . . and that was a close-run thing.

'By this stage I was getting towards the end of it. I'd been through the shakes, I really started to shiver and shake pretty badly, and the shakes were just going, and then all of a sudden I saw all these lights and I swam towards the lights. As it turned out, it was a bloody great big oil tanker and she was coming down at me. And I yelled and then I suddenly realised this thing's going to run over the top of me, so I ended up swimming away from the thing.'

There was another bad moment when the *Ampol Sarel*'s searchlight lost him. 'No sooner had the light gone off me and I remember going, "Oh, shit," and looking around and then I saw the . . . lights of *Atara* coming at me. So, they must've responded very quickly. There were a number of yachts hanging around the ship, that was part of the deal.' It was 5.09 a.m. when Quinn was pulled out of the water, 5 hours and 27 minutes after he went overboard.

'How could anyone do that?' said Braidwood, reflecting on Quinn's feat of endurance. 'And he was not a young man when this happened.' Quinn was 49 at the time. The crew of *Atara* got him, exhausted and hypothermic, into a bunk with one of the only crew who was still dry. 'We had the space blankets around him and that, jamming cups of tea into him,' said Braidwood as they resumed the passage home. They were ready for this – they had the equipment and knew what to do. Once again Quinn was lucky – lucky that the flotation vest had allowed him to handle the waves, lucky to be found before he ran out of the energy needed to help its limited buoyancy keep him afloat, and lucky to be found by a well-crewed and prepared boat, but again, only just . . .

'*Atara* was in a total bloody mess,' said Quinn. 'I don't

know what they were doing there . . . The mast had come down. She was totally delaminated, I mean, she was a total wreck. I don't think she ever went anywhere after that.'

Tom Braidwood was just as aware of the frailty of their position. 'We would have had two or three other boats all around, and I remember one of the boats shadowing us had a doctor on board. We had the life rafts up in the cockpit because we were not in a good way at all . . . The whole side of the boat's leaking water and we've got bunks chopped up, we've got sails bricked up [folded, rolled and tied into tight, brick-shaped packages] and we're taking shifts at standing up in the bow and leaning against the side of the boat to try to support it. We would lay up there and push against the sail to try to help the side of the boat. And I remember he [Quinn] came to, and he just turns around and he goes, "Oh, thanks, guys. Thanks, fellas." You know . . . And I turned around and I said, "Well, don't thank us yet, mate, because your fucking ambulance is about to sink."'

The indomitable streak that had got John Quinn to that point came out in his reply. 'When they told me that the ambulance wasn't in too good a shape, I think I said something rude. Like, "Can I wait for the next one?"' He didn't have to; *Atara* made it back to shore with one of the luckiest people alive onboard.

The fate of *Ragamuffin* was also decided while Quinn's rescue was going on. A routine check revealed that strips of the top layer of carbon fibre from which the boat was constructed were peeling back from a part at the very front of the boat. The bit in question was a part that was holding up the mast. It was an easy decision to turn back; any failure and the mast would come tumbling down on our heads and could punch a hole in the hull – as it had on *Atara*.

We turned the boat around, pointed it at Eden and Twofold Bay and everything changed. We were sailing with the wind now, so the boat came upright. We were no longer living at an angle of 20 degrees or more. And we were riding with the waves, not pounding into them, so the punishing heaving, rolling and crashing motion turned into a much smoother ride with long fast surfing sections.

I fell asleep. I woke up three times. The first time it was because I was cold, shaking uncontrollably. I looked around. Everyone else was asleep, still just a couple of people on deck sailing her home. Down below, the boat was a scene of complete devastation: people, sails, gear, food wrappers, ropes, buckets, tools – it was as though someone had turned the entire interior upside down and shaken it. Which wasn't far from the truth. Something in my head told me I needed to get up and get out of the wet clothes. The soaking-wet cotton layer finally came off, and just the thermals went back on. The effect was almost immediate. I couldn't believe then or now how stupid I had been not to do it earlier.

The second time I woke to a splash on my face. I opened my eyes thinking someone was coming down the hatch and a wave had followed them. I saw Syd Fischer at the bottom of the companionway ladder holding the pee bottle and looking pretty sheepish. I hadn't come across the pee bottle before; a bottle loosely tied to the companionway ladder. When it's rough you pee in it, then just pour it into the scuppers outside to wash away.

I've lost one friend and I know of two more people that have gone overboard trying to take a pee off the back of a boat in bad weather. If it's likely to get rough, getting the pee bottle ready is a pretty good metaphor for how you should go about life. However, on this occasion the pee hadn't made it outside. Syd had slipped and dumped it in my face. I was past caring, I shrugged, half smiled, rolled over and went back to sleep.

The third time I woke up because it was hot. It was also completely still. A few people were up and about; I went on deck and discovered that we were now becalmed. No wind at all, not a breath. We were about 12 miles short of Eden. And the engine wouldn't start. It felt like the final straw. We were exhausted, filthy and ravenously hungry in a way that damp two-day old sandwiches was not going to fix. We talked about trying to raise the Port of Eden harbour master to get a tow in. Syd Fischer agreed to pony up for whatever it cost. A few hours later I was in a taxi headed up the New South Wales coast, back to Sydney, a trip I remember absolutely nothing about. The rest of the race I've never forgotten.

Staying Afloat

> ☐   *We have a high capacity for missing or ignoring the things that are going to try to hurt us.*

CHAPTER 4

Overconfidence

Preparation And Luck

The life-long lessons that I took away from the 1993 Hobart were really about the critical roles played by both preparation and luck. These two things are interwoven. Sometimes, luck will let you get away with not doing the preparation. Not always: there will be times when all the preparation in the world won't save you, but often enough, it's the combination of a lack of forethought and chance moving against you that leads to bad outcomes. So do the preparation, because you never know when you're going to run out of luck. John Quinn was incredibly lucky to be found right at the limit of his ability to survive in those conditions, and it saved him from some poor preparation.

'Towards the end, it would have been nice to be able to go . . . and pump it [the flotation vest] up a bit higher . . .' he said, acknowledging his error. 'The first thing I did when I came back was, I threw out all the life jackets . . . and I put inflatable life jackets on board the boat for everybody. Because inflatable life jackets allow you to control your buoyancy in the same way as a diver can control their buoyancy. And that I regard as absolutely critical because I think with a full life jacket, those waves picking you up, I don't think you'd last very long. You would have to do what I was doing. But with an inflatable, you can get it to a point where you're comfortable about handling the conditions you're in.

'I made a number of fundamental mistakes,' Quinn continued. 'The first thing is that I shouldn't have been racing a boat that light in the Sydney to Hobart Race. They're a beautiful little coastal racing boat, the J/35, magnificent little boat, but they're not designed to go into that sort of weather. The second mistake I made was when I realised we were going into that sort of weather: I should have pulled the plug and just simply peacefully sailed into Twofold Bay. Shouldn't have allowed myself to get out of bloody control, I know better than that. They were the two fundamental mistakes.'[21]

John Quinn was a very long way from being the only one to make mistakes that night. I could have written this story about my own errors of judgement, except the consequences of them were a lot less dramatic – of course, that was just down to luck. The obvious mistake was leaving on the cotton clothes, but in reality, I probably shouldn't even have been out there. I knew I was prone to seasickness and combined with the cold it became completely debilitating during the second night, to the extent that I could no longer do my job. A crewmate, Peter Shipway, had to take over the radio watch. There was more though, and it was only once I'd heard the stories of others involved in that race that I realised I hadn't even been fully aware of all the risks, never mind prepared for them.

At one point, I'd unclipped and let myself slide across the deck to get to the other side of the boat. If a wave had hit us at that point I would have gone straight out the back. Was I ready for that? Well, no – I had an inflatable life jacket on, but that was all. I wasn't carrying anything that would help the crew of *Ragmuffin* find me in the dark, amongst the foam and the waves. I didn't even have a waterproof torch on me. Afterwards, I bought a personal emergency strobe light. I kept it in the pocket of my foul-weather kit, changed the batteries at the start of every season, and carried it on me for every overnight race.

And what if I'd ended up trapped in the water by the rigging, like Peter Messenger on *Atara*? I was carrying a knife, but it was on the belt of my shorts, under the foul-weather gear. I would have had absolutely no chance of reaching it in any kind of emergency that involved holding my breath. I was much more careful to put it on the outside layer of clothing after that experience. Previously, it had never occurred to me that I might need these things – just as it had never occurred to John Quinn that he wouldn't want to wear the life jackets he had bought for *MEM* when he most needed them, and that they would be a liability in breaking waves anyway. And this, it turns out, is a pretty normal way for humans to think.

Staying Afloat

☐ *If it's not possible to be great, at least be organised, be prepared – you will need it if you run out of luck.*

Overconfidence

Human beings are not naturally inclined to take a pessimistic outlook; we're much more likely to hope for the best. I doubt very much that John Quinn was the only one without a life jacket on that night. And I'm sure that I wasn't the only one sliding around the deck without being clipped on. The psychologists are all over this tendency; there is lots of data to support it.[22] Take marriage for instance, something we can all relate to, even if it's the marriage of our parents or grandparents. The 2021 figures for divorce in England and Wales[23] showed that for couples married in 2011, almost one in every five marriages ended in divorce before the tenth wedding anniversary. If everyone walking up the aisle really believed that they had just a four-in-five chance of making it to ten years, never mind 'till death do us part', I suspect many would not bother.

There is a similarly proportioned statistic about restaurant failure rates that's often quoted in relation to this topic, and this seems to derive from a 2005 study done in Columbus, Ohio.[24] It was based on health-department restaurant-operating permits over a three-year period. It showed that at the end of the three-year study, almost 60 per cent of the restaurants had closed or changed ownership in that time. Now, changing ownership doesn't necessarily mean a business failure – it could also mean retirement or a change of heart about life's vocation – but even allowing for that, it's probable that anyone staking their life savings on the opening of a coffee bar or bistro is actually betting everything on the equivalent of a coin toss. In those terms, it seems like a massive risk that can only really be reconciled if people just don't believe that the statistics apply to them.

A good example of the psychological studies that substantiate this view is a 1980 paper by Ola Svenson.[25] She questioned two groups of drivers – one in the US and one in Sweden – and asked them how safe they were as drivers relative to the others in the group. In the US, 88 per cent of those asked thought they were safer than the median driver in the group, while in Sweden it was 77 per cent. The median driver is by definition the one in the middle, halfway between the most dangerous and the safest. So, it's impossible for more than 50 per cent of the drivers questioned to be above the median, and yet, 88 per cent and 77 per cent of those asked thought they were. Similar experiments have repeatedly led to similar results, and this tendency to be over-confident about our own abilities and judgements has become a fundamental truth for psychologists.

Our predisposition for optimism has got us into all sorts of trouble, especially at sea. Too many people have been lost thinking that the weather wasn't going to be as bad as all that, or even as bad as the forecast, or – and this is worse – that they were a match for it. A deeply tragic case was the loss of the HMS *Bounty*, a three-masted replica of an 18th-century ship built for Marlon Brando's 1962 film version of *Mutiny on the Bounty*. The ship was famous, and had appeared in other movies, including Johnny Depp's *Pirates of the Caribbean.*

The Bounty's 63-year-old captain, Robin Walbridge, took the decision to leave the safe harbour of New London, Connecticut, for St Petersburg, Florida, when there was a hurricane in the Atlantic, moving north up the east coast. The *Bounty* sank in the storm on 29 October 2012, about 100 miles from Cape Hatteras, North Carolina. Walbridge and deckhand Claudene Christian were both lost while they were trying to abandon ship. The captain's body was never recovered. The

Coastguard rescued the other 14 crew members from the life rafts in a truly heroic operation.

The subsequent federal enquiry reported:[26] 'In fact, just before the shipyard period, the captain had told a local Maine television station that the *Bounty* "chased hurricanes," and that by getting close to the eye, sailors could use hurricane winds to their advantage.' It's a well-established technique to route sailing boats into the favourable sector of any weather system – but a hurricane? Why would you take that risk? Only because you believe the risk doesn't apply to you.

The enquiry ruled:

> The probable cause of the sinking of tall ship *Bounty* was the captain's reckless decision to sail the vessel into the well-forecasted path of Hurricane Sandy, which subjected the aging vessel and the inexperienced crew to conditions from which the vessel could not recover. Contributing to the sinking was the lack of effective safety oversight by the vessel organization.

It seems that Walbridge believed he and his ship could ride out the hurricane, and his over-confidence in both cost him and deckhand Claudene Christian their lives.

It should never have needed a hurricane to get me to think about how I might mitigate the risk of going overboard from a race boat.

Overconfidence can be blamed for many of the other dramatic disasters of the 20th and 21st centuries. Why didn't the *Titanic*'s Captain Smith slow down or change course when he was told there was ice in their path? Why weren't there enough lifeboats on board? Overconfidence is just as likely to be the cause of disasters small and large in each and every individual life, as it is to take hundreds of lives in a disaster like the *Titanic* . . . but of course, it's one thing to identify a problem, altogether another to find a solution.

Staying Afloat

☐ *We are all capable of overconfidence – believing that you are not is being overconfident.*

Understanding Overconfidence

Let's get some background. This tendency for overconfidence is another cognitive bias, our hard-wired predispositions to assess problems in a particular way. When the head of the TED organisation Chris Anderson interviewed Daniel Kahneman (who was responsible along with Amos Tversky for the original work on cognitive bias), he asked if Kahneman could 'inject one idea into the minds of millions of people, what would that idea be?' Kahneman replied, 'Overconfidence is really the enemy of good thinking, and I wish that humility about our beliefs could spread.'[27]

We need to start with a distinction that Kahneman and Tversky make between two modes of thinking. I'm going to use their terms and call the two modes of thinking System 1 and System 2.[28] They regard System 1 as the cognitive-bias mode; it's instinctive, unconscious and relies on patterns and prior experience. It uses a set of rules that psychologists call heuristics, or shortcuts: rules of thumb that help us to get quick decisions. System 2 is a much slower way of thinking; it's conscious, deliberate and self-aware – this is where the rational thinking happens.

There were excellent reasons for these two modes of thinking when we lived in the jungles, forests and on the savannas. Quick decision making was essential to our survival. If a bear appeared from behind a tree, the need to react was instantaneous; there was no benefit to calculating the probability that the bear was hungry. We also use heuristics to do things like catch balls and throw spears at moving targets – these are abilities that we could not have developed any other way. The need to hunt existed way before the maths required to work the answers out on paper, never mind that the antelope is long gone even before the pencil has touched paper.

The second reason for developing these modes of thinking was that thinking itself is hard; it takes energy as well as time. System 1 was developed to make fast decisions with minimal effort. If we engaged System 2 for every single decision, we'd get no further than a cost–benefit analysis of our breakfast cereal choice, and we'd be exhausted by the time we got around to eating. The world would grind us down to a gooey pulp. We've evolved for efficiency, for System 1 to make every decision for us, while System 2 monitors those decisions and intervenes when it thinks it should – which is not very often, because engaging in that extra effort is hard work, and hard work is something to be avoided when getting the next meal might involve a life-or-death struggle with a lion.

The most important point about all this is that these modes of thinking are powerfully ingrained in us and changing them will not come easily. There's an internal bias to overconfidence in all of us, and it's so hard to overcome because (like all System 1 thinking) it's instinctive – we don't stop to think things through properly. Any business start-up, particularly one that is likely to fail as regularly as a restaurant, needs the full engagement of System 2 from the outset. Unfortunately, the problem gets worse when the goal is a long-held dream, an object of great desire – like marriage or a new business venture. We are inclined to push ahead without thinking about the risks under normal circumstances, and it just gets worse when we desperately want something or want to do something.

So, it's not just a question of putting down this book and thinking: Right, I need to assess my decisions more carefully, and pick through them for an optimistic bias . . . and expect it to happen. Kahneman came up with this stuff, and he felt he was as prone to the errors as anyone. In the Conclusion to his book *Thinking, Fast and Slow*, he says, 'As I know from experience, System 1 is not readily educable.' Kahneman goes on to note that his own intuitive thinking is just as prone to the errors of overconfidence as it was before he started researching them.[29]

The first part of any solution is to ensure that System 2 is engaged when it needs to be, but we must accept that this is far from easy. It was Kahneman's central hope that while the future for individuals might be just as error-riddled as the past, organisational decision making could be considerably improved by better quality second-guessing and gossip in the proverbial water-cooler moments that happen in every organisation. The size and unwieldiness of most organisations mean that they have to make decisions more slowly than individuals, so there is time for both informal (water-cooler moments) and formal feedback with procedures that can be put in place to guarantee an orderly and relatively thoughtful process.

Staying Afloat

☐ *It takes time, effort and practice to become more risk aware.*

Building Risk-Aware Habits

We have seen that we have a capacity to ignore or miss the risk of things that might harm us, and we've learnt that there is much to be gained by a pause for reflection. So, despite Daniel Kahneman's pessimism – and speaking as an individual who's made some pretty bad choices – I'm going to keep trying to achieve that pause for reflection. It's surprising how often risk mitigation costs little more than a moment's thought. 'Which coat should I take?' is a popular question for my children before we leave the house for a day trip. The best answer (and not the one I always give) has nothing to do with the weather forecast: 'Take both, then you have the choice every time you leave the car.' It costs nothing to carry the extra coat around in the car. Often, risk mitigation is a simple as putting an extra coat, blanket or shovel in the car. It's as simple as putting a strobe light in the pocket of your foul-weather gear. It's a simple as taking a moment to think about whether you're going to wear the bulky life jacket when it matters.

There are a few strategies that we can employ to help us overcome the pernicious bias of overconfidence, ways to learn to slow down and pay better attention. One of them is to build habits to review risk *whenever* there's time to do so. By the time I next sailed with him, Neal McDonald (who was aboard *Ragamuffin* during the Sydney–Hobart) had developed the habit of playing an almost constant 'what if' game during any pause in the action. It might have been when the boat was sailing or motoring back to the dock after a race, or at a meal, or at the bar. At any moment he could start a pop quiz: 'What do we do if that sail breaks?' or 'What's the repair if the steering gear fails?'

McDonald was constantly looking for solutions to problems he didn't yet have, and it's a very powerful tool in raising everyone's awareness of risk. It's a great topic of conversation for the water cooler or coffee machine: 'What's the plan if the dollar drops ten per cent in the next month?' or 'What's plan B if the new widget design is late?' Asking risk-based questions in a playful way to a random group of people at a lunch or tea break can provide insights into whatever business you are involved in, insights that might not be gathered any other way.

Neal McDonald's habit of talking through problems out loud demonstrated to me how it can clarify them. And it always makes sense, ahead of any upcoming important action or decision, to talk it through with someone. It doesn't matter if they are independent and unaffected by the outcome (someone with less skin in the game can be more objective) or involved (they may have seen something that you have missed). If there's no one around to help, then pick up a pen or pencil and a piece of paper, turn on a smartphone or tablet, or open a laptop – whatever is the thinking tool of choice.

The good old-fashioned list of pros and cons goes a long way towards uncovering risks we were previously unaware of. Charles Darwin famously listed the advantages and disadvantages of matrimony, having a couple of goes at it in the months before his marriage to his cousin Emma Wedgwood in 1838.[30] He concluded, 'Marry–Marry–Marry Q.E.D' – his enthusiasm is somewhat ironic considering the current divorce statistics.[31] The consequences of a marriage failing are serious, and they are for System 2 to consider; Darwin's list and the prenuptial are both System 2 documents – but how many people have either? I certainly don't...

We can develop better habits, though; as well as discussing or listing risks, adopt a routine of analysing your performance each time you make a decision or do anything of consequence or importance. No one gets better at something without practice, and practice and learning are not effective without some sort of feedback mechanism. So, make it a routine to revisit events and decisions: look at how they played out – not just the outcome, instead focus on the process and thought that went into the decision.

The reason that we need to focus on the process and not the outcome is that when we assess a decision, we do it with the benefit of hindsight, and we are very prone to what's called hindsight bias. This is another cognitive bias stemming from the work of Kahneman and Tversky, but first identified and established in a 1975 paper by Baruch Fischhoff and Ruth Beyth.[32] Hindsight bias is the inclination to believe that the outcome was more predictable, that we 'knew it all along'.

This tendency to believe that we correctly predicted events when we didn't is another component of overconfidence. If we always look back at our decisions and hindsight bias makes us think we made the right one, then we're going to become overconfident. So, if we are going to make a habit of revisiting events and decisions to see how they played out then it's really important to focus on the decision-making process rather than worrying about the outcome. Did you pay attention, did you see the risks? Did you make good decisions once you had seen them? And if not, how could you do better?

Once we have learnt to pay attention and started to think about the risks involved in what lies ahead, we have made a significant step forward. There's still plenty of work to do though, not least is knowing whether we've found all the risks. Did we miss something? Have we covered all the possibilities? Are there tools that can help us in a more formal process of investigating risk?

It's ironic that when I google 'confidence' I get a list of links to articles and books exhorting me to be *more* confident[33] rather than less confident. Not only is overconfidence an inherent trait, but on top of that there's an entire industry of self-help and business books about bolstering confidence as a means to greater achievement. It's true that some of us have a predisposition to under-confidence, a lack of conviction about our own talents and abilities. I've chosen to focus here on overconfidence because this is the one that affects not just the individual with the bias, but those that work and live with them and the consequences of their actions. People that lack confidence don't often get into positions where they can, for instance, set ludicrous, under-resourced deadlines that wreck projects and ruin businesses ... or sink ships.

So, in the public domain – at least as it's represented by the search findings on Google – it appears that there has been much more energy put into boosting people's confidence than the converse. When you dig a little deeper though, there's a fair bit of pushback against the 'confidence' industry. I've already cited some of the published research and there's plenty more, along with popular books and articles: guidance for avoiding catastrophic overconfidence, particularly in the context of commercial project management. We're going to look at a couple of the suggested strategies for reining in an overconfident C-suite, as there's something in these for the individual.

Staying Afloat

☐ *Build risk awareness by building habits that will reveal risks.*

Premortems, Planning Fallacy And Prediction Markets

One idea that's been developed to help reveal hidden risks in a business environment is the premortem, an idea that came from research psychologist Gary Klein.[34] The principle is straightforward: before any major decision goes forward, all the people involved in it gather for a premortem in which they project forward a year after the decision was enacted. The basis for the meeting is that the decision was a disaster, and everyone must explain why.

Klein's work leant on research that showed that this idea of 'prospective hindsight' could improve the identification of the factors that would contribute to the outcome by 30 per cent.[35] The premortem's power lies in making it safe for doubters to speak up. The process can bring to the surface information and issues that might otherwise remain hidden, at least until it's too late. There's no reason why we can't individually do a version of this too – Gary Klein says that the format of the premortem is liberating, and this can be the case for individuals as well as organisations. Look forward a year, imagine it's all gone belly up and ask: What went wrong? In many ways, this is similar to the process that Neal McDonald was practising with his 'what if' games.

It should be no surprise that much of the literature about overconfidence is directed at business and commerce where the damage it can cause can be spectacularly expensive. It doesn't take more than a moment with a search engine to find some examples of the cost-overruns created by overconfidence. Pick your poison, but my favourite is probably the Sydney Opera House: ten years late and *14 times* over budget. Danish planning expert Bent Flyvbjerg argued that there's some necessary self-deception involved in budgets and timelines for the biggest and most political megaprojects, but that excuse isn't going to cut it for most of us in our daily lives.[36]

The planning fallacy is another idea that came from the fertile minds of Amos Tversky and Daniel Kahneman. In his book *Thinking, Fast and Slow* Kahneman says the planning fallacy captures the idea that most human planning is optimistic and unrealistic, often built on the unsteady foundation of a best-case scenario.[37] The solution that he proposed was to research the outcomes of similar cases and use those numbers for a reality check.

It was Bent Flyvbjerg who developed this idea into what's now called reference-class forecasting, estimate validation or more simply benchmarking. The goal is to better predict the outcome of a planned project by looking at a substantial database of previous examples. So, if the goal is to build a brand new, 25-mile strip of six-lane highway, the smart planner should start by finding as many comparable projects as possible and establish how long they took, and what they cost – this is the reference class. Any budget for the new project should be comparable to this reference class (with allowance for all the obvious differences like terrain, labour and materials costs, technical complexity and so on).

The reference class captures the risk involved in a project of that size and complexity – there will be examples that were delivered on time, on budget and to specification. There may even be a handful that overachieve by coming in under budget and quicker than expected. And there will be those that comply with what Flyvbjerg calls the Iron Law of Megaprojects: 'Over time, over budget, under benefits, over and over again.'[38] This distribution of outcomes will allow the savvy planner to adjust their own predictions to align with this spread of possible outcomes.

Professional planners embarking on big projects can now rely on the work of Flyvbjerg and others for databases of information on different reference classes. Those of us embarking on something smaller will have to get more creative in researching the outcomes of whatever project is being undertaken. It might be starting a business, rebuilding a vintage car, sailing around the world, competing in a world championship, or a house renovation – start online, and go down the rabbit hole (in the case of house renovation or building, watch a few episodes of *Grand Designs*). There will be plenty of people who have done it before: finding them and seeing what they have to say about it will help mitigate the risk of overconfidence.

Another good strategy for revealing the weakness of ideas or project planning is the so-called prediction market. Again, the idea is simple enough – a market is opened to trade on future events. Initially these were largely used for the prediction of political events; the Iowa Electronic Markets is an example, allowing people to trade contracts based on election results and economic indicators. More interesting to our goal of better risk awareness is the internal business prediction markets. They use websites or apps to allow employees to bet anonymously on outcomes that are important to the business. The idea is that the cloak of anonymity allows them to bet on what they think will really happen, rather than what they might tell the boss, or the outcome they might hope for.

The oft-cited case, and the example that introduced me to the idea, features US retailer Best Buy. The story was covered in a 2008 *New York Times* article by Steve Lohr.[39] He quoted Jeffrey Severts, the vice-president responsible for Best Buy's prediction markets, explaining how prices in a market on a new Shanghai store dropped from $80 to $40–50. The plunge in value gave executives a heads up on real doubts about the store's prospects held by those doing the work. And, while the management were unable to prevent it opening late, the warning helped arrest the slide. Other major companies also use internal prediction markets to support corporate planning and decision making, including Google, InterContinental Hotels and Hewlett-Packard.

There's another strategy more tailored to informal groups and individuals that does much of the same work by offering an opportunity to gamble on beliefs – winning and losing, especially winning and losing real money, does focus the mind. Annie Duke is a former professional poker player and her book *Thinking in Bets: Making Smarter Decisions When You Don't Have All the Facts* shows how the challenge to put money on an assertion can force a quick recalibration of beliefs. I had some experience of this in an America's Cup team in the early 2000s where there was a strong 'wanna bet' culture – any assertion from 'he'll end up marrying her' to 'that keel will never work' or 'that'll break' could be met with the riposte 'you wanna put some money on that?' And I can tell you, the prospect of losing cold hard cash forces you to reconsider your beliefs and any misguided optimism very quickly.

Staying Afloat

☐   *Formal strategies like premortems, reference-class forecasting and prediction markets can effectively reveal risk.*

Loss Aversion

We can take the lesson from the wanna-bet strategy to one final idea for curtailing overconfidence: utilising our powerful aversion to losses. This is another cognitive bias identified by Daniel Kahneman and Amos Tversky. It's part of prospect theory, the work that won Kahneman the 2002 Nobel Memorial Prize in Economic Sciences (Tversky's early death at 59 meant that he couldn't receive a prize that is not awarded posthumously). Their finding was that our dislike of losing something is about twice as strong as the love of gaining it, and this can help in moderating our overconfidence and making us more risk aware.

This concept is often demonstrated with a simple bet: I'll toss a coin; if it's 'tails' you pay me £10. The question is: How much would I have to offer you for a 'heads' to get you to take the bet? When it's tested on large groups the answer is usually around £20. People need to have a chance to win double what they could lose to take a 50/50 bet like a coin toss. The pain of potential losses is felt powerfully, so think about them: what's at stake if a project or decision goes bad? The idea of the loss could energise plans to fully understand what's being undertaken, to enhance our knowledge of both the project and the limits of our abilities.

Staying Afloat

☐ *We can use our aversion to loss to energise our search for the risks in any venture or decision.*

Making The Horse Drink

We have learnt that we are disposed to be overconfident and the key message has been to work at overcoming our natural inclinations by stopping to think and becoming more aware of risk. In the aftermath of the 1979 Fastnet Race there was an inquiry, and it had many precise, careful recommendations that set offshore racing on to a path of much greater safety. One of the legacies was a set of rules about safety equipment that should be carried by yachts for different types of races, and the manufacturing and quality standards for that safety equipment. These were all very positive outcomes; the problem is that while you can take a horse to water, you can't make it drink.

There were (to push the metaphor too far) a lot of thirsty horses out there in the 1993 Sydney–Hobart Race and it shouldn't be surprising that recent research finds that a culture of overconfidence is contagious. If the environment is overconfident, then there is more chance that the individual will become overconfident.[40] One of the good things about sailing, and one of the reasons I would encourage my children into the sport, is that it builds confidence and independence. There is inherent risk in sailing and negotiating that is one of the things that's so satisfying about it – but you can have too much of a good thing.

We were all fortunate that there was no loss of life in 1993, but the lesson really wasn't learnt. What happened next was painful and tragic. In 1998 another storm hit the Sydney–Hobart fleet, and this time the outcome was much worse. Six sailors died; one of them was a friend, the British Olympian Glyn Charles. Seven yachts were abandoned from the 115-boat fleet and five of them sank. In all, 55 crew members were pulled off boats and out of the water by helicopters and other vessels. This time a Race Review Committee was set up, led by a former Commodore of the Cruising Yacht Club of Australia, Peter Bush.

When the report was published, Bush summarised the key findings and recommendations and one of the points he made was:

> After the 1993 SHYR [Sydney–Hobart Yacht Race], when only 38 out of 104 starters completed the race, the CYCA circulated a questionnaire to competitors. The results found safety equipment was satisfactory but recommended that a series of actions be taken by the Club. These included the improvement of some safety equipment and the skill level and education of sailors in the use of safety equipment and heavy weather sailing. While some of the issues identified in the survey were addressed and implemented, many of the same issues emerged again during the investigations into the 1998 Race. These particularly relate to training and education. The CYCA should have pursued these issues more rigorously.[41]

The 1993 experience was a warning, but there was no loss of life and no formal inquiry, just a questionnaire sent out to sailors. The conclusions of this were not fully implemented, and while the central criticism for this failure was levelled at the CYCA by Peter Bush and his colleagues on the Review Committee, the sailing community as a whole should take some responsibility. We were overconfident. We believed the myths and not the facts. Despite John Quinn for one, trying to get us to see the light.

'I mean, the good thing was that I learnt from the experience, I lived through the experience, and more importantly, it was me that went over the side instead of one of the crew. If it'd been one of the crew and they didn't get through it, Christ, I wouldn't be alive today,' Quinn told me, before adding: 'There was a point when, quite frankly, I should have said, "This is beyond the capacity of this little boat." But you know what it's like, I guess that's what happened . . . Well, I don't guess, I know that's what happened to the guys in the '98 Hobart race, the adrenaline's pumping and you're doing pretty well so you keep on bloody well going, which was a bit crazy.

'I did a lot of talking about it; I did presentations to the club. I avoided the general press . . . but I did a lot of talking at [sailing] clubs . . . I guess the main things were the life jackets, the boat, how important it is to feel . . . not go into conditions that are beyond the capacity of the boat and the crew. That was pretty important. And in retrospect, unfortunately, very few people actually understood it, I suppose, because '98 shouldn't have happened . . . Anyway, it did.'

To mitigate against this sense of overconfidence, the clubs that run the big ocean races like the Sydney–Hobart and the Fastnet now insist on certain experience levels; maybe a number of miles raced together as a crew, along with requiring a percentage of people who have had formal rescue training. It shouldn't be necessary for the clubs to mandate these things, but it is, and we can see why. Sometimes you have to make the horse drink – but don't be that horse.

Staying Afloat

☐ *Overconfidence is contagious – make sure you are not infected.*

Self-knowledge is as important as any other kind and understanding that you may be prone to overconfidence about your abilities (or the abilities of those around you) is a critically useful piece of information. It will help you build your awareness of risk – but this isn't the whole story; awareness isn't enough. We also need knowledge and understanding of risk, because it's a complicated world, with some complicated risks.

CHAPTER 5

Cape Horn

Taking On Cape Horn

It's important to become more risk aware, whether the risk is of falling overboard, getting seasick or not completing a project in time. Improved risk awareness is not going to be enough on its own though. We are always at the mercy of random events (that luck thing again) and in this next story we're going to look at what happens when even the best prepared get caught out by the unexpected. And where better to do that than on the way to Cape Horn?

If there is a single point on the planet that figures in the imagination of every sailor, it is Cape Horn. The source of its notoriety is its physical position. It lies at the southern end of the South American continent, the tip of the Andean finger pointing towards the Antarctic. It reaches through the Roaring Forties and deep down into the Furious Fifties – the Horn is just short of 56 degrees south – squeezing the wind and waves of the South Pacific Ocean into a 500-mile gap between South America and Antarctica called the Drake Passage. Few would willingly sail down into these latitudes, but for almost 300 years – from the first rounding of Cape Horn in 1616 to the completion of the Panama Canal in 1914 – the Drake Passage was the main route from the Atlantic to the Pacific Ocean.

It was named after the buccaneering Englishman, Sir Francis Drake, who had traversed South America via the Strait of Magellan, a channel between the mainland of Chile and Tierra del Fuego, the archipelago of which Cape Horn marks the southern tip. Drake was then forced south and east by a storm, eventually realising that Tierra del Fuego could not be part of the postulated southern continent, and that there must be a way around the bottom of South America. It was left to a Flemish expedition led by Willem Schouten to fully investigate Drake's discovery, rounding and naming the great cape for his hometown, Hoorn, in 1616.

But it's not enough that Cape Horn is lodged firmly in some of the worse weather systems on the planet. The deep water of the South East Pacific Basin shallows into the Drake Passage, and particularly on to the continental shelf that extends south of the Horn. We already know what happens when waves hit shallow water from the Bass Strait. When you add together the weather, the size of the Southern Ocean seas and the shallow water with the fact that primary trading routes ran past the Cape in both directions, it's hardly surprising that the place has the reputation it does.

Despite the opening of the Panama Canal, square riggers continued to trade around the Horn right up until 1949, when a four-masted barque called *Pamir* was the last commercial sailing ship to pass that way.[42] Appropriately, she was under the ownership of Gustaf 'Ploddy' Erikson, the same master mariner who ran the *Moshulu*, the boat that Eric Newby shipped aboard and wrote about in his famous book about the end of commercial sailing, *The Last Grain Race*. After that, Cape Horn was left to the yachtsmen – Conor O'Brien's *Saoirse* had already been first. He departed from Melbourne and successfully rounded the Cape as part of a solo circumnavigation, and his book, *Across Three Oceans*, records his 1923 achievement.

It was 35 years before another yacht, the *Tzu Hang*, would clear customs in Melbourne with Montevideo in mind, and with good reason. It was an obviously risky venture, and the fact that no one had tried it for such a long time speaks volumes to the risks, and the widespread appreciation of them. In the end though, someone did take on Cape Horn and their adventure can tell us a lot about risk awareness.

Tzu Hang

The *Tzu Hang* was a 46-foot-long yacht, originally built in Hong Kong from teak and copper fastenings, and in 1951 it was bought by Beryl and Miles Smeeton. They were the kind of redoubtable British adventurers that belong in *Boy's Own* annuals. Nevil Shute wrote the foreword to Miles Smeeton's account of their voyage to Cape Horn, *Once is Enough*.[43] Shute picks out a telling story – when asked if they had had any trouble crossing the Atlantic, Miles allowed for a three-day period in bad weather when the toughest thing had been keeping their 11-year-old daughter, Clio, to stay at her lessons.

Even before she met Miles, Beryl had done her share of adventuring, travelling on four continents, as likely on foot or horseback as in the comfort of a railway carriage – think rainforests with a pith helmet and an umbrella and you'll get the spirit if not the letter of Miss Beryl Boxer's endeavours. Once they had teamed up, they attempted Tirich Mir – a 25,263-foot peak in the Hindu Kush – with a young Sherpa called Tenzing Norgay (who was, along with Edmund Hillary, the first to climb Mount Everest). Miles and Beryl didn't get to the top of Tirich Mir, but it was the highest altitude achieved by a woman at the time.

Miles was a career army officer, and it was after his service in the Second World War that they took up sailing, beginning with that voyage back across the Atlantic in which Clio had tried to skip school. They were on their way home to Canada after buying the *Tzu Hang* in England. Four years later, in 1955, they sold the farm in British Columbia that had been their home since the war and took off in the boat. Like so many people before and since, they set off across the Pacific. Unlike many others, on reaching Australia they turned back east, sailed down into the high latitudes and attempted to round Cape Horn, which is where their story joins this one.

It all started well enough; Miles Smeeton's descriptions of life on board are idyllic to anyone familiar with the privations of a modern racing boat. They had the fire stoked up like a country pub on a winter weekend, with the cat curled up in front of it.

Beryl Smeeton had taken to knitting jumpers, and her breakfasts of porridge, bacon and eggs, toast and home-made marmalade all washed down with tea would have shamed some British bed-and-breakfast hotels. The bunks were real beds, oatmeal cakes were baked, pudding was cooked at any excuse and the England versus Ireland rugby match was on the radio: blissful really (unless you're prone to seasickness) – until 12 February 1959.

Like *Saoirse*, *Tzu Hang* was a very slow boat to Cape Horn by today's standards; modern monohull offshore racers can reel off one 400-plus-mile day after another – fast enough to almost pick and choose the weather. The Smeetons were hoping for an average of little more than 100 miles a day. At that speed, they were sitting ducks – the proverbial fish in a barrel: whatever weather came along rolled right over the top of them.

By 12 February things had been deteriorating for a while. The Smeetons and their crew mate, John Guzzwell, had reduced the sail of *Tzu Hang* and were trailing over 100 metres of 8-centimetre-thick cable out of the back of the boat. The idea was to slow her down and help keep her in line with the breaking waves. The swell was bigger than they had ever seen before – Miles Smeeton described a seascape that was as different from a normal rough ocean as a winter landscape is to a summer one. There was white foam and spume everywhere, showered like confetti by the breaking crests of the huge waves; it lay over the ocean like Christmas snow. And for the first time since the Tasman Sea, the albatrosses had disappeared – this, it turned out, was ominous.

Miles was in his bunk reading when it happened, his wife on deck at the helm. He described what she saw:

> Close behind her a great wall of water was towering above her, so wide that she couldn't see its flanks, so high and so steep that she knew *Tzu Hang* could not ride over it. It didn't seem to be breaking as the other waves had broken, but water was cascading down its front, like a waterfall.

After that, Beryl Smeeton remembered thinking that she could do nothing else with the helm, then the sensation of falling and no more, until she found herself floating alone, in the Southern Ocean, with just the broken tether of her lifeline for company. It was only when she was lifted by the following wave that she saw the boat just 30 metres away, both masts gone and very low in the water – which was unsurprising, when you consider that a substantial part of the deck (the deckhouse) had been ripped off.

It's arguable whether Miles Smeeton and John Guzzwell were any better off down below. They were hurled around the cabin along with everything that wasn't tied down and quite a bit of what had been. Then the vanishing deckhouse had allowed the cold black sea to pour in, as the *Tzu Hang* was rolled over and under that huge wave. They both surfaced into waist-deep water, awash with cushions, mattresses and books – and one seriously unhappy cat. Miles made it on deck in time to see his wife swim to the remains of the mast, from where she pulled herself to the boat on the still-attached rigging and was hauled back on board by the men.

It seemed that they had only saved Beryl for a few minutes – both men felt the *Tzu Hang* would sink at any moment. Their home was full of water, and there was a two-square-metre hole where the deckhouse had been. Both masts were gone, as were the rudder, dinghies and the cabin skylights. The rigging, guardrails and stanchions were a mass of twisted metal. There was no life raft, and no hope of rescue. The men just stood and stared in despair, but Beryl went for the buckets. She galvanized them all, and their energy was rewarded with luck. John Guzzwell quickly found nails, a hammer and wood in the chaos below. He worked like a demon to make the Tzu Hang watertight again, before another wave took her down for good. Meanwhile, Miles and Beryl bailed, and bailed, and bailed. It took twelve hours to get the water down to the level of the floorboards – had there been any floorboards left. Then, exhausted, they managed to heat some soup, and slept.

The storm abated the following day, and they were fortunate that the sturdy teak hull had not sprung a leak. Slowly, the chaos was cleared – amongst the casualties was the stuffed blue bear they carried as a lucky mascot. Headless, he was thrown overboard, judged to have been no help at all. The boat had been pitch-poled, or somersaulted end-over-end. The evidence was a tin of make-up that had slid forward as the boat sat on its nose, then slipped into a gap in the wooden hull's structure that had opened with the force of the masts hitting the water. As the masts had sheared off at the deck, the load had disappeared, and the make-up tin had become trapped. And there it stayed, proof of their experience and of the forces involved. They built a temporary mast to pull up a small sail on, along with a steering oar. Mostly the *Tzu Hang* sailed herself though, with just changes to the sails to keep her going in a straight line. Enough navigational equipment had survived for them to take position fixes, along with a pilot book for South America and 23 unbroken eggs. It took almost a week for the cat to dry off and recover her good humour.

They made a landfall near the Chilean naval yard in Talcahuano, and with a great deal of effort and patience *Tzu Hang* was rebuilt. Then the Smeetons – alone this time – went back to the south, intending to run into the Chilean Channels and round the tip of South America through the Magellan Strait. There was also a sense that they had some unfinished business down south, and Miles allowed for the possibility of another crack at the Horn if the opportunity appeared. So, they sailed west, offshore, to clear the southerly wind and northerly current that tore up the coast of Chile. And they found another storm. This time, they let *Tzu Hang* lie 'a-hull' – that is, all the sails down and the rudder tied in place to keep the boat facing into the wind. It was a technique that they had used many times previously, but not in the Southern Ocean.

After ten hours of riding out the worst of the storm, the boat was hit by another monster wave and rolled – this time it went sideways, tumbling through a full circle with both the Smeetons down below. Despite the stove breaking free and being thrown around the cabin, neither of them was badly hurt in the carnage. And so, a year after their first crushing defeat by the Southern Ocean, they found themselves in remarkably similar circumstances – a little further north, but a lot closer to the coast. The radio, chronometer and barometer were all gone, and so they had much less in the way of navigation aids. Otherwise, the damage was not as bad, the new deckhouse – built by John Guzzwell in Chile – was cracked and crushed, but still in place, and a stump remained of one of the masts, along with the rudder. Their new dinghy, which they had never even used, was gone, but at least the cat seemed a little less disgusted than the first time. They built another temporary mast, and once again turned back to the north. This time they were insured and used the favourable wind and current to reach Valparaíso, from where *Tzu Hang* was shipped back to England to be repaired.

Staying Afloat

☐ *Rogue waves can come from nowhere and present an unpredictable challenge and risk to any venture.*

Rogue Waves

When it was all done, Miles Smeeton described the encounters with the rogue waves in his book. He then put himself at odds with the received wisdom of the sailing fraternity of the time when he concluded that there are some waves that a yacht; 'will be lucky to survive whatever she does.'[44] These days, such an opinion is mainstream, but prior to *Tzu Hang*'s experiences, yachtsmen had believed that a well-sailed, well-founded yacht was safe in any deep-water sea. They were wrong. There are rogue waves out there that don't seem to belong to any ocean or storm, monstrous waves created by some unknown collusion of the elements. 'With more experience I do not think these waves are so rare,' commented Smeeton.[45]

The Smeetons' experience can teach us something important about risk – we can't know them all. When Miles Smeeton published his book, it joined a building folklore about rogue waves. There are many accounts of huge waves dotted throughout the logbooks and tales of seafarers,[46] one of the most famous being Ernest Shackleton's account in his book about the voyage from Antarctica to South Georgia, *The Voyage of the James Caird.* They were almost swamped by a rogue wave that Shackleton initially mistook for a line of clear sky in the storm. It turned out to be a white-topped wave that was bigger than anything Shackleton had previously seen.

Then there was the *Esso Languedoc*, caught in a storm off South Africa in 1980. Philippe Lijour, the first mate aboard the oil tanker, was fortunate enough to have a camera handy when the breaking crest of a wave roared past, just short of the top of the ship's cranes some 25 metres above the waterline.[47] At the time, Lijour reckoned the *average* wave height to be somewhere between five to ten metres from trough to crest. So where did this monster come from?

Despite the stories and even despite Lijour's photo, oceanographers and meteorologists refused to believe these freak waves existed in any number – their theories simply didn't predict them. Conventional, linear mathematics states that waves should vary in a pattern around the average, called the significant wave height, defined as the mean of the largest third of the waves recorded. According to this analysis, in a storm sea of 12 metres, a 15-metre wave will pop up about once every 25 years. A rogue wave – one defined as twice that of the significant wave height – is theoretically possible, but you'll have to wait about 10,000 years to see one. It seemed to the seafaring community that they were appearing a lot more often than that, but the scientists were about as interested in the anecdotal evidence as they were in reports of the Loch Ness Monster. And that's how things stood when, on New Year's Day 1995, the equivalent of the dead bloated body of Nessie floated up on the shore of the loch.

The winds howling down the North Sea had peaked at hurricane force that afternoon, when what's become known as the New Year Wave roared under the Draupner oil platform just after 3 p.m. It was measured by a laser wave sensor at a maximum height of 25.6 metres – twice the size of the average wave at the time.[48] If that wasn't enough, five years later a British oceanographic research vessel, the RRS *Discovery*, was in the Rockall shipping area, to the west of Scotland. Caught in another horrendous storm, their onboard recorders measured a wave 29.1 metres from the crest to trough.[49] Suddenly, the accounts of walls of water approaching at twice the height of the waves around them were no longer quite so unbelievable – even to the scientists.

The immense extra force of these waves does not have good implications for the safety of ships and oil platforms – their design had always been based on the assumptions of linear mathematics. But the maths was flawed, and the theory shot to hell, so the science community went back to its other mainstay: observation. The European Union started up a project called MaxWave, which used images from satellite radar to 'measure' wave height across broad swathes of ocean.[50] I've used quotes, because there's a fair bit of theory between the radar images and the computed wave heights. Nevertheless, from three weeks of images taken from a period and place when two cruise ships had almost been sunk by rogues, the project measured ten waves bigger than 25 metres – and that kicked the linear maths model into touch once and for all.[51]

We still don't have an explanation for why these waves occur. Counter-currents and the seabed provide known mechanisms for throwing up bigger waves, but that explanation only works in areas like Cape Horn, where an easterly gale can meet the westerly Antarctic circumpolar current across an area of shoaling water. It doesn't tell us why some waves roar under North Sea shipping platforms at twice the height of all those around them. The most likely explanations use the same equations as quantum mechanics – those of non-linear mathematics. It seems that somehow, the energy from several separate waves is being focused into just one or two of these monsters, but until these theories are better refined and established, our best chance of predicting these waves is radar tracking.

The research and results from the MaxWave and subsequent programmes have essentially upended hundreds of years of design assumptions about the conditions that ships will meet at sea. It turns out that a newly built and apparently well-founded, well-prepared ship and crew leaving harbour in 1980 to cross the North Atlantic were in fact not prepared at all to face the conditions they might encounter.

There is a lesson here for our knowledge of risk – it's difficult to properly prepare for and mitigate all the risks when we can't be sure what they are. The Smeetons' experience was completely unforeseeable at the time. A rogue wave – of a size that was believed by the planet's top mathematicians to be physically impossible – appeared from nowhere and rolled their boat, destroyed their home and threatened their lives. Nothing in their experience or anyone else's had given them any expectation of this event, so how could they have been aware of this risk, never mind fully prepared for it?

Staying Afloat

☐ *Rogue waves show us that we cannot have perfect knowledge of all the risks we face.*

Unknown Unknowns And Different Risks

Rogue waves happen in many different fields and areas of our lives. Donald Rumsfeld famously labelled them the unknown unknowns in his reply to a journalist's question in 2002.[52] 'There are known knowns; there are things we know we know. We also know there are known unknowns; that is to say we know there are some things we do not know. But there are also unknown unknowns – the ones we don't know we don't know . . .' because we haven't thought about them.

In the latter category we could include cataclysmic economic events like the US housing market crash in 2008 – believed to be impossible by many, but a handful of people knew better.[53] There are also those sudden, violent outbreaks of war, like the Second World War starting just twenty-one years after the end of the 'war to end all wars'. Tsunamis qualify; so does being bitten by a poisonous snake in central London. Volcanic eruptions and earthquakes don't really qualify – unless they happen in places where science hasn't predicted them. The question we must consider is whether – and how – we can prepare for the unknown unknowns? Is it even possible to prepare for the implausible, improbable or 'impossible'?

We can't plan in any detail for something that we can have no possible knowledge of, an unknown, unexpected and unpredictable event – but we can plan flexibly, we can be open to the potential for the unexpected and we can prepare for it in some ways. The Smeetons and Guzzwell had a hammer, nails and wood on board *Tzu Hang* and that was enough to get them through an experience they had no expectation or even comprehension of when they left Melbourne. This is what we're looking for when we're preparing for something with full appreciation of all the risks, known and unknown – the wood, hammer and nails, the tools that will get us through the unexpected crisis.

There was a cost to the Smeetons in carrying those tools though; *Tzu Hang* was a fixed size and had a limited carrying capacity. So, what did they leave behind that they might have needed in some other crisis? More food? More fresh water? Instead of meeting that rogue wave, they might have been becalmed for an extended and unexpected period. It does happen even at Cape Horn, as we will see in Part 6. The hammer, wood and nails wouldn't have been much use then.

Any endeavour will face many different kinds of risks, and the real world is a world of limited resources. So, while it's a good start to overcome our natural instinct to believe that we're different – that it'll be all right on the night – there is a lot more to risk awareness. We've already seen that there can be risks that no one has even imagined yet. This takes us into the territory of assessing risk: the balancing of resources – of time, energy and money – against an array of different risks (known, known unknowns and unknown unknowns) that might overwhelm any given endeavour.

Staying Afloat

☐ *Learn to assess the likelihood and impact of different risks, to respond correctly and create the best chance of success.*

A sound knowledge of risk and how to assess it is one of the keys to success in life. It's the knowledge we need to make good decisions. Ironically, it's also one of the most difficult things to do; not least because it involves knowing the future . . . and because it involves maths. Fortunately, in many instances of our social activity as humans (as opposed to those occasions when we go up against nature) it's not necessary to assess risk perfectly; it's enough to just do it a tiny bit better than most people. It's like the old story of the bear chasing two hikers through the woods. It's not necessary to out-run the bear, just out-run the other guy.

Part 2: Staying Afloat Summary

☐ *We have a high capacity for missing or ignoring the things that are going to try to hurt us.*
☐ *If it's not possible to be great, at least be organised, be prepared – you will need it if you run out of luck.*
☐ *We are all capable of overconfidence – believing that you are not is being overconfident.*
☐ *It takes time, effort and practice to become more risk aware.*
☐ *Build risk awareness by building habits that will reveal risks.*
☐ *Formal strategies like premortems, reference class*

forecasting and prediction markets can effectively reveal risk.
- *We can use our aversion to loss to energise our search for the risks in any venture or decision.*
- *Overconfidence is contagious – make sure you are not infected.*
- *Rogue waves can come from nowhere and present an unpredictable challenge and risk to any venture.*
- *Rogue waves show us that we cannot have perfect knowledge of all the risks we face.*
- *Learn to assess the likelihood and impact of different risks to respond correctly and create the best chance of success.*

PART THREE – PREDICTION

No one can see the future perfectly, but some can see it better than others

It is difficult to make predictions, especially about the future.

KARL KRISTIAN STEINCKE, FARVEL OG TAK: MINDER OG MENINGER

CHAPTER 6

Decisions and Consequences

Fight Or Flight?

If we want to make good decisions in our life, we need to understand and assess the risks. Many different kinds of knowledge are needed to do this well: if we knew the future there would be no risk, we could take every decision knowing the outcome. We *can't* know the future, but for many of the decisions we make in life we have to act as though we do. Part 3 is about that process – finding and trusting the knowledge we need to help us understand risk and make decisions for an unknowable future.

In this chapter I want to focus on the importance of knowing and fully understanding the consequences of a decision, because this is often enough for us to make a choice. When we know and understand all the possible gains and losses, the upsides and downsides, it will sometimes reveal that one of the outcomes is completely unacceptable. In these cases, the decision becomes very simple. Other times, an assessment of the consequences may not weigh quite so heavily but may still tip the balance firmly one way.

I want to start this exploration with a story about the different choices made by different skippers at a crucial moment in a race. The story is about the Volvo Ocean Race, a race around the world that took place across 2017–18. After I discovered that my weakness for motion sickness prevented me from racing around the world in sailboats, I started doing a lot of commentating on the races instead – particularly writing blogs on strategy (ground-breaking in 1997–8 and becoming passé by 2017–18). In the latter case, I was writing a weekly strategic review for the Volvo Ocean Race website. So, I watched this incident unfold in detail, in real time and in dangerous weather conditions – British sailor John Fisher was tragically lost overboard from one of these boats later in the race in very similar conditions.

The Volvo Ocean Race always consisted of several stages (or 'legs'), with breaks (or 'stopovers') for rest, repair and recuperation in between. The third leg of the 2017–18 race was sailed between Cape Town and Melbourne, from the southern tip of Africa to the south coast of Australia. A quick glance at a globe will show that the shortest straight-line route between these two points goes directly through the Southern Ocean, around a section of Antarctica.

The westerly storm track marks the path of powerful weather (or low-pressure) systems as they circulate west-to-east around the South Pole, and the fastest route to Melbourne followed the storm track around Antarctica. The closer to Antarctica the boats went, the fewer miles they had to sail, but the further south they ventured, the higher the risk of a collision with icebergs large and small. It's an accident waiting to happen, and so when technology gave race officials the opportunity to make it safer, they took it.

Icebergs are now tracked by satellite as they break off the ice sheets of Antarctica and start to drift north. Information on the position of the ice in the Southern Ocean has allowed race officials to set exclusion zones (the Ice Exclusion Zone or IEZ) to prevent the boats from going too far south, thus keeping them away from the ice. If a boat crossed into the IEZ and ended up to the south of it, it would get a penalty. The seriousness of the offence would be judged by the race's International Jury, depending on the circumstances of the infraction. The Exclusion Zone was there to keep them safe from the ice, but it was also an element in the strategic game: the 'pitch' now had an extra border.

It was 12 December when the storm that caused all the problems started to appear on the weather maps; at this stage the whole fleet was in the storm track, heading east and going fast. The new weather system was predicted to form behind them, to the west of the fleet's position. The forecasts had the storm growing with a spectacular speed and violence; by the 13th it would be a fully formed monster with winds up to 65 knots at its centre. It would come at them from the north-west; if they held their course it would chase them down and run them over, bringing winds in excess of 50 knots. There were seven boats in the fleet and each of them had to make the same decision – fight or flight?

I mentioned in Chapter 5 – Cape Horn that a modern ocean racing boat is fast enough to pick and choose the weather that it sails in – and this is a good example. Flight was an option; unlike *Tzu Hang*, these boats weren't just rolling around waiting for the storm to hit. Modern satellite communications and weather-forecasting technology enabled all seven boats to know that the storm was forming, and the VO65 boats that they were sailing had the speed to get them out of the way. So, who chose flight and who chose to stay and fight, and why?

The navigators had computer software that could calculate what's called the optimal (or fastest) route. The optimal route is calculated from knowing the boat's straight-line speed in different conditions and the weather predicted by the forecast. And the optimal route took them south to the very edge of the IEZ and into the heart of the storm. Once they got there they would ride with the storm, executing one manoeuvre after another to keep as far south as possible, and stay out of the Ice Exclusion Zone. These manoeuvres are called gybes, and they are one of the most dangerous things you can do on a sailboat. In this case the crews were going to have to gybe over and over again in storm conditions.

I'm going to skip right over the reasons why gybes are required (leaving them safely buried in the physics of aero- and hydrodynamics) and state as a fact that a gybe entails swapping the wind from one side of the boat to the other, moving the sails across the boat, and so creating a series of zig-zags towards the destination. Each zig or zag involves turning the stern (back) of the boat through what's called the eye of the wind (so the wind is momentarily blowing up the centreline of the boat). The sails all swap sides in this moment, resetting on the new side. The boat then resumes straight-line sailing with the wind blowing at 20 to 30 degrees to the centreline, but on the other side of the boat.

The dangerous part of gybing in lots of wind is swapping the sails from one side to the other. When sailing with the wind blowing on to the back of the boat, the sails are all eased out almost as far as they will go. So, they have to be pulled on to the centreline of the boat and let back out on the new side. At all times the wind is pushing on the sails, and so if this process isn't controlled, then the wind will fling them across the boat with a speed and violence that has to be experienced to be believed. In this moment, the force can snap rigging, tear sails, break the supporting battens that help hold the sail in the right shape, damage or bring down the mast and throw people overboard.

So, while the prediction was that the southern route would be quicker, this wasn't the whole story. The computer programs weren't assessing the risk of a mistake in a gybe and the potential for damage (or worse) that might be caused. They are a bit like those frictionless surfaces so beloved of secondary school Newtonian physics problems – an important piece of information was missed out. Following the advice of the computer program greatly simplified the problem – the southern route to the IEZ was a lot quicker so that was the way to go – but it ignored the potential consequences: the upsides and downsides of the decision.

The other option was flight, to get the hell out of Dodge, to head north where conditions were forecast to be much less intense. It was a detour – more miles, so, everything else being equal, it would take longer. And going north would also take a boat into more moderate conditions. Well, that was the idea after all; the point was to find less wind and avoid the storm. But once the storm had passed by there was a risk of suffering significantly less wind and getting slowed even further. However, there was a much smaller chance of damage.

Choices

There were seven boats in the fleet. Two of them chose flight and took the opportunity to get north before the storm hit them. *Turn the Tide on Plastic* was the first to make the move. The boat was a late and underfunded entry put together by Dee Caffari. Now Caffari is no slouch (she was the first woman to sail alone around the world going both west-about and east-about), but *Turn the Tide on Plastic*'s entry had come together at the very last minute, and they were still announcing crew just weeks before the start. It was also a very inexperienced group, mostly consisting of rookies and sailors under 30 years old. Dee Caffari understood that her team lacked experience in those boats and in those conditions and the potential consequences of that. She headed north to avoid the worst of the storm.

The second boat to go north only did so after their first taste of the bad weather. This was *Team Sun Hung Kai/Scallywag*, the first ever Hong Kong entry into the race. It was led by David Witt, a skipper with a lot less experience in the Southern Ocean than Caffari. It was his second race, the first being almost 20 years earlier. In between he had been successful on the professional 18-foot skiff circuit in Australia. The skiffs are very light and powerful boats, with just three crew. In the skiff, Witt had a reputation as a wizard in strong breeze downwind – a reputation helped along by a famous video of him dominating a race in extreme conditions in Auckland Harbour[54].

Witt had then moved on to bigger boats, done lots of Sydney–Hobart Races, and eventually moved to Hong Kong to skipper the 100-foot 'super maxi' *Scallywag*. It was this team that he'd brought to the Volvo Ocean Race. Despite a lack of personal experience leading a boat in those conditions and several young and relatively inexperienced crew, it still wasn't much of a surprise when Witt – just as famous for his bravura as his sailing skills – initially chose fight over flight, staying south as the storm approached. They stuck it out until 14 December, from which point they chose a more northerly strategy.

In both cases, the decision to go north feels like the correct one. There was a very small upside to the southerly route for these boats. It was very unlikely that they would do better than sixth or seventh even if they had chosen to stay south. They could get that result by going north with much less risk of damage, and they might pick up a place if any of the boats that stayed south suffered damage in the storm.

The opposite was true for the top three boats on the overall scoreboard. They had previously taken all three podium places in the first two legs. They were all contenders for the main prize and so the downside of the northern route was much greater. It would likely relegate them to a fifth place and drop them from contention for the overall lead. They also had more reason to think they could handle the storm and avoid the worse consequences.

The three boats were *Dongfeng Race Team*, *MAPFRE* and *Vestas 11th Hour Racing*. The first two had been the first and third boats to launch their campaigns and both had raced in the previous edition with much the same leadership and management. They had talented and very experienced sailors onboard and had spent plenty of time training. If anyone could have had confidence in their ability to weather the Southern Ocean storm that hit them, it was *MAPFRE*, *Dongfeng* and, to a slightly lesser extent, *Vestas 11th Hour Racing*.

This was how it played out – *MAPFRE* and *Dongfeng* both stayed in the south, executed two days of a masterclass in high-wind sailing and, once the storm had passed, led the fleet by over 50 miles. *Vestas 11th Hour Racing* played it a little more conservatively, repositioning slightly to the north until the cold front – the thing that defined the leading edge of the storm – had passed. Once the worst was over, they moved back to the south to take a very solid third place with a lead of over 100 miles from the fourth-placed boat. In all three cases it was clearly the right decision to stay south; they were all contesting the overall lead so the consequence – the downside – of going north was serious.

They also had good reason to believe that they could manage the conditions in the south and avoid a bad outcome.

This left two boats: *Team Brunel* and *Team AkzoNobel*. Neither crew lacked experience. Skippering *Team Brunel* was Bouwe Bekking, who was on his eighth attempt at winning the race. And while *Team AkzoNobel's* skipper Simeon Tienpont was a first-timer in the role, he had won a couple of America's Cups and been around the world twice before. Tienpont's crew also included Chris Nicholson, a six-time world champion in high-speed skiff classes and a two-time Olympian for Australia, who counted a second-place finish as skipper amongst his six previous Volvo Ocean Races.

The crews of *Team AkzoNobel* and *Team Brunel* nevertheless faced a more difficult choice than the others. On the one hand they had every right to regard themselves as peers of those on *Dongfeng Race Team* and *MAPFRE*. On the other hand, *Team Brunel*'s crew had sailed together a lot less than those two boats', while *Team AkzoNobel* had management issues that had disrupted their preparation. The navigator onboard *Team AkzoNobel* was British-born Jules Salter. He was on his fourth race around the planet. One of the world's top offshore racing navigators, he had abandoned a legal career to become a professional sailor. He already had a second place and a win in his previous three races, and after missing the 2013–14 race, he had returned in 2017–18 for a fourth go-around.

Salter explained how the team had been unsettled in their preparation. 'There were two management groups trying to work out how they were going to run the team and they couldn't quite see eye to eye on how it was going to work.' It was a diplomatic description of an argument that had ended with the Dutch Arbitration Institute. 'In the end the negotiations impacted on the team and didn't allow us the best preparation . . . It was ultimately resolved, but it didn't get resolved soon enough [for me] to start the race. I didn't do the first leg. The boat did, and they did all right; Brad [Jackson, originally a watch captain] was made skipper and then didn't continue [once Tienpont resumed control], and Joca [Signorini, also watch captain] didn't continue. So, there was quite a big crew change: you lose both your watch captains a couple of days before the start [in Cape Town] . . . You can't instantly replace those two people . . . If you look at this race again and again, no one has thrown the boat together six months before the start and gone out and done really well.'[55]

Despite this inauspicious background, *Team AkzoNobel* and *Team Brunel* both decided to stay south on what was – in the view of the weather-routing software – the optimal course. By 14 December, *AkzoNobel* was sailing fast, riding the storm with winds gusting more than 40 knots. They were about to meet the man-made, invisible limit of the Ice Exclusion Zone and they were going to have to gybe. The crew on *Team AkzoNobel* had known that this moment would come – they knew that the southern route meant they would have to execute several of these gybes in very difficult conditions. They had backed themselves to do it and now the moment had arrived. What would be the consequences?

The Gybe

The preparation began about 07:00 UTC on 14 December 2017 and it started with navigator Jules Salter. He had been monitoring the boat's progress towards the IEZ and he felt that they were getting close enough. 'We were trying to do the gybe as close to the ice gate as possible. So, you're doing twenty-five knots towards it and closing a bit obliquely – but it only needs a slight shift in the wind and suddenly you're sailing straight at it and you've got a lot less time. So, you want to plan a bit of an extra factor in there, just in case you can't complete the gybe the first time,' Salter explained.

'There are various techniques to gybe a VO65 in full-on breeze. You basically need everyone on deck. So, to gybe takes an hour – you've got to decide when to gybe and then you've got to get everyone up [on deck]. It's starting to get cooler down there so everyone has to get their gear on. It's quite early in the leg . . . so people probably haven't slept or got into their Southern Ocean rhythm or routine yet. So, there's that to allow for – it takes a good hour to do it.' Meanwhile, the clock was ticking and the IEZ was getting closer. 'It was thirty-five to forty [knots of wind speed] with maybe some lulls of thirty – so it was pretty windy. The sea state was starting to get bad. There were no big waves; the problem was trying to get the right wave, one in your direction . . .'

There are a couple of things that can help to make the gybe safe – firstly, it's critical to pull the sails in as the boat turns, so that they are always under control. This limits the distance they can be flung across the boat and stops them slamming into the mast and the cables that hold it up. The other thing is speed. Remember that the boat is travelling with the wind, so the faster it goes, then the lower the wind speed felt by the sails. If you drive down a road at 30 miles an hour with a 30-mph tail wind, then the wind felt by those aboard the car – the apparent wind – will be zero.

This would be the perfect moment to gybe: when the boat is moving as fast as the wind, and the apparent wind is zero. At this moment the sails can be pulled across the boat and let out on the new side with almost no effort and no risk. How do you get the boat going that fast, or at least as fast as possible in a big breeze in the Southern Ocean? Surf a wave. The trick to a good, safe gybe in these conditions is finding just the right wave to surf, so that the gybe can be carried out with the boat accelerating down the wave face. This is not easy to pull off – first the wave has to be caught, then it has to be moving in the right direction to allow the gybe to happen on the wave without prematurely ending the surf. 'We had a couple of goes trying to find the right wave,' explained Salter, and each time they failed to complete the gybe, the psychological pressure built a little more as they roared towards the IEZ.

And so it was that with all nine of the crew in position and on deck, *Team AkzoNobel* finally went for the gybe. It always starts with the man or woman on the wheel. They have to make the call on when to start, they have to believe they've caught the wave, that they will have the speed when they need it. 'We were a bit unlucky with the wave, I think there was a gust at the time so we couldn't steer it exactly as we wanted to steer it,' said Salter.

The boat didn't pick up speed, and the wave went by unridden like some clean-up set on Hawaii's North Shore. At this point there is sometimes a choice – the driver might be able to back out, keep going straight. They had already done that a couple of times, missing two waves and bailing out to try again. Now they were running out of time and space. The IEZ was rushing up on them, and the man on the wheel decided to commit anyway . . . and, for a moment, it looked all right.

And then the mainsail came crashing over, all the power of the sail was transferred from one side to the other in a fraction of a second, threatening to take the mast with it. It was a piece of cable or rigging called the running backstay (or runner) that both saved them and hurt them. There are two runners, one on each side of the boat, and they provide support for the mast when sailing downwind. During the gybe one must be released and the other pulled on – with the new one coming tight before the old one can be released, or the rig can lean forward and bend or break.

The mainsail on *Team AkzoNobel* slammed across the boat before the runners had been swopped and it hit the one that should have been released. It was this impact that did most of the damage: breaking the carbon-fibre battens that ran across the sail. At the same time the leverage of the battens caused the track (which holds the sail to the mast) to break away from the main section of the spar.

The mainsail was also trapped against the runner, and nowhere near its proper setting. This had another immediate knock-on effect, changing the delicate balance of forces between the sails, the rudder and the keel, throwing them off-kilter. The boat started to lean over and the newly asymmetric shape of the hull flowing through the water added a further force, pushing the boat more out of whack, adding more heel which quickly took the rudder out of the water – making the steering useless.

It was a vicious circle and the boat skidded on to its side, with a torrent of white water rushing down the deck. Everyone hung on for a few grim seconds in which anything could have happened. Anything could have broken; anyone could have been hurt or washed overboard. And everyone was trying to ease, pull, push or otherwise wrestle whichever part of the boat they were closest to that would bring it back under control.

'There're seven reasons or ten reasons why it tripped out,' said Salter. 'Maybe we should have been more patient [and waited] for the biggest, biggest wave and the best, best surf, rather than trying to hurry into it, but we'd had two or three goes already and it's hard to be patient in that wind speed. There was another cloud coming that we didn't want to gybe in front of ... All the usual reasons for not doing a good gybe whether it's in your Feva [dinghy] or a VO65. If you can go fast enough before the gybe, then it doesn't matter where anything is . . . you get away with it.'

It could have been a lot worse. They could easily have lost the mast in the manoeuvre, or a man overboard – it wouldn't have been the first time in this race that a gybe had been disastrous. However, it was still bad enough. 'On another day we might have just got away with it, we might only have broken a little bit of track and one batten, and thought, Oh, that was a bit on the edge, and off we go. I've done that before many times,' said Jules Salter. Instead, a crippled *Team AkzoNoble* limped into Melbourne in last place, three days and almost eight hours after the leader, and immediately started the next race – against time, to get the boat repaired and ready before the start of the next leg.

Consequences

Team Brunel fared much better than *Team AkzoNobel* – they kept it together through the storm and finished in fourth place less than two hours behind *Vestas 11th Hour Racing* and just over a day ahead of *Team Sun Hung Kai/Scallywag*. There will be no problem with hindsight bias here, we have two decisions made by the crews aboard two separate boats in very similar circumstances, with polar opposite outcomes. We are not going to be over-influenced by the outcome in assessing the decision. Both outcomes occurred. So, we must concentrate on an assessment of the process. They both chose the fastest, southerly route; one came fourth, the other seventh and last.

If we weigh potential outcomes I think there's an argument to be made that both boats made the wrong decision and took an unnecessary risk; it worked out for *Team Brunel*, but that still doesn't make it the right decision – and here's why. I don't think the crews fully set what might be gained by their choice against what could be lost. In both cases, the potential losses of going south outweighed the potential gains.

The upside of staying south was limited – could either crew realistically hope to beat the much better drilled and prepared *Dongfeng Race Team*, *MAPFRE* and *Vestas 11th Hour Racing* in those conditions? Maybe later in the race, yes, but on this first excursion into the Southern Ocean it was very unlikely that they would suddenly make the jump to the podium that had eluded both of them in either of the first two legs.

So, if there was little to no chance of a third place or better, why not go north with the other two – *Turn the Tide* and *Scallywag*? They could expect to beat both of them on that same northern route, which meant that they would finish fifth at worst, with every chance of moving higher should any of the leaders have a problem or break down in the storm. And if both *Team Brunel* and *Team AkzoNobel* had chosen to go north they would have been racing for exactly the same fourth place that they were effectively contesting in the south, but in much milder conditions with much less risk of damage or worse.

The potential downside of staying south and incurring damage outweighed the upside, which was a potential gain of just one or two places. The upside of going north and having a high confidence that they would complete the leg outweighed the downside of losing just one or two places. When I put this to *Team AkzoNobel*'s navigator Jules Salter he wasn't convinced . . . or maybe he was.

'There is a balance – I think that showed in the next Southern Ocean leg where we went a very similar way again and we got to a point where we thought we're just going to back off a bit here because we know what damage can do . . . We did and we dropped back a bit, not a big distance but fifty or a hundred miles behind the leading group, and on the approach to Cape Horn we gradually caught them all up again. *MAPFRE* broke the mast track and the mainsail . . . and *Vestas* lost the rig soon after that as well. So, you get yourself up to third by doing that. It's just picking the right time to play that strategy – and offshore sailing is so much about that.'

In Leg 7 (the one that Salter was referencing), *Team AkzoNobel* used the strategy that I'm suggesting. They weighed the small gain of pushing as hard and going as fast as they could against the potential downsides of damage to boat or people. On this occasion they decided to ease off, and they gained against those that kept pushing and ended up damaged. Balancing the downside against the upside is a sound approach to assessing the risk and making the decision, and often it's the only thing that you need to consider.

Sometimes the potential downside is so great that it's completely unacceptable and makes the decision really easy. This is the case with the insurance[56] of very valuable possessions, like yachts, or houses. Our family home represents well over 50 per cent of our accrued wealth. If anything were to happen to it, such as fire, flood or storm damage, it would be a financial disaster that we would probably never recover from. So, we insure it. The potential downside of not having house insurance (losing the house) vastly outweighs the downside (the cost of a few hundred pounds) of having it. The likelihood of something happening to the house is not relevant. The chances of something bad happening are not zero, and that's enough for us to feel compelled to insure the house because the consequences of losing it are too great.

Staying Afloat

☐ *When faced with a decision about the future, always assess the possible gains and losses first – this might be all you need to make your choice.*

Expected Value

We cannot expect every decision to be driven by the consequences of one of the potential downsides or upsides. Often, we need a more analytical approach that will allow us to weigh the potential outcomes against each other. There are formal decision-making systems that provide tools to do this, and they go all the way back to ideas developed in the seventeenth century.[57] The theory of expected value assesses the value of all the possible outcomes for each decision, and multiplies them by the likelihood (the probability) of those outcomes. The results of each of these multiplications (Value (V) x Probability (P)) are then added together to give the expected value (E) for that decision.[58]

Once all the expected values have been calculated, then the decision with the highest expected value is the one to go for . . . and while it's not always that simple, as we will see, the concept of expected value is very useful in all sorts of situations.

Before we look at examples though, we need some understanding of the maths that underlies all numerical risk assessment. This is the maths of probability: the measure of the likelihood of any given event happening. If you took secondary school maths, then you might remember the basic method of calculating probability. The easiest example is flipping a coin. There are two sides to a coin – the head and the tail in regular parlance – and when we flip it there is (unless the coin has been tampered with) an exactly equal chance of both outcomes.

Let's say someone has offered us a £50 bet that rests on the toss of a coin, and we've chosen heads. We want to know the probability of a head; what is the likelihood of a head being the outcome? It's calculated as the number of outcomes that constitute a head – which is just one – divided by the total number of possible outcomes – which is two (head or a tail). So, the probability of flipping a head and winning £50 is 1/2 or, written as a decimal, 0.5.

We can convert the fraction or decimal into a percentage just by multiplying it by 100, so expressed as a percentage the answer is 50 per cent. We often see the likelihood of something happening described as a percentage: a 10 per cent chance of rain today, or a 1 per cent chance of developing an illness.

A slightly more complex case is rolling an odd number with a regular die. There are six numbers on a die (1, 2, 3, 4, 5, 6), so six possible outcomes, and this time there are not one but three outcomes that would give us what we want: an odd number (rolling a 1, 3 or a 5). So, the probability of rolling an odd number is 3/6 or a 1/2, or again as a percentage it's 50 per cent.

We can use simple probabilities like these to calculate expected values and assess the strategic choices for *Team AkzoNobel* and *Team Brunel* as the storm approached. A simple analysis might look at three possible outcomes: the probability of them racing hard all the way to the finish; suffering moderate damage; or suffering more serious damage and not finishing the leg or starting the next. We can assign a probability to each of these outcomes for both the northern and southern route, as well as using the points available for each position in the leg as the outcome. If we do that – and make some assumptions about the choices made by the rest of the fleet – an expected-value analysis for the northern route scores 5.54 points compared to 5.0 points on the southern route.[59]

Any decision based on expected value would be in favour of the northern route, supporting the earlier conclusion. Now, maybe others would score the probabilities of damage differently – and it's fun to play around with the numbers to see how the outcome changes – but there's no doubt that the analysis helps to clarify the choices.

An expected-value analysis can also help with some of the issues of overconfidence and planning that we came across in Part 2. Sailing is a very complex sport and one of the big problems facing any race-boat campaign – be it an America's Cup team or a small keelboat shooting for a top ten at the national championship – is that there are more ways to improve performance than there is time or money to pursue.

This problem can also be approached using expected value, calculating an expected cost for each unit of performance gain. The process starts by creating a list of the performance projects that are under consideration – let's say that they are practising for a weekend, buying new sails, or hiring a coach for the season. We could then calculate the expected value by assessing the value of these projects for each of the possible outcomes and assigning them a probability to complete the calculation.[60] The expected-value approach tackles the issue of balancing resources, it's a way to balance risk that incorporates the investment of time and money, and it can be useful in revealing the trade-offs involved in any decision. It's a great way of tackling the problem of how resources are utilised, as the whole team can be brought into the discussion on the performance gains to be made, their cost and the likelihood of them being fulfilled.

Now, this is not the whole story; for instance, there's no allowance for how these gains will degrade with time. The benefits from the new sails and the coach may well last longer than the practise.[61] High-risk, cheap options with big potential gains also test this analysis since the risk element isn't fully captured. There might be a new keel shape available at low cost with great potential performance gains, but it also might not be faster at all – if there was an 80 per cent risk of failure, but a similar cost-effectiveness ratio to the option of running a practice weekend, which would you choose?

The subjectiveness of the risk to the individual is what is lost. Let's say I've helped a crazy billionaire yacht owner win a few big races and she offers me one of her two $100-million yachts.[62] I can accept the offer and walk away with the keys. Or she offers a gamble: she will flip a coin and if it comes up heads then she'll give me both $100-million yachts. If it comes up tails I get nothing. If we work out the expected value for each case it is exactly the same, and so theoretically I could take either. However, most of us would prefer to take the guaranteed $100-million yacht, rather than risk walking away with nothing. It's the risk that's not being captured in these examples.

The theory of expected utility seeks to take this into account by substituting utility for value, where utility is a measure of the subjective preference of the outcome – and that will vary with the individual's circumstances. Someone with $20 billion in the bank may well prefer to take the coin toss with a chance to win $200 million or nothing. The utility of $100 million will feel very different to them, compared to someone who has little or nothing. The problem is putting a number on this subjective utility – risk can be an emotional subject.

There are going to be difficulties using either expected value or expected utility to help with our decision making. In the first case there's the difficulty of deriving realistic probabilities for the expected outcomes (no surprise, since we are trying to predict the future), and the problem of not fully capturing the risk in the decision process. And in the second case there's the difficulty of making good judgements about the subjective utility of an outcome.

So, in Chapter 7 we're going to look in more detail at our attempts to model outcomes and derive their probabilities using data sets and computers, before moving on to more general issues with how predictions are presented and used in society. And then in Chapter 8 we'll tackle the issues surrounding our perception of risk, and how it can distort even the best-intentioned assessment of an outcome.

All of this is why, when it comes to the big decisions, I try to weigh the outcomes against each other first, balancing the upsides against the downsides of each choice in the hope that one or the other will weigh so heavily that it will make the decision for me – because if it doesn't, I know it's only going to get more complicated after that . . .

Staying Afloat

- ☐ *Expected value and expected utility can be useful concepts but should be used cautiously.*

CHAPTER 7

Predicting the Future

Probability, Prediction And Understanding Risk

It's no coincidence that most of us gained our understanding of probability through rolling a die; the roots of modern mathematical theories of probability lie in the analysis of simple games of chance like flipping coins and playing dice. This is the way most of us think about a probability when we see it – as akin to the chances of flipping a head or a tail. This was just the start though; the usefulness of probability quickly became obvious beyond the gaming tables, particularly when it was allied to concepts like expected value and expected utility. It should come as no surprise that the use of probability has been significantly extended from these simple games, as we seek to quantify the likelihood of our predictions about the future.

One of the biggest developments that has come with the staggering increases in computer power over the last few decades has been the advances in data science – 'big data' as it's been dubbed – and its use to make predictions. There's always been a powerful need for prediction, beginning with soothsayers and crystal ball readers, and no one should be surprised at the way that big data has developed to fill our need to know what the future holds. The collection and analysis of huge data sets has flooded our lives with probabilistic predictions of outcomes for every decision from the trivial to the existential.

Should I take a coat with me today?
Check the forecast on your smartphone or laptop and discover there's a 10 per cent chance of rain.

Should I buy a house now with the deposit I have saved, or wait

and save more?
Search the internet for 'should I buy a house now' and you will find any number of websites with predictions on what the housing market is going to do over the next year.

Should I take statins?
Once again, search for the answer to that question on the internet and you will find that, for instance, the British Heart Foundation suggests 'If your 10-year risk of having a heart attack or stroke is greater than 10 per cent, you will be asked to consider taking a statin.'[63] That's a prediction based on data analytics, and the advice relies on more data analysis to predict your 10-year risk.

All of the answers to these questions rely on an algorithm, or what's also called computer modelling. I'm going to use the terms interchangeably; they are just names for some – admittedly often complex – maths that calculates an outcome based on the best science available in whatever area we are trying to predict.

While we can't all be data scientists, we all need to understand the output from the big data industry. It really does pay to know where the numbers come from, what they can say with authority and what they can't – and in this respect the education of the majority has nowhere near kept up with the advances and insights of the specialists who work in this area.

If there is one piece of knowledge that we need in order to make better decisions, it's a better understanding of the flood of data predicting risk. A basic knowledge of how these data sets are collected and analysed, and how the conclusions are reached and presented, is absolutely fundamental to good risk assessment and to making good decisions in the modern world. It's not necessary to be a data scientist, just to understand what it is that they are doing, and what they mean when they present their results. And that's what I want to look at in this chapter.

Modelling Everything

It's hard to open a news website without seeing at least one home-page story about algorithms and computer models. People are using the power of computers to build mathematical models to describe and predict all sorts of systems from the weather to the transmission of disease. And now, with the development of machine learning and artificial intelligence (AI) we are using the computer models to allow the machines to make decisions about everything from who gets a bank loan to who gets probation.

There are many issues with this, including ethical issues, but I want to stick with the things that we need to know to understand what these models are doing, when they are doing it well, and when they are doing it badly. The first point already came up with the navigators and skippers in Chapter 6, deep in the Southern Ocean and picking a route through the storm to Melbourne. The central tool they had at their disposal was the weather-routing software that I described in the previous chapter. The output of this software, the computer model, was an optimal route for their boat based on their starting position and the weather forecast.

We've seen how the weather-routing software was just calculating the fastest route. It was not doing an expected-value calculation. It wasn't saying we can expect 5.2 points on the scoreboard if we take the northern route, and 4.6 points if we take the southern route. Instead, it just shows the fastest way to sail from A to B based on the parameters that it's given (weather and accompanying boat performance). It doesn't do any more for a very good reason – in the limited world view of the weather-routing software there is no uncertainty about getting to the destination.[64] There's no chance of a boat-breaking crash. It doesn't take sufficient account of the cost of the manoeuvres in the real world. It just assumes that each gybe or tack can be executed with zero loss – and the crew of *Team AkzoNobel* would beg to differ.

And that's the first point I want to make about modelling – the algorithms very rarely, if ever, take everything into account. The first question that needs to be asked when presented with the output from any algorithm that's predicting the future is: What's missing?

Staying Afloat

- ☐   *Consider whether a prediction includes the influence of everything that might affect the outcome.*

Mature Science

The weather forecast is probably the most familiar example of computer modelling and algorithms in our daily lives, and I'm sure we're all aware of its practical limitations. Who's not left the house without an umbrella or jacket and needed both before the end of the day? There are many good and well-understood reasons why weather forecasts are inaccurate. These throw light on more systemic problems with many of the other things we try to model.

Firstly, the atmosphere is an incredibly complex system with many different variables: temperature, pressure, humidity, wind speed, wind direction and so on. The models must combine all these variables in complex calculations based on our understanding of the physics that controls their interaction. Unfortunately, we still don't completely understand all the physics of the atmosphere. We're going to look at the status of scientific knowledge in a lot more detail in Part 4, but for now we should just remember to ask the question about how well developed the science is that lies behind the prediction.

Staying Afloat

- ☐   *Always ask if the science behind a prediction is well developed and effective.*

Data Accuracy

The next point is that even if we did completely understand all the processes in the weather down to the molecular or atomic level, we still couldn't model and predict the weather perfectly because we don't have enough data, enough detail in the measurement of the weather when we start the model running. We are getting better at this, with satellites, weather balloons, aircraft and drones all adding to the traditional stalwarts of global meteorological data collection – the land stations – but it's still a far from complete picture. And if we don't know the full set of starting conditions, and know them accurately, then our predictions will have limited accuracy.

It is generally true of data that the bigger the data set the better. Any experiment repeated a thousand times is more likely to provide a useful answer than one repeated five times. However, resources are not infinite, and no one is going to collect data indefinitely. So, data sets will be limited, and we have to decide whether the size of any particular data set is sufficient for the analysis to be credible.

It's also true that there are many more ways to generate bad data than there are to get good data. If instruments are involved, they need to be of an adequate quality, properly calibrated and maintained. If people are involved then anything that they report themselves, by filling in a form or survey, is less reliable than that obtained by experiment. The people that collect the data may imprint their own biases on it in the way that they frame experiments or survey questions. And experiments with people are better when they are double-blind (so both experimentor and experimentee are unaware of what's being done and to whom), and randomised (so the experimental groups are selected at random) to limit the chance of confounding variables (see below) and psychological distortions like the placebo effect.[65]

Staying Afloat

☐ *Check if the data used in a prediction is accurate and comprehensive enough to make it useful.*

Chaos Theory

It would be bad enough if accurate and comprehensive data were the only problem. Unfortunately, there is an even worse problem for weather forecasting (and some other predictions) in the so-called butterfly effect. This is an idea developed by an American mathematician and meteorologist called Edward Lorenz, who first observed Chaos Theory while working on weather forecasting models.[66] Chaos Theory describes dynamic systems that are particularly sensitive to the starting conditions, so in weather terms, the classic example is a butterfly flapping its wings. This tiny effect subsequently influences the creation of a tornado several weeks later, as it ripples out into the atmosphere.

It's not just that a tiny change in the atmospheric starting conditions can radically alter the outcome, but that even with perfect knowledge of every single molecule in the atmosphere at any given moment in time, we *still* couldn't forecast the weather completely accurately because we can't control all the butterflies, birds, people, animals or volcanoes that can influence the outcome as time goes on. So, in the case of the weather forecast and many other unstable systems, *there will always be limitations on the accuracy of the predictions.*

Staying Afloat

☐ *Consider if the science behind a prediction allows for a completely accurate answer, or is the system unstable?*

Having Confidence

When we look at the prediction that there is a 50 per cent chance of rain in three days' time, it doesn't stand up to the scrutiny of the tips I've outlined above particularly well. However, the claim that there is a 50 per cent chance of a coin flip delivering a tail *does* stand up to the same scrutiny. The prediction includes everything that might affect the outcome. The science behind it is well developed and effective. The data used is accurate and comprehensive and it's a stable system.

The point I want to make is that while the output from the weather forecast looks exactly like the output from our earlier probability calculation – both involve maths, both give us a percentage chance (50 per cent) of a particular outcome occurring – they are *completely different*. It's really important to recognise this fact, because it's unlikely that anyone will point it out to you alongside a prediction they are selling.

If you want to make good strategic decisions based on high-quality predictions, then it's essential to recognise the difference in the way predictions like these are derived. In the case of the coin flip it is a cast-iron fact that the chance of a tail is 50 per cent – bet the house on it if you fancy betting the house on a one in two chance. The amount of risk that's being taken is known very precisely and with certainty.[67]

In the case of the weather, the 50 per cent is a best estimate based on a lot of complex maths with known flaws. The amount of uncertainty in the forecast is not known with much precision. Bet the house on it if you want to bet the house on what might be a 50 per cent chance, or might not – depending on the quality of the computer forecasting model, the data set and whether or not a butterfly flapped its wings over Tokyo three days ago.

The two '50 per cent' chances look the same, but they are very different. The toss of a coin or the roll of a die is a precise probability. Forecasting the weather also gives us a probability as the answer, but it's far from certain or precise. Both are presented in exactly the same way, and it's very easy to think that they mean the same thing when they don't.

This problem would be fixed in a heartbeat if everyone who published any kind of measurement, data, or result from a calculation or output from an algorithm also quoted some measure of the potential errors associated with it – a measure of the confidence that the reader can have in the number. This is standard practice in mature sciences. In physics, for instance, there is an established methodology for analysing the potential errors in experiments. These assess both random and systematic measurement errors[68] and they are always published with the data. There are other techniques in other disciplines. The simplest is probably the standard deviation,[69] which provides a measure of the scatter in the data set. The general principle is that the more scatter there is, then the greater the likelihood of error in any conclusions drawn from the data. A more sophisticated statistical measure is the confidence interval,[70] which more clearly allows you to assess the accuracy of, and potential errors in, a number or prediction. Some techniques for error analysis are better than others, but it's more important that some attempt is made to indicate the potential accuracy of the forecast. It should be made mandatory to provide this kind of information with any published data or prediction, even when it's presented to a general audience.

A number looks very different with an error attached to it; a weather forecast that states there's a 50 per cent chance of rain with a 40 per cent confidence interval gives us a much better feel for what might happen. It also clearly distinguishes the prediction from the 50 per cent chance of a head or a tail – a prediction that has a 100 per cent confidence interval. If you are using a prediction – or indeed any number – in making an important decision, try to find some measure of the potential error or confidence in that number. If there is nothing available, then downgrade its importance in the decision-making process.

Staying Afloat

☐ *If there is no measure of the confidence or potential error in data or a prediction, treat it with suspicion.*

Causation And Correlation

We've taken our first step away from a world of coin tosses and what we might call certain uncertainties or known unknowns and moved into a world of uncertain uncertainties and unknown unknowns – as exemplified by the weather forecast.

Unfortunately, the reliability of predictions only gets worse from here. At least there's real science in the weather forecast, an attempt to match cause (like a temperature change over the land) to an effect (like the wind increasing) and to describe that change consistently with a mathematical model. In the case of a lot of predictions and data output that we see, there's no understanding of causation at all, just a correlation.

Now, anyone familiar with the terms correlation or causation will see from the length of this section that I'm not so much skimming the surface on this topic as waving at the surface from a safe distance. Both causation and correlation are important subjects in many disciplines such as physics, logic, philosophy and statistics.

All these disciplines require very precise definitions of terms that – it turns out after several thousand years of pondering – are hard to pin down. Physicists have spent a great deal of time trying to be clear about what is cause and effect; in the case of a man pushing a bike up a hill it's clear that if the effect is the bike moving up the hill, then the cause is the man. It was less clear when they turned their attention to things that rely on forces like gravity that appear to act at a distance. Gravity isn't visibly the cause of the earth's orbit around the sun, but we certainly believe it to be so.

I'm not going to go into this in any more detail – fascinating as it is – because some simple definitions will suffice for this discussion about prediction. Let's define causation as *a person or thing that gives rise to an event.*

If a coin landing heads up is the event, then the cause is someone flipping it into the air. There is a clear and unambiguous relationship between the two. And if we knew the starting conditions with sufficient accuracy – the precise force vector that was applied to a precise point on the coin to propel it upwards, the density of the air, the distance to the floor below the launch point and so on – then we could (theoretically if not in practice) calculate which side it would land on.

Now, let's take a look at correlation, starting with a simple definition: *a mutual relationship, interdependence or connection between two or more things*. The place to find lots of examples of correlation is health research. There are sound ethical reasons why we don't do direct testing of many medical hypotheses – no one would directly test whether poor diet is a cause of heart disease by forcing a group of people to eat badly for long enough to prove the theory one way or the other.

And so, in its place we have epidemiology. This discipline uses or collects data from existing populations of people and attempts to interpret and analyse that data to work out the factors contributing to health. Epidemiology often goes looking for correlations, and no one needs to go very far to find the results of an epidemiological study.

While I was writing this chapter, there was a flurry of news stories based around some research into the health benefits of dog ownership. Here's a typical headline, this one from the Daily Mail: 'Owning a dog could extend your life: People are 24% less likely to die after a heart attack if they have a furry friend at home.'[71]

Anyone reading this could easily be left with the impression that the advantages of owning a dog had been established beyond any reasonable doubt. Unfortunately, that was far from the case. The study that had established this correlation in the data was what's called a meta study, or a study of studies where all the relevant studies in a particular area are put together for a combined assessment.[72] In this case, ten studies were included, amassing data from 3,837,005 people. And yes, it did establish that amongst that number of people those who owned a dog were 24 per cent less likely to die (during the period of time being assessed) than those who didn't own a pooch.

The problem comes from one short sentence in the paper: 'A possible limitation was that the analyses were not adjusted for confounders.' A confounder is the scourge of correlations: a confounding variable or factor – one that has influenced both of the apparently related or dependent variables.

So other explanations for this decrease in mortality were possible – including the rather simple one that elderly people are less likely to own a dog than younger people. And elderly people are more likely to die than younger ones. It's quite possible that owning a dog had nothing to do with the decrease in mortality, that the two things were correlated through a third variable that was related to both – age – that hadn't been accounted for in the analysis.

An apparent correlation – in this case between dog ownership and decreased mortality – might indicate an important and useful relationship that we can use to predict outcomes; it also might do the opposite. Owning a dog might not help you live longer at all. In fact, a frail 85-year-old trying to look after a puppy might have an increased chance of mortality from a fall.

Any prediction or analysis based on a well-understood causal link is more likely to be useful than one based on a correlation. This is not to say that correlations can't be useful; we just need to be more wary of them – after all, correlated variables may actually be causally linked in ways that we just don't understand yet.

In some cases, the causal link is obvious and can be established beyond doubt – as in the case of the coin; in plenty of other cases the link is less obvious and might only become clear with time. If we return once again to the sea and ships, then we find an excellent example of how this works: the planetary observations that underwrite celestial navigation.

Inspired by Plato, the Greeks did an immense amount of observational work on the heavens, work that sadly only survives to us through Ptolemy's book *Almagest*. This observational work allowed these ancient civilisations to predict with great accuracy many of the movements of the planets. And they did it well enough for ancient Greek voyagers to use the knowledge to navigate the seven seas, or a couple of them at any rate.

This is despite the fact that Ptolemy's model of planetary motion was based on a fundamental misunderstanding. He believed that the planets revolved around the earth. He was wrong, but there was an adequate correlation between Ptolemy's model and the observed data to make further predictions that were sufficiently accurate to the naked eye to be useful.

The correlation between Ptolemy's model of planetary motion and the data was sufficient to get the job done and allow Greek sailors to navigate the Mediterranean more or less safely. Eventually, the model would be revised by Copernicus, and then by Johannes Kepler to match the better data derived by Tycho Brahe and made possible with the telescope.

Once we had a model with the earth and all the planets rotating around the sun the correlations between the observations and the theory got a lot tighter. We have gone on from there to determine a cause and effect – gravity – for planetary motion. The full explanation is both more useful and more accurate than Ptolemy's misjudged model with the earth at the centre of the universe – but it doesn't mean that his work wasn't helpful in its time.

So, I'm not suggesting that all causal relationships provide gold-standard predictions – while we broadly understand the factors that contribute to fog (humidity, temperature, particles in the air) we still struggle to predict its formation. And a correlation may well be indicative of a causal relationship that we have yet to explain. *But* . . . in general, it pays to be more wary of predictions based on correlations than those based on causal relationships.

Staying Afloat

- *Be more wary of predictions based on correlations than those based on causation.*

Data Sets And Distributions

I want to finish this chapter by moving away from questions about the accuracy of data analysis, modelling and algorithmic prediction, and looking at some of the more general issues around data and prediction – and how they are presented to us by the mainstream media. We've already seen how important it is for high-quality data to be used in generating predictions, in particular the need for large data sets wherever possible. There's another important quality to the data that we need to be aware of though, and that's the distribution.

Distribution means the way that data points are spread out through the data sample, and there's one kind of distribution that has dominated most of our experience for most of human history. It's called a normal or Gaussian distribution, and it is sometimes referred to as the bell curve because that's what it looks like when plotted – a bell.

This distribution describes a great many things in the natural world, like human height and weight, or the age at which women have their first child. There's no one at the age of one getting pregnant and no one (unless medically assisted) doing so above the age of 60. Most women are clustering around the peak at 30 years old (at least in urban, educated populations) and then tailing off to either side.

The statistics that most of us were taught at school were applied to normal distributions or approximations to them. For instance, the three most common types of average that we can calculate – the mean, median and mode – are the same for a normal distribution.[73] All are meaningful values on this type of data set, as is the standard deviation which is primarily useful on normally distributed data. The ubiquity of the normal distribution in the natural world, along with the fact that it's the core of secondary school statistics, tends to make us think that everything is distributed in this way, and to treat any analysis of a data set as though it were. Unfortunately, it's not, and it's useful to understand that there are other data distributions and that many of those familiar numbers – like the mean – tell us something different when they are applied to these distributions.

The other relevant and important distribution in our contemporary, hyper-connected world is the power law. Data following a power law has a very distinctive plot, starting high on the left-hand side, close to the vertical y-axis, and diving down quickly, before shallowing to a long sloping tail almost parallel to the horizontal x-axis, as we see in Fig.1.

Fig. 1

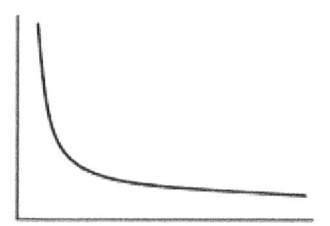

It's this plot that describes many of the things that we care about, like income distribution. While I was writing this there was a big news story that referenced power-law data – a well-reported claim from US Senator and Presidential candidate Bernie Sanders, who wrote in a *Wall Street Journal* article in June 2019 that 'The wealthiest three families now own more wealth than the bottom half of the country.'[74]

It's a claim that happens to be true – those three wealthy families are all up there, riding high on the y-axis (net worth) at the left-hand end of the x-axis plot, while the poorest half of the US population fill out the shallow, low sloping tail to the right of the graph.[75]

The importance of power-law distributions has been known for a while; the Pareto principle or 80/20 rule follows a power-law distribution. It was named after Italian economist Vilfredo Pareto. He demonstrated at the turn of the 18th and

19th centuries that 80 per cent of the land in Italy was owned by 20 per cent of the population – *plus ça change*. Nassim Nicholas Taleb's book, *The Black Swan*, railed against our preoccupation with bell curves, while power-law distributions describe much of the unfairness baked into modern life. Unfortunately, since then they have only become more important; they now describe many of the things that preoccupy us – like bestseller lists for music, movies and even books.

A handful of the most successful people take the vast majority of the rewards in many of the highest-profile endeavours – culture, sport, entrepreneurial business. Power-law distributions have been an increasing feature of the internet age for well-documented reasons (a process called preferential attachment that distributes more wealth to those who already have more),[76] even while the internet has allowed the development of the long tail – a notion that was introduced in another popular book, *The Long Tail* by Chris Anderson.

Power laws are important in the modern world, and we need to understand when we are dealing with one. Let's take an example with which I am painfully familiar, writers' incomes. In figures from Nielsen BookScan showing the data of sales at bookshops, it was reckoned that the top 50 authors sold more than 13 per cent of all books in bookshops in the UK. When you consider that there are 55,000 authors selling books through that survey, it means that the top 0.1 per cent is collecting 13 per cent of the income.[77]

Top authors earn tens of millions of pounds, while the average annual income for an author in the UK was found to be £12,500 by a European Commission study, also in 2016.[78] At the time that was 55 per cent of the average earnings in the UK, and below the minimum wage for a full-time job. And if that average salary was a mean, rather than a mode or median, then it's being dragged higher than it should by the massive earnings of a handful of authors. This is a power-law industry. It will appeal to those with one or all of the following: a healthy appetite for risk, a massive dose of overconfidence and/or an inexplicable feeling that nothing else is worth doing.

In contrast, the salaries for vets in a 2010 report for the Royal College of Veterinary Surgeons shows a very close approximation to a normal or bell curve.[79] Over half of the full-time workers within the profession earn between £30,000 and £50,000, with a healthy few making up to and over a £100,000 – but no one is earning millions and the average basic salary for those same full-time workers is £49,951, enough to live comfortably on.

This is the kind of profession that will appeal to those who want to know that their hard work is going to be properly rewarded, rather than hoping that it might . . . if they come across the right combination of luck and good timing. Anyone choosing a profession would be wise to check how the income is distributed because it will have a big impact on salary estimates. If you go into a profession that has a power-law distribution hoping to make the mean income (the sum of all the salaries divided by the number of them), then you are very likely to be disappointed. The median (the middle number when the data is sorted and ordered from low to high) would be a much more useful guide. However, if the income is normally distributed then the mean will be an accurate reflection of expectations.

Staying Afloat

☐ *Always consider the way the data is distributed; it's vital to gaining an understanding of what you are dealing with.*

Absolute And Relative Probabilities

One phrase that I used to hear a lot when I was in my twenties was 'lies, damn lies and statistics' – its popularity around that time was probably due to the 1976 publication of a book called just that: *Lies, Damn Lies, and Statistics: The Manipulation of Public Opinion in America* by Michael Wheeler. I don't hear the expression much any more, but data is still being manipulated to prove just about anything.

So it's important not just to understand the source of the data, the characteristics of the data set, the type of relationship between the variables and the nature of the modelling – but also whether someone is deliberately presenting the data for 'impact'.

The biggest culprit for this is medical statistics and the use of relative rather than absolute probabilities to scare the living bejeezus out of people. The absolute probability is the probability. So, if one person in a thousand will get lung cancer in a particular demographic then the absolute risk is 0.1 per cent. If that absolute risk changes to 0.2 per cent, so now two people in every thousand will get it, the relative risk is doubled. There's twice as much chance of getting lung cancer for anyone in that demographic.

This is a good example of a headline using relative rather than absolute risks for impact: 'Breast cancer risk from using HRT is "twice what was thought"'.[80]

It's from *The Guardian* – and they really should know better. Maybe they thought it was acceptable as they were quoting someone. The headline is followed up with the lead paragraph that includes this: 'The risk of breast cancer from using hormone replacement therapy is double what was previously thought . . .' Double the risk sounds terrifying – but what's the absolute risk that the doubling refers to, and under what circumstances?

The answer is in the fourth paragraph, where it explained that research published in *The Lancet* had claimed that one in 50 women of average weight that were taking combined daily oestrogen and progestogen over a five-year period would get breast cancer.[81] So that's a new absolute risk of 1 in 50, or 2 per cent for women taking the drug for five years. The article goes on to explain that the increased risk is smaller when the drug is taken for shorter periods, or when one of oestrogen or progestogen is taken.

So the headline writer took the worst case from the article in the medical journal, and then made it look worse still by using the relative risk increase – DOUBLE! – rather than stating the new absolute risk factor, which was the far less scary (but not insignificant) 2 per cent or 1 in 50.

Notice how much easier this last number – one person in every 50 – is to understand. No statistical knowledge is required here at all. This is what's called a natural frequency and it's the only way that risk should be communicated to an audience with no statistical background.[82]

Switching from absolute to relative risk is one of the simplest ways to manipulate the data to change the message. I see it used less than I used to, but I suspect that rather than being good news, it just means that more sophisticated methods to massage the message have been adopted. Different answers can be got from the same raw data by slicing it selectively, choosing particular time periods and ignoring others, for instance. This has come to be called p-hacking – adjusting the data set until you get a result at a level of statistical significance that will get the research published.[83] Lies, damn lies, and statistics.

Staying Afloat

☐ *Is the raw data telling the same story as the media?*

Pundits And Superforecasters

This chapter has been largely devoted to understanding and critiquing the tidal wave of data-based predictions that threaten to swamp our ability to make sensible choices. However, there's another source of prediction that we have not yet considered: the expert pundit. These people are everywhere, but their natural habitat is the 24-hour news channel, where they can fill endless hours telling us what's going to happen next, and what to think and do about it.

The first point about these folks is the wiggle room provided by the imprecision of language – 'There could be a recession' is open to a lot of interpretations: a 10 per cent chance? A 50 per cent chance? If a lack of information on errors or confidence intervals is a problem with a lot of published measurements and data, then the imprecision of the language of punditry is at a whole new level of unhelpfulness.

Over the years, I've gone from being interested in expert punditry (after all, what 25-year-old doesn't want to know what the next hot trend is going to be?) to suspicion, then disinterest and finally disdain. All of which might explain why they've been relegated to this final section of the chapter.

The most well-known study that has been done on the quality of expert predictions bore out my disillusion on roughly the same timescale that it occurred – Philip Tetlock, a writer and professor at the University of Pennsylvania, conducted his famous experiment between 1984 and 2004 using a series of forecasting tournaments. Tetlock and his team concluded – after about 28,000 predictions – that most were just a tiny bit better than chance.[84] Or, as he rather memorably put it – about as useful as having a chimpanzee throw darts at a board.

The one thing to remember when you come across expert punditry is that very, very few people are any good at forecasting, and experts are worse than most. Tetlock and his team did identify people who were good at forecasting, and he put a group of these people together and went on to win an independent forecasting tournament run by the Intelligence Advanced Research Projects Activity (IARPA) in the US.[85] Tetlock and his collaborators now run the Good Judgement Project, which has a commercial forecasting arm and was the subject of a further book by Tetlock and Dan Gardner called *Superforecasting: The Art and Science of Prediction*. If you are interested in making your own predictions, rather than just assessing the quality of others, then *Superforecasting* is a good place to start.

Philip Tetlock's central point is that good forecasting requires intellectual humility and the recognition that 'reality is profoundly complex . . . and that human judgment must therefore be riddled with mistakes.'[86] This quote from *Superforecasting* brings back to mind what Danny Kahneman had to say about overconfidence, back in Part 2: 'Overconfidence is really the enemy of good thinking, and I wish that humility about our beliefs could spread.'

There's one more point that I'd like to leave you with just in case, despite all that has been said in this chapter: you should never take a prediction at face value and without further thought. The Good Judgement Project has compared the predictions of two personality types, usually identified as 'foxes' and 'hedgehogs'. The hedgehogs have one single big idea, they are specialists, often ideologues. The fox takes a little something from everywhere, is more open-minded, and more likely to draw on a range of experiences and concepts. The fox is by far the better forecaster.[87]

Staying Afloat

☐ *Always be suspicious of the predictions of pundits; be very wary if they are self-described experts; and run a mile if they come from people with an ideological standpoint.*

Decision Paralysis

There are times when we have too much data, too much analysis and it seems impossible to cut our way through it to a decision. There are also times when predictive modelling is inadequate, the science half-baked, the data set small and the measurements flaky. Or even worse, the unknown unknowns seem overwhelming and the whole problem beyond rational analysis. It's moments like these that the right answer can seem a long way away, and the sleepless nights start. Sometimes the data is good enough: it doesn't have to be perfect and what we need to do is just . . . *decide*. We are stuck in a costly loop of decision paralysis. To cut through this it can sometimes be useful to turn away from the analytical approach and accept that there are some decisions for which analysis simply doesn't work well enough to help. So, what does work?

I find that the moment I know whether or not a decision

is right is the moment that I enact it. Sometimes I just feel overwhelming relief. And sometimes my stomach starts to churn with anxiety. In the latter case it's time to backtrack – if that's possible; sometimes it's not ... And so now I do my best to imagine myself into that state – without actually committing – as a way of getting a take on how I really feel about the decision. I don't have to follow these feelings, but they are an important input into the process.

The best trick I've come across to achieve this is to make the decision with a coin toss, or a dice roll if there's more than one option. It's important to believe that this coin toss is decisive. Don't just do it, take some time over assigning the options, build up to it, make yourself believe that you are going to follow through on the result – channel your inner Dice Man.[88] Roll the dice, flip the coin and then see how you react to the result. It can reveal a lot about what your real instincts think about the options.

There's been some research on this, the most well known of which has shown that it can also help people get past an internal resistance to change. Steven Levitt is a University of Chicago economist and co-author of *Freakonomics: A Rogue Economist Explores the Hidden Side of Everything*. Levitt ran an experiment on a website called *www.freakonomicsexperiments.com* (still there at the time of writing).[89] The website would flip a coin for anyone facing a decision that they were struggling to make. The question and the result were recorded, and researchers would follow up two months and six months later.

The experiment concluded that those who were instructed by the coin toss to make a change were both more likely to do it, and to be happier six months later, when compared to those that stuck with the status quo. The suggestion was that people are too cautious about making big life decisions. So, flipping a coin works for most people, even if you just accept the result.

There is also research into the use of a coin flip to support decision making in the way that I have described. A paper by a team at the University of Basel concluded that using coin flips or dice rolls: 'can function as a catalyst in the decision-making process' by bringing to the surface emotions revealed by the coin flip's result.[90] These are particularly good strategies when you've hit the buffers on the 'rational' decision-making process and still not come to a conclusion. As Danish philosopher and mathematician Piet Hein said in his short poem: 'solve the dilemma by simply spinning a penny'.[91]

It feels more than a little ironic to finish these chapters on risk assessment and knowledgeable decision making – a sales pitch for rational thinking in an increasingly irrational world – by recommending a coin flip. There are two important points about this though, beyond it being a good route out of decision paralysis. We must recognise, and will investigate in more detail in Part 5, that however good our risk assessment and decision-making process is, nothing can eliminate the role of chance in the outcome – and sometimes it's all right to embrace chance in the decision making. And, finally, our feelings about decisions, consequences and risk matter, which brings us to Chapter 8.

Staying Afloat

☐ *A coin flip can be a catalyst for a decision – it can tell us how we really feel about the choices.*

CHAPTER 8

Risk Perception

Perception Is Everything

I have always wanted to be rational about risk, to apply a sensible, knowledgeable process to my decision making. The previous chapters have revealed what that means in practice, but it's also revealed how difficult it is to achieve – we have just looked at many ways in which badly collected or analysed data and inadequate modelling can distort the choices that we face. And in Part 2 we previously saw how a psychological bias to overconfidence makes us less aware of risk, and perhaps less fearful than we should be. So – while my objective has been to develop ways of making more rational assessments of risk – I'm conscious that the emphasis so far could be making people more anxious. A knowledgeable and rational approach to risk should make us less anxious, which is why I'm going to finish Part 3 with a review of some of the things that drive our anxieties, in the hope that greater knowledge of the mechanisms working on our subconscious will give us some tools to defuse them. There is a very emotional element to knowledge and decision making, and the more we can acknowledge and understand that aspect, the smarter we will allow ourselves to be.

We've already briefly introduced one example of a psychological bias – loss aversion – that makes us more averse to risk, more fearful than we should be. Daniel Kahneman and Amos Tversky also discovered the 'availability heuristic', which can also drive us to being more fearful. The availability heuristic is a predisposition to make decisions based on how readily an example of something comes to mind. So, if you ask someone to judge the risk of losing their home to a fire, they will assess the risk as a lot higher the week after news of a big house fire than during a period without such a tragedy. Remember, the risk of fire hasn't changed just because someone is more aware of it, any more than the number of Honda Civics on the road has changed because I'm driving one and tend to notice them more.

This is a particular problem in the world we now live in, filled as it is with news channels clamouring for our attention with clickbait headlines. An overwhelming amount of this is bad news. Kahneman and Tversky's work would lead us to believe that this constant exposure to bad news is more likely to make us risk averse as it makes us constantly aware of bad outcomes.

I've already seen news of four murders today; one was featured on the home page of the news website that I use, and another three were in the news bulletin I was unfortunate enough to catch on the radio. Only one of these was recent – the other three were reports on investigations and prosecutions – and none of them happened locally. If I lived in a world without mass media and global communications, I'd got through my day without being reminded of the possibility of a violent and brutal end at the hands of another human being. And I'd be less worried about it as a result.

Staying Afloat

☐ *A world saturated with bad news can make us anxious about the wrong things, because the most recent information has the strongest influence on our decision making.*

Bayesian Thinking

There's another interesting analysis of how this constant exposure to bad news works on our risk perception in Brian Christian and Tom Griffiths's book *Algorithms to Live By*.[92] It reaches the same conclusion as the previous section, but I'm going to repeat it here anyway – much more briefly – because it also introduces another very important tool in the prediction business. Bayes' theory is an immensely useful piece of mathematics and it will be behind forecasts that we see and use every day. While its essence is relatively simple, its full application can be complex – this has led to some unjustified bad press, particularly in the legal profession.[93]

Criminal justice cases can often pivot on evidence dependent on technology like blood, fingerprint or DNA matches. The perpetrator's DNA might have been found at the scene and been tested, coming up with a match to the DNA of the accused. The prosecutor's fallacy is a name for a courtroom strategy used by prosecutors to convince juries that the probability of the accused being innocent is tiny, because the chances of a random match with the general population is tiny.[94]

This ignores the main insight of Bayes' theory, which is that the final probability of an event is a combination of both the general probability (also known as the prior probability or base rate), and any information or probabilities specific to the event. Let's say that the chance of a random DNA match in the general population is one in three million. The wayward prosecutor will want to paint this statistic as meaning that the chance of a match is so remote that the accused just *has* to be guilty.

This is not necessarily the case, since the odds also depend on the specifics, like the size of the potential pool of perpetrators. If that pool is large enough (which it will be if the DNA match has been found in a search against a national database), say 36 million people, then the number of other possible matches is actually quite high. In this case, with the chance of a match set at one in three million, then in a population of 36 million people there could be 12 other people out there with a DNA match that would put them in the dock.

When looked at in this light it quickly becomes clear how important all the other evidence in the case will be – eyewitnesses, alibis and so on – and Bayes' theory provides the maths to combine the different evidence and calculate a probability for the individual's guilt. It's been used in this role in court cases with mixed results,[95] not least because the maths and its complexities and subtleties can be hard for jurors to understand.

Fortunately, all we need to take away from this is an awareness of the theory's efficacy and our intuitive use of its fundamental principle – always start with the prior probability and update and revise probabilities based on each new piece of evidence. If I see blue ink on the wall of the dining room, I might suspect my youngest son based on earlier instances of ink on walls. Let's say that there have been ten events where there's been writing on the wall in the house and six of them turned out to have been the youngest son. In this case the prior probability or base rate is six out of ten, or 60 per cent, and it's a fundamental number to understand when assessing any kind of risk or prediction.

If I then go looking for the youngest son and find him with blue ink-stained fingers I'd quickly reassess the probability of his guilt upwards. I may even think it's 100 per cent until I find that his older brother also has blue ink on his hands, at which point I'd be forced to conclude that the new evidence told me nothing, and that I should return to the prior probability (60 per cent) of it being the youngest son. I've now combined the prior probability or base rate with all the specific features surrounding a particular event to arrive at a sound Bayesian prediction.

If we return to the problem of calculating the best way to spend our money on improving the performance of a sailboat, then we can enhance our assessment of the probabilities by including Bayesian thinking. For instance, a little research might give us a general probability for the effectiveness of coaching in a sports environment. This number would be the prior probability. The specifics would be any data we had on the actual coach under consideration for employment – perhaps he had taken another team from a string of mid-fleet results at major championships to a top-ten place at the worlds. Bayes' theorem allows us to combine these two – just multiply them together – to get an updated probability.

One easy mistake to make is to ignore the base rate and just look at the specific CV of the coach that's under consideration. This is easy to do because the specifics of a case are often the most readily available information – the coach may well be pitching for the job by providing their CV and giving a sales chat. It's easy to be dazzled by the details of a specific event and ignore the prior probability, but it's going to lead to poor predictions and risk assessment, something called base-rate neglect.[96]

Another problem arises when, instead of ignoring the prior probability completely, we replace statistical facts with a stereotype or distorted world view. The argument made by Christian and Griffiths suggests that a world saturated with bad news distorts our set of prior experiences. These distorted experiences replace facts as our base rate and that magnifies errors in risk analysis.

Let's say I'm lucky enough to live to be a frail old man, I may well think twice before heading out to the local shop late in the evening to get some milk. I might think it too risky, the chances of being mugged or assaulted too high. This judgement would start with a view on my personal risk of being attacked. I'd see this as relatively high; frail old men (and women) are easy targets. I would then combine this with my opinion of the general risk of being mugged. Where I'm lucky enough to live this is so close to zero that it matters very little whether I'm an easy target or not. The chances of being mugged are still incredibly small.

Unfortunately, by then, I'll probably be a *Daily Mail* reader and willingly submitting myself to a daily deluge of stories of assault and robbery. The fact that none of these events has happened anywhere close to me will go unnoticed. Instead, I will come to believe the general risk of attack – the base rate – is very high: I hear about it happening all the time in the news, after all. Now my prior experience has been distorted by the reported experiences of others. And when I combine this with my specific risk (relatively high compared to the general population) I will likely decide it's safer to stay indoors and drink my tea without milk.

It's sad, because I'm sure the consequences of this unnecessary fearfulness can be a lot more serious than black tea – the loneliness and isolation of many elderly people. Unfortunately, it's a long way from being the only mechanism by which we become too fearful.

Staying Afloat

☐ **Bayesian thinking can improve the way we assess the probability of an outcome.**

Dread Risk And Unknown Risk

There are two other types of risk that we are unnecessarily averse to – 'dread risk' and 'unknown risk'. These were identified and analysed by Paul Slovic and Elke Weber in a paper published in the wake of the tragedy of the 9/11 attacks on the World Trade Centre.[97] They were grappling with the way that this tragedy had distorted risk perception. Dread risks are the kind of events that could kill lots of people all at once, risks we can't personally control, the ones that evoke terror – like plunging to death in a burning plane with hundreds of other people. This is why people refused to fly after 9/11. It might seem a sensible reaction, but they turned to what was actually a much more lethal mode of transport: driving. It was a choice that almost doubled the number of deaths due to the 9/11 attacks, thanks to the increase in road fatalities in the ensuing years.[98] Real people died in real crashes as a result of dread risk – so don't avoid flying because it's dangerous, avoid flying because it's a massive burden on the environment.

Slovic and Weber also established that unknown risks trouble us disproportionately; these are the things that we don't understand, that are new, or whose consequences we have yet to comprehend. There are regular scares that play to this fear – the one in the news at the time of writing is the potential health harm from the roll-out of new 5G mobile-phone networks.

There have been thousands of papers assessing the risk from mobile-phone radiation in the three decades or so since they arrived on the scene. The arrival of 5G has led to renewed calls for the authorities to take another look, presumably because it's a new technology. The advice at the time of writing on the World Health Organisation's website states[99] 'To date, and after much research performed, no adverse health effect has been causally linked with exposure to wireless technologies . . . Provided that the overall exposure remains below international guidelines, no consequences for public health are anticipated.' There are good reasons to have a fear of the unknown, there are also good reasons to revise those fears when the evidence tells us to.

Staying Afloat

- *We have an irrational fear of both dread risk and unknown risks, which can leave us more exposed to other more likely dangers.*

It's time now to acknowledge the elephant in the room: science. We've been looking at ways to better understand and assess risk, and the source of much of the knowledge about those risks has been science. In the discussion about strategy before the storm that hit the Volvo Ocean Race fleet, we were relying on science for the weather forecast. When we worry about health and medical risk, we're relying on scientific research to investigate and clarify those risks. We've looked in some detail at how to assess the data from that research, and now it's time to take a broader look at the status of scientific knowledge – because if there is one area where we consistently misunderstand what's known and what's not, it's science.

Part 3: Staying Afloat Summary

- *When faced with a decision about the future, always assess*

the possible gains and losses first – this might be all you need to make your choice.
- *Expected value and expected utility can be useful concepts but should be used cautiously.*
- *Consider whether a prediction includes the influence of everything that might affect the outcome.*
- *Always ask if the science behind a prediction is well developed and effective.*
- *Check if the data used in a prediction is accurate and comprehensive enough to make it useful.*
- *Consider if the science behind a prediction allows for a completely accurate answer, or is the system unstable?*
- *If there is no measure of the confidence or potential error in data or a prediction, treat it with suspicion.*
- *Be more wary of predictions based on correlations than those based on causation.*
- *Always consider the way the data is distributed; it's vital to gaining an understanding of what you are dealing with.*
- *Is the raw data telling the same story as the media?*
- *Always be suspicious of the predictions of pundits; be very wary if they are self-described experts; and run a mile if they come from people with an ideological standpoint.*
- *A coin flip can be a catalyst for a decision – it can tell us how we really feel about the choices.*
- *A world saturated with bad news can make us anxious about the wrong things, because the most recent information has the strongest influence on our decision making.*
- *Bayesian thinking can improve the way we assess the probability of an outcome.*
- *We have an irrational fear of both dread risk and unknown risks, which can leave us more exposed to other more likely dangers.*

PART FOUR – SCIENCE

Understanding science means understanding the role of doubt

It is imperative in science to doubt; it is absolutely necessary, for progress in science, to have uncertainty as a fundamental part of your inner nature.

RICHARD FEYNMAN, THE PLEASURE OF FINDING THINGS OUT

CHAPTER 9

The Wind Direction

The Nullarbor

Science powers discovery, it powers understanding about the world and it powers the technology that surrounds us. Scientific knowledge deserves a book of its own, and many of them have been written. *Bad Science* by Ben Goldacre is one; using Goldacre's specialist subject (medicine) it covers most of what needs to be said about scientific knowledge and its problems in the 21st century. It gets deep and dirty into examples that affect us all: alternative medicine, vitamins, nutrition, mendacious pharmaceutical companies and the ridiculous way that most science stories are covered by the mainstream media.

I've already covered some of the same ground, particularly the ideas of cognitive bias and the way statistics can be used to misrepresent data and risk – but you probably know that. I suspect that if you've picked up a book called *Knowledge 2.0* then you have already read *Bad Science.* If not, I can recommend that you do.

The point I want to make about science is a little more abstract and reflects my own background in physics (although I'm going to come on to a healthcare example in Chapter 11 because it is the point where science most directly and immediately touches all our lives). Physics is often held up as the main paradigm for science, it's thought of as the application par excellence of the scientific method, revealing extraordinary truths about the universe. The reality is different, and it can show us all a better way to think about science and scientific theories.

I'm going to start with a story about a lack of doubt,

a quality that is both fundamental to the scientific endeavour, and its Achilles heel. It was the inciting incident (as they say in creative writing classes) for this book, and the insight gained is going to take us to a place where we can better understand what science is doing. Part 4 is going to show us that we should forget our ambition for scientific knowledge to be true, and instead understand that it is temporary, always in doubt and to be judged by its utility. This approach will enable us to properly understand the knowledge that science is producing and how best to judge it.

This story is going to start on the dockside in Fremantle, Western Australia, in early April 1986. To arrive at that moment, I had hitch-hiked 2,398 kilometres along the Eyrie Highway and across the Nullarbor Plain from Port Augusta in South Australia. I was just another backpacker seeing the world on a budget, 18 months on the road. A backpacker who had gone to a lot of trouble to get to Fremantle for a very particular reason. The America's Cup was due to be held there in 1987, and the teams had started to arrive at the venue in the late (Southern Hemisphere) summer of 1986. I wanted to see the Cup boats, particularly the British boat, so after arriving in Fremantle I found a job and waited for my countrymen to show up.

The America's Cup

The America's Cup is sailing's premier trophy and it's almost as old as the sport, beginning back in 1851, the year of the Great Exhibition at Crystal Palace. A group of wealthy New York Yacht Club members had built a boat – a black schooner called *America* – and sailed her across the Atlantic to show the world what Yankee shipbuilders could do. They were hoping to win back in wagers the money that they had put into the build and the cost of their British expedition.

America was a very different boat to the British yachts of the time and, even before she arrived in Cowes, she had gained a reputation as fast. None of the British owners wanted to sail against her, so in the end it was left to the Royal Yacht Squadron to invite *America* to join one of the club's annual races, a lap around the Isle of Wight. The trophy was a silver ewer called the 100 Pound Cup.

The *America* won this peaceful contest of maritime supremacy, outclassing the rest of the field to be first at the finish line off Cowes. The yacht and her owners returned to the New York Yacht Club in triumph, and a few years later they gifted the trophy to the club as the prize for a challenge competition open to sailing clubs of all nations. They called it the America's Cup.

It took 132 years to wrestle the trophy back out of the hands of the New York Yacht Club. It was 1983 when the Cup finally went to Australia after a match of such drama that it could never have been scripted as fiction. The backroom dealings were every bit as brutal as the contest on the water, as the Americans tried to have the Australians' innovative keel declared illegal. Warren Jones, the Executive Director of Alan Bond's Aussie team, fought a brilliant tactical and strategic battle. And eventually he ensured that the decisive move was made out on the water. That came as the Aussies passed the Americans on the final lap of the seventh and final race.

It could not have been any closer – but after 132 years in the hands of the New York Yacht Club the America's Cup finally left America. And it was the upstart Aussies that were taking it away. On the night of the victory, their Prime Minister, Bob Hawke, declared that 'Any boss who sacks anyone for not turning up today is a bum.'

I had processed the Australian's successful challenge via newspapers and magazine articles. They were devoured in lunch and tea breaks snatched from 12-hour days in a summer job, running machines and moving metal around a sports equipment factory. However, once my degree was complete (concluding my obligation to my parents' expectations), I was free to see the next contest up close. And so it was that when the brand-new British boat arrived at the Cup venue in Fremantle, I was able to go straight down there to have a look.

In those days America's Cup boats were built to what was called the International Twelve Metre Class Rule. The boats were 65-foot-long monohulls, built from lead and aluminium to structural guidelines laid down by Lloyd's Register. The rule produced boats that were very staid by today's standards. However, at the time there were questions as to whether a day racer designed for the sheltered waters off Newport, Rhode Island, could be raced in the open Indian Ocean off Perth. To me, the boat just looked huge; I'd done all my sailing in small boats, starting at the local sailing club, then around the UK and eventually a couple of international events.

It was an expensive sport and as a family we had limited resources – that's what I was doing in the factory, eight weeks' work during the summer holidays would pay for two or three weeks of competitive sailing. I raced with my sister and we'd made it into the Royal Yachting Association's (RYA) first foray into race training, the National Youth Squad. We stretched the money as far as we could. I'd hitch-hike to events, and on one memorable occasion (mostly because none of my friends from that era will let me forget it) I managed to do this with the boat on its trailer. My main life goal at that point was to go to the Olympic Games. Back then, Team GB was pretty hopeless at Olympic sailing and going to the Games was about as good as it got.

It was one of the RYA youth squad's former coaches that spotted me gawping at the British America's Cup boat the day after the team arrived in Fremantle. His name was Jerry Richards and he was a sail trimmer on the crew. He came over to say hello and – understandably, as Perth is a hell of a long way from anywhere else – asked what I was doing there. I told him: sweeping up in a shop, and tutoring.

'How much are you getting paid?' he asked.

'I make about two hundred dollars a week,' I replied.

'If we can match that . . . will you come and work here? We really need some help.'

Oh, yes, and I'd do anything. And over the next couple of months I did. The team was setting up its operations base on a plot in the boatyard not far from the Fremantle Yacht Club. It was a little ring of converted shipping containers and Portakabins circled around a couple of piers and a crane to get the boat in and out of the water. They added a chain-link fence for security. I added red, white and blue stripes around the top of the Portakabins. I painted a sign for the front gate. I swept and cleaned and tidied, lifted and carried, sanded and even painted, unless it was raining, and it rained a lot. I worked hard, bloody hard, at anything that needed doing.

Slowly, the team imposed some sort of order on their new home and I got the opportunity to help in other areas, like the boat electronics and in the sail loft. I even went sailing. Well, almost. The long, cold and wet Fremantle autumn was taking its toll. I was pulled on to the boat to make up the numbers. In those days – when the boats were simpler – everyone, and that included the back-office staff and the chefs, could end up doing some sailing. But it didn't happen for me that first time I made it on to the boat: someone wasn't concentrating when the mainsail was pulled up; it went too far and we broke a part on the mast.

An Opportunity

I soon got a second chance. On a particularly cold wet day in late May 1986 I was asked by Harold Cudmore – the skipper of the boat and the very same man who starred in the Fastnet story about the flares – if I would go out on the tender and operate the coaching video, to film the crew training. I had been reading and hearing stories about Harold Cudmore for more than a decade, and now here he was, larger than life, asking me to help his 12-metre crew. I didn't need to be asked twice. I went once, and then again – soon, I was a regular on the tow boat, or tender, taking video, working the tow rope, and helping move spare sails around. And eventually another opportunity came up to sail on the boat. David Arnold, who was both Chief Financial Officer for the team and a potential navigator for the race crew, showed me around – the computer was his tool. I was fascinated from the get-go; simple though it was, the boat's track was plotted on a monochrome screen – one of those early IBM monitors with green pixels – displayed beside a few numbers.

It happened to be the day when *Australia II* – the boat that had won the America's Cup in 1983 – was out for what we were told was her final sail. Alan Bond's team were about to pension her off, replaced by new boats. She came and lined up beside us for a few minutes in about 12 knots of wind and bright blue, late autumn sunshine. It's a cliché, but it was one of those 'pinch me' moments. Somehow, I'd gone from sitting in a factory tea room – in grease-stained overalls and oily, steel-toe-capped boots– reading about this boat . . . now here I was sailing beside her. I had come a very long way, both literally and metaphorically . . . and yet, it still felt a long way from the real deal.

At the first opportunity I went to the library and got books to try and learn more about the computer onboard; the only one I had seen before was housed in a building on the Nottingham University campus. We had communicated with it via terminals and tape cassettes – this desktop was something quite new. And installing it on a boat was even newer, only a couple of people on the team seemed to have a clue what it did or even what it was really for . . . it seemed to me that I might be able to help out there, what with having a degree in Physics.

The team had installed the same computer on the tender — same hardware, same software – and from then on, I took every opportunity to fire it up. It even had a wireless connection to the sailboat, and when there was someone onboard who knew how to switch it on, I could see the sailing data. My interest was clear to everyone – I was a very ambitious cleaner and deckhand.

A few days after the sail with *Australia II*, it was announced at a team meeting that the navigator flying out from England to join the crew wasn't coming after all. Over the next few days Eddie Warden-Owen and Chris Law asked me about my sailing. Along with Cudmore they were the team's three most senior sailors and in rapid succession I had conversations with all three of them, before getting another chance to sail on the boat. After that, Harold called me over to talk to them together. Cudmore told me they were considering taking me on to the sailing team to run the computer. It wasn't so much a question as a statement, and even if it had been a question my answer was clear. My slight build and lack of height, Cudmore told me, was a disadvantage, but 'you've got the ability'.

Many of the guys on this boat were heroes of mine, defined by all those stories, like the one about the flare gun. It was as if I'd been plucked from cleaning boots or selling programmes outside the stadium to playing in the Premier League. No one really mentions it in those Roy of the Rovers narratives but let me tell you that this is not an easy transition to make. I was still expected to clean up after everyone – and there was no general announcement about my new role. My status was uncertain in my own head, never mind everyone else's.

I worked hard to prepare. All sailing tactics and strategy are determined by the wind (speed and direction, present and future), the boat's position relative to the course markers, and the position of the opponent or opponents. My job was to keep track of all these things. I already mentioned that when armed with perfect knowledge of them, race strategy reduces to a geometry problem. Since perfect knowledge is impossible (in life as in sailing, otherwise no one would need this book), knowing what you know and what you do not, and to what degree of certainty, is where the skill comes in. Once again, it's just like life.

I'd spent all my time sailing small boats, where the wind's behaviour was something we could only feel and guess at through intermediaries like flags, the waves on the water, the performance of other boats and maybe a compass. Now I was to be aboard this fabulous America's Cup boat with an electronic display that would tell me exactly what the wind speed and direction were at all times. The computer would show me a graph of historical wind data, and exactly where the boat was on the racecourse.

All I had to do was to learn to set it up properly and operate it quickly. I thought I could do it. The question in my head was whether anyone else *really* thought I could do it, or if this was just some crazy experiment that would soon end in a humiliating return to the hot tarmac and the road north to the Kimberley.

A Lack Of Doubt

And so, the moment came when the tender pulled us into the wind and the covers came off and the sails started to go up. I'd watched this process dozens of times from outside, and even from onboard a couple of times. And I'd asked the right questions of the guys that were interested in helping me out with advice. I knew how to operate the winch I would be responsible for; I knew that the rope I would be handling held the mast up and that the consequences of screwing up would be catastrophic to the programme. I knew what I was supposed to do, where I was supposed to be . . . and none of this knowledge helped.

It was breezy, bright sunshine flashing off white-capped waves. The sails seemed huge and barely controllable, the noise as the wind caught them overwhelming. I focused on trying not to do anything stupid. I didn't have to be brilliant, just not dumb. Once we were sailing it quietened down, the boat seemed more manageable, the situation more familiar. It was a sailboat, a racing sailboat, and I knew about that. We started the first training exercise.

'Keep me updated on the wind direction,' said Eddie Warden-Owen as he steered the boat into the first manoeuvre. No problem, I thought, reading the number off the electronic dial. I had too much to do on my winch to keep watching it, but once we were settled again I glanced up and saw that there had been a big change, a shift in the wind, and one that we could take advantage of . . . but only by a second manoeuvre. It's a simplification, but in general a boat takes advantage of a 'heading' wind shift by changing direction, and a 'lift' or lifting wind shift by carrying on.

'We're "headed" on this one,' I called out, slipping into jargon to get the message across above the crash of waves, the groaning of winches and wires.

'Ok, let's go back,' said Warden-Owen.

And back we went. Once again, I was focused on my winch, fast learning just how much more load there was on these ropes compared to the ones on a dinghy. I glanced up at the wind-direction dial. Another heading wind shift – it meant another manoeuvre to take advantage of it. My heart was pounding, my arms already struggling, and I spoke without really thinking . . .

'Headed again!'

'Going back as soon as we get up to speed,' called Warden-Owen to the crew forward.

I noticed a couple of people raise their eyebrows. The manoeuvres were hard. I was the reason we were doing more of them. I felt out of my depth. I was the cleaner and this wasn't an easy audience.

There was more crashing and groaning, wire whipping through the wind as the sails flogged from one side of the boat to the other.

'Are we up?' called Warden-Owen as we settled out of the tack.

I looked up. It was another heading wind shift. How could this be, how could we tack on to three consecutive heading shifts? This pattern of changes in the wind direction wasn't just unusual, it was implausible.

'Are we lifted?' called Warden-Owen again, patience clearly wearing thin with the strange pattern of wind shifts.

I only had one answer, it didn't feel right, but I had no idea why. 'No, we're headed again,' I said.

I caught the look, he didn't have to say it, but he did

anyway. 'What the fuck, how does that happen? Where are we getting this information from?'

I waved at the digital display.

'Oh . . . that thing's useless,' he said. And with that, Eddie Warden-Owen turned his attention back to steering.

In that moment, the scale of my failure seemed unfathomable. It felt as if it reached all the way to the very bottom of that dark blue Indian Ocean . . . and then carried on through some fissure that led all the way to the boiling centre of the earth. They say that luck is where preparation meets opportunity. I had been incredibly lucky to be in the right place at the right time to get that opportunity, to be magically lifted up – just some guy that had hitched across a desert to see some boats – on to the crew. All the way up from a casual interaction on the Fremantle dockside to a shot at the America's Cup.

It wasn't all luck: I had seen the opportunity; I had worked hard to open it up and make it happen. I thought I was prepared to take advantage of it, to jump straight into the most elite level of sailing. And then, in a moment, it felt as though I had surely blown it. I was on the boat because of the computer, but the computer's usefulness was completely reliant on accurate data from the boat's sensors – in particular from the anemometers. It turned out that this data was at best poorly calibrated, and at worst outright rubbish.

My failure to check the accuracy of the wind information was that much worse because this was something I should have thought about, something that I should have checked. I was trained to do just that: I knew about sensors, I knew about calibration – I'd had it drummed into me for the best part of five years of training as a physicist. The anemometer is a scientific instrument, a simple and well-understood one, but a scientific instrument nonetheless – without it, the atmospheric physics on which meteorology is based would be stuck back in the Middle Ages.

When I studied it, a big part of university experimental physics was (and hopefully still is) learning to calibrate and understand errors in sensors. All our secondary school and university lab work needed notes on instrument calibration and errors; all the data and graphs needed visual error bars to show the limits of accuracy. Teachers (one in particular whom I will come to shortly) that had grown up in an analogue age were particularly scornful of digital displays. Just because it said 32.04 on the dial didn't mean that it was really accurate to a hundredth of a degree. So, if I'd been *properly* prepared and had viewed the instrument with a healthy dose of doubt, then I would have done the error analysis that I mentioned in Chapter 7 – Predicting the Future, and known that while the wind-direction display said '235 degrees' the data being displayed was '235 □ 12 degrees'.

This means that if the dial said 235 degrees, the actual wind direction could be 223 degrees, or 247 degrees, or anything in between. These error bounds are doing the same job as the measures of confidence in data discussed in Chapter 7. And when the errors are included in the number then Eddie Warden-Owen nailed it. It was useless. Nassim Nicholas Taleb makes a similar point in his book *The Black Swan*. There's a section called 'Don't Cross a River if It Is (on Average) Four Feet Deep'.[100] The point being that the error in the measurement is important because no river is four feet deep everywhere, it's four feet some places, and in others it's two, or three or eight or even nine. The detail of what the measurement means, and the potential errors, cannot be ignored.

So why had I not given these sensors any thought? I'd believed the digital display with its apparent precision. I'd taken the measurement at face value. This is a mistake – sometimes trivial, sometimes serious – that we make all the time with all sorts of scientific information. I hadn't doubted the data on that wind-direction display, and I really should have known better.[101]

Staying Afloat

☐ *It's important to fully understand scientific information before we rely on it.*

CHAPTER 10

Scientific Truth or Scientific Instrument?

The Problem Of (Scientific) Knowledge

I'm sure that most of us have at some point relied on information that didn't hold up to scrutiny. It might have been a statistic in a presentation, or data that we relied on for an important decision – such as whether or not to get vaccinated. It could have been knowledge that we used for a purchase or an investment. Or maybe it was just a fact quoted during a discussion in a bar. The outcome could have been anything from mildly embarrassing to expensive or even life-threatening. Many of these pieces of information will have been outputs of one sort or another from the most pervasive knowledge source of our time: science. The wind direction that let me down was measured by a scientific instrument; the cup anemometer has been a part of the basic meteorological toolset for almost two hundred years.

    Science has built the world around us, with all its glories and all its problems. Its very majesty and ubiquity mean that we look to it for truth, much as previous eras looked to gods and kings for answers. It's one of the reasons why the first reaction to scientific knowledge is often the same as the response that I had to the wind direction on the boat. I accepted the data on the display without doubt or question. The second reaction – which usually follows a disappointment just like the one I suffered – is often to start to approach all such information with a much higher degree of scepticism. Both reactions are unhelpful, and in the last few decades they have both become downright dangerous.

    Our confusion over science has serious, real-world consequences, and the main goal of Part 4 is to propose more helpful ways to think about scientific knowledge. We need this and we need it soon because of the status that science holds in our society, and the importance of scientific information to our security and health. Many of the facts and information – and almost all the contentious stuff – that we use in our decision making comes to us labelled as science. And before long, even the people who are doing a good job of processing that information are going to find that the negligent inaction – or reckless action – of others is going have serious consequences that no one can avoid.

Let's be clear, our confusion about science is widespread; science, particularly physics, is often held up as a paradigm of how knowledge should be sought and verified. I regularly hear smart people from other fields (economics, social sciences) aspire to the methods of physics – a process that has come to be called the scientific method. The scientific method is understood to be the way that we can distinguish scientific knowledge from other information. The implication is that scientists turn a crank on a machine called the scientific method, and out pour scientific truths.

The philosopher of science Lee McIntyre wrote his book *The Scientific Attitude* to examine the argument that 'there is a "scientific method" . . . such that if we could just apply the standard rigorously enough, good science would bloom as a result.' McIntyre concludes that 'there is no such thing as scientific method' and – worse – that those thinking deeply about the philosophical underpinnings of science have concluded that it's impossible to come up with any criteria that will allow for a rigorous demarcation between what's science and what's not.[102] It's a measure of our confusion that the people who have tried have found it so difficult to capture what's special about science – while everyone else is still extolling the specialness of the scientific method.

If we can't define a scientific method that differentiates the way scientific claims are produced, then what is special about science? Why do we accord it the status that it has?

The status of different types of knowledge is something that philosophers have been arguing about for a long while. They call it the *problem of knowledge.* My preoccupation with this predates my unfortunate experience with sailboat instrument systems. I bailed out of a pure Physics degree within a couple of weeks of arriving at university, switching to a joint honours with Philosophy instead. I did all the 'problem of knowledge' classes – on empiricism, scepticism and idealism – and I can tell you with some authority that the problem of knowledge is huge. Many famous and smart books have been written about what can be called knowledge. I think it's fair to say that the general argument is still ongoing.[103]

It's a discussion that I made a tiny contribution to when I finished up my degree with a dissertation on the status of scientific theories. It was called 'Instrumentalism Realised' and it asked a fundamental question: When I refer to elements of a theory – say an electron or a quark – am I referring to real things that correspond to an independent reality? This belief is called realism – it states that the truth (or otherwise) of any statement about (for instance) an electron is resolved by whether it matches an independent reality. If it does match reality, then it can be said to be knowledge. This is the way that most people think about science and, along with the scientific method, it's the thing that gives scientific knowledge its status.

The alternative that I considered was called instrumentalism – this is the idea that scientific theories are just useful instruments. To an instrumentalist, these things – electrons or quarks, or whatever – are just devices that we can manipulate to achieve a desired outcome. To the instrumentalist, we can manipulate the equations and ideas of modern physics to practical effect – building smartphones and supercomputers – but the theory says nothing about the underlying reality. Truth or falsity of the theory does not matter, it's left open.

I'm not going to get too deep into the weeds on this one, but I am going to show you an example which establishes that the only practical way to think of scientific theories is as instruments, whose central quality is their usefulness, their ability to help us manage and understand the world. Some people might argue that this would undermine the status of science on (to pick topics at random) climate change or vaccine efficacy.[104] I'm going to argue quite the opposite – that science makes a lot more sense when usefulness is the central quality. I'm going to make the case that we need to stop worrying about truth, start worrying about utility and evidence, and understand the central role of doubt in the whole process.

In the words of physicist and science writer Carlo Rovelli, 'To the very last, doubt. This permanent doubt, the deep source of science.'[105] If we can understand the centrality of doubt in the scientific enterprise, we're going to find we have a far healthier relationship with science, with a much better chance of correctly assessing scientific knowledge when it really matters.

Staying Afloat

☐ *No one has yet successfully defined what it is that makes scientific knowledge special, but the idea of science as a powerful arbiter of truth and falsehood is still very prevalent.*

Why We Are Mixed Up About Science

The idea that scientific theories are 'matching an independent reality' is the way most people tend to think of them. It's a simple vision, what's called a correspondence theory of truth[106] and it's implicit in the version of physics still taught in British schools. It would be no surprise if the vast majority of people – if they think about it at all – believe that gravity is an invisible force (whatever that might mean), and that electrons and protons are solid particles that bounce into one another like billiard balls. Unfortunately, neither of these things is true and in letting people believe this version of science we are giving them an entirely false view of the whole enterprise.

If we want to create significant change here, then we really need to think hard about the way we teach science. This is the start of the misapprehensions and the errors that the media subsequently amplifies. And in our ever more complex society these errors are going to get increasingly serious. The British GCSE (General Certificate of Secondary Education) syllabuses for Physics that I checked made no mention of either quantum mechanics or relativity and only one that I could find (the OCR Twenty First Century Science Suite) has coverage of data collection, analysis and the process of science. It's hardly surprising that people misunderstand the scientific enterprise and the information that science provides if they still think that Newton has had the final word on gravity[107] and that Laplace's Demon[108] can predict the future.

Newtonian physics still flourishes and has such a powerful hold on so many people because it perfectly explains the forces and motion in the world that we see with our own senses. And it does so simply and coherently. Who needs anything more? Only the people building telecommunications networks, nuclear power stations, supersonic planes and any number of other vital modern technologies. For better or worse, we are now reliant on these technologies and they have created problems that we can't escape or fix without the help of the science that lies beyond Newton. We need a much more widespread understanding of how advanced science goes about its business, because we can't run and we can't hide from these problems. We desperately need science to fix the problems it's created and it's never going to do that if too many people have got the hump with the scientific endeavour because they don't understand the way it works.

The way that science is taught – at least up to the age of 16 in British schools – encourages a belief in its output as permanent truths. This idea is promulgated by the media, by experts from other fields and sometimes by scientists themselves. But it's setting us up both as individuals, and as a society, for a crashing fall. We will always be disappointed with science because it's complex, difficult and uncertain and its wisdom is temporary. Science will always disappoint us the way that the anemometer disappointed me on that boat. The answer is not to turn away from science, to throw our hands in the air and declare that we know nothing, because we do – we can see just how much we know reflected back at us in the world around us: planes fly, cars do 300 mph and nuclear power stations generate electricity.

Instead of turning away from science, we need to remember that as humans we need and want the simple stories that we discussed in Part 1. Science doesn't have simple stories, it has complex ones, and the most important one to grasp is the one about how science works, how we should view its theories and how doubt is at the core of the whole process.

Staying Afloat

☐   *Science does not provide us with permanent truths.*

What Science Gives Us

My secondary school science teacher was a wonderful man by the name of Norman Simister, and he took every opportunity to ram a couple of things down the throats of his A-level students. The first was his little green men theory. 'Remember,' he would say, 'this is just an explanation and a set of equations that works – it gets us to the right answer. The real explanation for Brownian motion/gravity/friction could be that little green men are doing it.' Norman Simister was definitely an instrumentalist.

Norman Simister's other bugbear was measurement accuracy. On one occasion he had walked into class and announced that there had been an academic paper published with a new measurement of the speed of light. Of course, we had pretended to be interested and asked the value of the new measurement. It was a trap, giving him the opportunity to explain that everyone knew what the speed of light was; that this was not what was interesting about the new experiments. What was exciting was the confidence and accuracy that the authors of the paper were claiming for the measurement. This was what physics was all about: measurement, but not just measurement, the really important lesson was to understand both the measurement *and* the limits of its accuracy.

We can see the importance of scientific measurement accuracy in the progress made by celestial navigation that I described in Chapter 7. Ptolemy's model worked well enough for the sailors of Ancient Greece because they could only see the stars with the naked eye. Once telescopes were invented, the anomalies in Ptolemy's predictions became more obvious – Ptolemy's theory (that the planets revolved around the earth) worked with measurements of limited accuracy. It failed when better data became available, and a new theory was required. This is how science works; at one level, physics is all about better measurements.

One of the ways that physics moves forward is because better sensors and better measurements produce data anomalous with the current theory. And so, the theory must be changed. Or conversely, a theory will propose a new understanding of how the world works, and it will make predictions that can be verified by measurement. This isn't always how change comes about in scientific theories, which is why Lee McIntyre feels that philosophy of science has given up on defining a scientific method. However, measurement has been important in verification of new and important theories, including one that's probably the greatest achievement of modern science: Albert Einstein's theory of general relativity.

It was Isaac Newton's equations for gravity, developed towards the end of the 17th century, that had accurately explained all the available astronomical observations for a couple of hundred years – until better telescopes and measurement revealed a little problem with Mercury's orbit of the sun. The issue was that the closest point of Mercury to the sun altered slightly with each orbit. Newton's theory predicted this effect – called a perihelion precession – but not the scale of it.

Einstein's equations of general relativity finally explained the full amount of the perihelion precession of Mercury about 60 years after it was noticed. It was one of the first and most important confirmations of his theory, and one of the reasons that general relativity's explanation of how gravity acts in the universe came to replace Newton's theory.

There have been many other confirmations of Einstein's theory over the intervening decades. The equations of general relativity predict that space curves close to massive bodies like a star, and that the sun should cause light to curve around it. This was measured in 1919 exactly as Einstein had predicted. And then there's the prediction that the universe is expanding, a conclusion that Einstein himself resisted, only to have it established beyond any doubt by measurements made in 1964. Perhaps most spectacular was the existence of black holes, created by the collapse of burnt-out stars. Once an apparently wild prediction, now an observable phenomenon. This extraordinary vision of the universe comes from a simple set of ideas and equations; it's a theory of remarkable cohesion and elegance.

So how should we think of this incredible theory? Is this *knowledge*? To get an answer to that we need to look at general relativity in relation to the other great pillar of 20th-century physics. We touched on quantum mechanics in Chapter 2. It has been remarkably successful in describing observable physical phenomena at the level of the smallest particles and is used daily by scientists and engineers to build real stuff that really works in the real world.

Quantum mechanics spawned (in conjunction with special relativity) something called quantum field theory, which became the basis of our current particle physics, and that in turn led to something called the standard model of particle physics.[109] The standard model has been just as successful as general relativity and quantum mechanics in predicting observable, confirmable phenomena, one of which made international news in recent years: the Higgs boson.

During the period when the standard model was being developed there was a long-standing problem; it was to do with the mass of particles, a problem that Peter Higgs solved with an idea called the Higgs field, proposed in a paper back in 1964.[110] The Higgs field explained the mass of particles in a way that made all the equations of the standard model work consistently. It was effective and it became part of the furniture of particle physics – widely accepted. Nevertheless, for 48 years there was no way of confirming the existence of the Higgs field.

The maths predicted that its existence could be confirmed by particularly violent particle collisions that would produce what became called the Higgs boson. It took a 10-billion-dollar international investment in the construction of the Large Hadron Collider at CERN to finally confirm the existence of this little sucker in 2012 – only possible once we had achieved the ability to create the immensely high-energy particle collisions required to create the Higgs boson. Another remarkable confirmation of another incredibly useful theory that has helped us to build the extraordinary technologies all around us.

It would seem, then, that all is well and good in the world of advanced physics. If these theories are so successful, then surely the world of particles and interactions that they describe (however weird and counter-intuitive) must exist. So . . . can we regard all these extraordinary theories as knowledge?

No. There are contradictions in these theories that turn out to be quite significant. Eventually they may well lead to an entirely new physics, in the same way that measured errors in Mercury's elliptical orbit of the sun ushered in general relativity and ended the primacy of Newtonian physics. Carlo Rovelli makes this point in his book *Reality Is Not What It Seems*: 'And yet between the two theories there is something that grates. They cannot both be true, at least not in their present forms, because they appear to contradict each other.'[111]

Rovelli is a theoretical physicist who's spent most of his

life trying to find a solution to this contradiction, so he should know. My favourite example of the schism at the heart of modern physics is dark matter, which was originally proposed as a solution to a problem with general relativity. There didn't seem to be enough ordinary matter in galaxies to stop the fastest-moving stars from leaving, from flying off and leaving the galaxy. The observed force with which gravity was 'pulling' on stars meant that there needed to be a lot more matter in the galaxy than astronomers could see. The name they adopted for the extra mass that was required for general relativity to remain consistent was 'dark matter' (well, these are the people that brought you the 'gluon' after all).

If the predictions of general relativity are correct, then dark matter ought to exist. The problem is that all we can see of dark matter is its gravitational effect. We cannot 'see' it directly; it does not appear to be made up of the particles described by the standard model.

But if general relativity is correct then dark matter must exist, in which case we will need to modify or even discard the standard model for whatever new form of matter that dark matter turns out to be.

Alternatively, if the standard model is complete and correct, then there is no new form of matter, dark or otherwise, and we are going to need a new account of gravity to explain the movement of those fast-moving stars.

The very best we can hope for is that an explanation will emerge that leaves the current theories intact – so we are adding rather than modifying – but as it stands, these theories cannot be regarded as 'true' in any meaningful sense of the word.

This is just one of the fundamental contradictions between the most successful scientific theories that have ever been developed. It will come as no surprise that physicists are tearing at this and other problems every which way, both experimentally and with new theories. String theory is one; quantum gravity is another; both attempt to eliminate the contradictions between general relativity and quantum mechanics, and both currently lack experimental confirmation. Of course, that may come in time, as it did for Einstein and relativity.

Meanwhile, new experiments mean that new data is coming from all over; like ever more powerful telescopes that monitor the behaviour of faraway galaxies. Or experiments that 'drop' anti-matter particles to see if gravity acts differently on them compared to regular particles. Everyone involved in these fields of research anticipates that eventually something will point us to a solution, a new and better theory of gravity, a new and better particle physics or a synthesis of the two.

The problem is that while we are waiting for something to turn up to decide this one way or the other, how should we think about general relativity, quantum mechanics and the standard model? They are incredibly useful in the domains in which they work, the very large in the case of relativity, and the very small in the case of quantum mechanics and the standard model. So, we keep using them because they work, while having to acknowledge that they cannot all be 'true' at the same time. And if they are not true, then what are they? How should we regard them? They are useful; this is the central quality and the only one that we need to care about because . . . *this is how science normally works.*

A theory is useful until a better one comes along. One theory gives way to the next and the process of 'giving way' can be contradictory, messy and very prolonged; and all the while we must live with the doubt about the outcome. Philosophers of science like Karl Popper and Thomas Kuhn and their intellectual heirs have argued[112] and will continue to argue over how that process happens, but no one is denying that it does – and it would be incoherent to think of these theories as true during this process.

The realist might respond that we understand that the current theory is conditional and may be over-ruled, but the whole purpose is still to find out the truth . . . about nature, about reality, about our bodies. It may be that it's useful to think of the ultimate goal of the scientific endeavour as the discovery of truth, but we are so far from getting there that I don't personally believe it helps. We already understand that in many areas of science there are limits to what we can know. The potential for Laplace's Demon and Newtonian mechanics to predict the future has long ago melted into uncertainty and this is a long way from being the only 'edge'[113] to our knowledge.

It's even true in mathematics. If you didn't know any better this surely would be the place to find certainty: 2 + 2 = 4, right? Well, yes, but we don't have to get too much more sophisticated than that before there are problems. In a very famous paper, the Austrian mathematician Kurt Gödel established that any mathematical system derived from a consistent set of axioms (rules or assumptions) will contain theorems that cannot be proved.[114]

In other words, there are things in our maths that we cannot know. And if we can prove everything in an axiomatic system, then Gödel also established that this system is inconsistent, and so will contain theorems that can be shown to be both true and false. However you slice it, 'truth' and 'knowledge' are hard to come by in maths as well as physics. In such a world the only coherent way to think about scientific theories is in terms of their usefulness, in terms of their ability to predict and help us understand the world.

I suspect that most scientists aren't worrying unduly about all this, they are just doing science, getting published, getting cited and getting on with their careers. They judge theories by their success in making predictions that can be published, confirmed, or in producing coherent sets of equations or ideas. They are looking for the best explanation we have for any phenomenon at any given moment in time. A theory is what we know, but judged against a standard of usefulness, an ability to explain and predict, rather than against an immutable gold standard of truth. Any other outlook makes contradictions like the one between quantum mechanics, the standard model and general relativity very hard to live with and work alongside.

This is a long way from the popular idea that scientific truth must correspond to an independent reality. The danger of this difference in approach is the cognitive dissonance when scientists speak to non-scientists about their work. There isn't just the understandable issue of making technical subjects clear to people that aren't versed in the technicalities or jargon that often goes with it; there's also the problem that two sets of people can be talking yet have a completely different view of these things. While one is talking about truth, the other is talking about the most useful and predictive explanation that they have, fully expecting that at some point another one will come along.

It's as though one group is talking about baseball, the other group about cricket. It's no wonder that they rarely make any sense to each other. The result is often that people end up yelling angrily across the divide, unable to get the discussion on to any kind of common ground.

Staying Afloat

☐   *The status of scientific theories is undecided, with little understanding on either side of the argument that an alternative view exists.*

The irony is that none of this really matters for most of us when it comes to physics. At best, I'm an interested spectator – I have no skin in the game. Few of us care about which of quantum mechanics and the standard model or general relativity turn out to be right. It would be nice to be alive when someone finally says, *Eureka, I've got it, I understand the fundamental structure of the universe* . . . but I'm not holding my breath.

However, while I'm happy to stand by and watch while others arbitrate the best available physics theory, I'm not so happy to stand by and watch while others arbitrate the best treatment of a medical condition that affects me. So now I want to take this idea of scientific theories as instruments with a sell-by date on their utility, and consider it in the context of things that really do affect us, like healthcare and climate science. I want to show that non-scientists (and I include myself in that category) will get a lot more out of the scientific information we use if we start to understand it in this way – science is temporary, in doubt and only measured by its utility.

CHAPTER 11

Science in the Real World

A Question About Food

Two centuries of remarkable advances in medical science have given us longer, less painful and much more productive lives than at any other time in human history. It is one of humanity's most effective applications of a scientific approach, so it's particularly important to understand how science works in medicine, particularly when you consider that healthcare is a huge global marketplace predicted to be worth $11.9 trillion by 2022.[115] Where there's money there's both the best and worst of humanity,[116] so we all need to be able to process medical knowledge effectively to protect ourselves from the snake-oil salesmen.

Let's look at an example: food intolerance, the idea that some people find some foods difficult to digest. These people aren't allergic to those foods but eating them nevertheless results in pain and discomfort.[117] The existence or otherwise of food intolerance has been a controversial issue in medicine for at least a couple of decades, partly because it's given rise to an industry providing products that are 'free from' certain foods, the most common being gluten and dairy products. Is this snake oil, or is it useful in treating a real condition?

Dr Steven Novella is a sceptic and academic clinical neurologist at Yale University School of Medicine. In August 2019 he wrote on his Science-Based Medicine blog 'the gluten-free craze continues, despite a lack of evidence that anyone other than the 1% of the population who have true Celiac disease, are harmed by gluten or benefit from removing it from their diet.'[118] Gluten is a component of wheat and other cereals, and coeliac disease is the name for the (non-controversial) allergic reaction to gluten for which there is a blood test. However, there are plenty of people who believe they are intolerant of – rather than allergic to – gluten and avoid eating it.

It's these people that Dr Novella is taking aim at and his comments are pretty typical of the criticism of non-coeliacs who choose to be gluten free. And yet, Britain's National Health Service has a page on their website devoted to food intolerance. And it states, 'A food intolerance is when you have difficulty digesting certain foods or ingredients in food. It's not usually serious, but eating the food you're intolerant to can make you feel unwell.'[119] After listing the symptoms, it warns against paying for a diagnostic food-intolerance test and suggests that 'If you have a food intolerance, try to avoid or reduce eating the food you're intolerant to, including foods where you're intolerant to any of the ingredients.' Who to believe? A clinical neurologist at Yale University School of Medicine or Britain's National Health Service?

Non-coeliac Gluten and Wheat Sensitivity (NCGS) is a condition that I believe was first described by that name in a research paper published back in 1978.[120] It's defined as an adverse reaction to gluten in people that test negative for coeliac disease. And this is the real problem with NCGS amongst the medical community; a patient's self-reported symptoms are the only way to diagnose the illness. At the moment there are no other tests (like blood tests) that can indicate the presence of NCGS – this is referred to as the lack of a biomarker, something that has changed in the bodies of people with NCGS that sensors can measure.

The lack of a biomarker has led to a great deal of work to develop test criteria that will consistently establish the level of symptoms produced in NCGS sufferers when they eat gluten. These are called the Salerno criteria after a meeting in October 2014 in Salerno, Italy.[121] This established a procedure for a double-blind, randomised clinical rechallenge trial of the type that I described in Chapter 7 – Predicting the Future. The criteria have a patient eat a gluten-free diet for a period before gluten or a placebo is introduced into the diet in such a way that neither patient nor researcher are aware of the new food's contents. The subsequent recurrence or otherwise of symptoms is recorded against a defined scale.

The hope is that the criteria will lead to more consistent diagnosis and perhaps, one day, much more convincing evidence for the condition – but at the moment the evidence is still limited. There is an acceptance amongst sceptics like Dr Novella that something is going on. 'This does not mean that NCGS does not exist, and certainly does not mean that patients with possible NCGS do not have real symptoms.' But the hypothesis of NCGS may be incorrect – perhaps something else is causing the symptoms. 'There is probably a reason the ducks are not all lining up. We need to discover what that reason is.' [122] So, researchers continue to work on understanding and testing these ideas, and the hope is that one day they will find a biomarker that will put the matter to rest.

So we have a theory, we have lots of research, and while there is a lack of evidence either way for the existence of NCGS this could just be that we don't yet have the tools, sensors or instruments to convincingly establish the hypothesis one way or the other. The biomarkers could be there – we might be looking in the wrong place, or not have the tools to measure the right things, or not measure them sensitively enough.[123] Does this sound familiar? What if the NCGS idea is like the Higgs field – a working hypothesis that takes a very long time to prove? We waited 48 years for confirmation of Higgs's theory: what if it takes that long to confirm NCGS?

French physicist and Nobel Laureate Louis de Broglie wrote, 'the actual state of our knowledge is always provisional and . . . there must be, beyond what is actually known, immense new regions to discover.' [124] The difference between waiting 48 years for confirmation of a theory in physics and the confirmation of a hypothesis about an illness is that we have to decide how we treat the people that are suffering in the meantime.

The NHS has decided that even though the ducks aren't all lined up, that while the evidence for food intolerance is weak when judged by their normal standards of evidence (randomised, double-blind clinical trials), it is advisable to discuss both the condition and treatments for it on their website. There is enough evidence that something is going on and so – whatever the eventual fate of the specific NCGS hypothesis[125] – there is an acceptance that until we have a better explanation, we will use this one for treating those people. The theory is useful, going gluten free helps people get well, so they support the idea on the basis of that utility. The alternative is to demand a level of evidence that's impossible to achieve with current technology and would meanwhile prevent people from receiving a potentially useful treatment.

We learnt in the previous chapter that Lee McIntyre and his fellow philosophers of science were struggling to define the process, 'the scientific method' that could separate science-done-well from science-done-badly or non-science. Now we see that even when there is an agreed process in a specific field – the randomised, double-blind clinical trial in medicine – problems still get stuck without an answer because not everything can be easily tested using that process. And there are many areas of medical research like this because many medical experiments are impossible for ethical reasons. I mentioned this in Chapter 7 when we were discussing the issues with epidemiology.

In every field of scientific research there are theories that cannot be tested in a straightforward way. If we could devise and run an experiment to definitively test the existence or otherwise of dark matter, then we would. In the case of NCGS it's very difficult, or even impossible to run a gold standard, double-blind, randomised control trial to prove or disprove the theory. These are the difficult cases, the edge cases, and they exist in all fields of science. They are more pressing in medicine because there are people who need treatment right now. So, when we find these cases do we change our evidence base, change the rules by which we judge them, or do we ignore the treatment or new technology?

This is where we have to get comfortable with doubt – particularly if you are one of those cases that needs treatment right now – and understand that we will have to do some work ourselves because there is no single answer. We don't want illnesses being mistreated or patients being taken advantage of by unscrupulous practitioners offering snake-oil solutions. Nor do we want people being turned away by doctors when there's a treatment that shows potential but doesn't yet fit into the mould for the required evidence base. There will always be some level of uncertainty about results. So, there will always be a need for judgement, with the accompanying risks of making the wrong choice when choosing which lane to pick.

When you look at it in this light, the NHS solution is practical and pragmatic. In the case of gluten intolerance there is little (medical) downside to cutting out gluten to see if it helps – perhaps that's why the NHS is ready to publicise that option on their website. Other cases will not be so easy to referee. If we want an answer that we can act on, we have to accept that sometimes we're going to have to figure it out for ourselves – and we're going to have to do it when we have no educational background in the subject. The key to finding an answer is to understand that good science is messy, often incomplete and constantly in flux; remember that there will always be doubt.

Staying Afloat

☐ *We should all judge scientific information by its utility and understand that this utility may be undermined at any moment if another, better theory comes along.*

Living With Doubt

At this point the centrality of doubt to the scientific enterprise should be clear. It is impossible to make any scientific progress without it. If we are using utility to judge our theories, then we are constantly searching for greater utility – and that entails doubt in all existing theories. It's baked into the scientific enterprise and this is understood – whether explicitly or implicitly – by all those involved in it. The rest of us need to get on the same page, and stop regarding science as 'groundless, incomprehensible, didactic truth statements' as Ben Goldacre rather memorably put it.[126]

Doubt is also important and necessary for each of us as individuals as we try to deal with scientific knowledge, because science has many flaws – like any human endeavour it can be done both well and badly. Scientists are human. They can be plain wrong or driven by unconscious bias[127] – not least the bias to publish only what's new and what's different.[128] They can also be motivated by their ego or poor incentive structures. Sometimes the results can be distorted, or even bought by those with a vested interest in their outcome.

So, what are we looking for when we try to assess a piece of science? We've already got a list of things to look for in data from Chapter 7. We can add to that a few more rules of thumb, most of which inevitably relate to healthcare. To start with, if it's in the mainstream media, I'd avoid any science story that's not written by a science journalist. Second, if it sounds too good to be true (*Alzheimer's cure!*) it probably is. Always look at the actual evidence, how the new information was derived, ask how the experiment was conducted. Was it a randomised, double-blind, controlled trial with lots of participants – and if so, is it the only one of its kind to have this result, or have there been many others, and this is just more supporting evidence? Did the experiment get conducted on cells, animals or humans – if it's either of the first two then it's going to be a very long time before anything useful emerges from the lab, and there's a high probability it never will.

All this is explored in greater detail elsewhere; apart from *Bad Science*, there's *Trick or Treatment* by Simon Singh and Edzard Ernst, which is a more specific analysis of the potential benefits of alternative and complementary medicines. Tim

Harford's book *How to Make the World Add Up* is also strong on this stuff. I'd also suggest Stuart Ritchie's book *Science Fictions: How Fraud, Bias, Negligence, and Hype Undermine the Search for Truth*. While I'd question the fact that science is a search for truth, Richie highlights the structural issues with science as it's practised in the 21st century.

If these books take us deep into the cancerous bowels of the nadir of scientific uncertainty, then I shouldn't move on without pointing in the direction of the Cochrane Collaboration. This is an international organisation with members and supporters across more than two hundred countries. It gathers, reviews and evaluates medical information, providing some of the highest quality advice for anyone trying to make decisions about treatments. To quote the website: 'Our global independent network gathers and summarizes the best evidence from research to help you make informed choices about treatment and we have been doing this for 30 years.'[129]

While everyone screws up now and again,[130] there are many sources of scientific information that can usually be trusted. *Scientific American*, *Nature*, *Wired*, Smithsonian.com, *Quanta* and the *National Geographic* are a handful of them. Along with the Cochrane Collaboration, these sites and publications, and others like them can answer many, many questions that you or I might have. And there is always a greater chance of finding a way to a solution if we understand the process by which science proceeds. We need to embrace the uncertain, work-in-progress nature of scientific knowledge and understand that there are no truths chiselled into stone that will stand for all time. We cannot take scientific knowledge for granted. This is the mistake I made on the boat with the wind direction. I expected too much, and I took it for granted. I lacked the doubt that I needed to get the science to work for me. Those numbers mattered to me, and I should have doubted them, I should have paid full attention – I should have checked the utility of the instrument before it really mattered.

Staying Afloat

☐ *Doubt is central to the scientific process; realising this is necessary to gaining an understanding of the information that science is telling us.*

Weaponised Doubt

Almost every human construct and activity has both a positive side and a negative one, like nuclear bombs and nuclear power plants, biological warfare and medicine. Doubt is no different. It drives the whole scientific process, but those who seek to undermine that process also want to make it a weapon. Scientific research doesn't take place in a political and economic vacuum. Maybe it once did, back in some supposedly golden age when a privileged few 'gentlemen' enquired into nature out of nothing more than curiosity . . . although I have my doubts about that idealised version of the past, given that everything is ultimately political. These days there's no question that science is political; it's big business and it's life and death – and the doubt that is so fundamental to the entire scientific process has been seen as its Achilles heel.

The problem with this vision of good science as messy, uncertain and driven by doubt is that it makes it easier to undermine. The fundamental need for doubt in science, the very fact that doubt, uncertainty and renewal of ideas and theories is what drives the whole process forward, makes it that much easier for bad actors to undermine good science, and to make bad theories look good.

The space between the messy reality and our traditional expectations of scientific certainty and truth is where the snake-oil merchants, the peddlers of perfidy, can stick a tyre iron in and lever us open. The charlatans have a great advantage: they can offer certainty, and human beings love certainty, a bias that Daniel Kahneman called the certainty effect.[131] In contrast, science offers only doubt, uncertainty, risk and humanly flawed practitioners. It would be possible to undermine scientific research even if it were published with the force of absolute truth. It's much easier to undermine good science when scientists speak in the expectation that doubt is a core part of the whole process: that a debate will ensue, that more evidence will come to light, and that other newer theories may develop in time and become the best available thinking.

This has given rise to an effective strategy to oppose any scientific theory. Everything possible is done to encourage the public's belief that the matter is not yet settled, that there is more evidence to come, and that the 'truth' that the public seek is actually still in question. At the same time, as much confusing or contradictory evidence as can be squeezed out of the fuzzy edges around the research – and there will always be fuzzy edges[132] – is pushed out into the public domain to further muddy the waters. In this way, doubt is weaponised by political opponents of scientific research.

Scientists have an expectation of an on-going debate that will provide more evidence and reduce uncertainty in the theory, so initially this just looks like the first round of that process – but it's a process that bad actors, determined to obscure the truth about cigarettes or asbestos or climate change can spin out way past the point when sufficient evidence has been collected to convince any independent thinker.

Unfortunately, most independent thinkers never go and look at the evidence, they just wait for the process to end with a final concrete answer from the scientists, an absolute truth. Or, as Ben Goldacre put it; 'absolute truth statements from arbitrary authority figures in white coats'.[133] Science doesn't work that way; it works by amassing sufficient evidence to establish the utility of a theory. So, let's finish by looking at an example of evidence amassing in support of a scientific theory: the climate science models that predict a warming planet.

One of the earliest climate predictions came in what's now called the Charney Report.[134] This report came about as a result of a request from the USA's Office of Science and

Technology Policy to the National Academy of Sciences. They wanted to know if there was any basis to the thesis that increasing amounts of carbon dioxide in the atmosphere would lead to a warmer earth. The idea had been gaining ground since the 1950s. In 1972, John Sawyer, the head of research at the UK's Meteorological Office, had published a paper in *Nature* predicting that an expected 25 per cent extra CO_2 in the atmosphere by 2000 would lead to a global temperature increase of 0.6 °C.[135] The actual global temperature rise over that period was 0.5 °C.[136]

Back in 1979, this verification was still to come though, and the Office of Science and Technology Policy wanted their own high-quality assessment through an independent study of the issue. So, a distinguished group of atmospheric scientists, led by chairman Jule Charney, gathered under the umbrella of the Climate Research Board of the National Research Council at the NAS Summer Studies Center at Woods Hole, Massachusetts, on 23–7 July 1979. The resulting report stated in its summary and conclusions: 'We estimate the most probable global warming for a doubling of CO_2 to be near 3 °C with a probable error of ± 1.5° C.'

After reading Part 3 we should all recognise this for what it is, an excellent verifiable prediction – no woolly punditry here. They knew that they couldn't adequately predict the amount of carbon dioxide that was going to end up in the atmosphere over time as this was dependent on so many unknowable factors. They did think they could predict the temperature rise for a given amount of carbon dioxide though, and that would be verifiable at any point in the future. They also knew the limits of their modelling, and so the error bounds are quite wide.

The NOAA (National Oceanic and Atmospheric Administration) has data showing the monthly mean carbon dioxide concentrations for atmospheric carbon dioxide at Cape Matatula in American Samoa, and this shows a change from 336.3 parts per million (ppm) in 1979 to 409 ppm in 2019, a rise of 21.6 per cent.[137] If we use the Charney Report's prediction that a doubling of carbon dioxide would produce a rise of 3 °C (± 1.5 °C), then a (roughly) 20 per cent increase in carbon dioxide ought to produce a rise of 20 per cent of 3 °C – or 0.6 °C.

The National Aeronautics and Space Administration's (NASA) Goddard Institute for Space Studies (GISS) provides data on global temperatures[138] and their data for the same period shows an increase in the global land-ocean temperature index of 0.79 °C (I've averaged 1978–80 and 2018–2020 to provide some smoothing). This is very close to the best estimate of 0.6 °C and well within the error bounds.

This prediction was based on a forty-year-old and very limited model, but I've picked it for two reasons. The first was its independence from the actual amount of carbon dioxide pumped out, so it was verifiable over time regardless of how much carbon dioxide actually ended up in the atmosphere. The second reason is the time that has elapsed since the prediction was made. In Chapter 7 we saw how chaos theory undermined weather forecasting, but these chaotic short-term effects average out over time.

This is what the Intergovernmental Panel on Climate Change's (IPCC) Fourth Assessment Report (AR4) has to say about it:

> The chaotic nature of weather makes it unpredictable beyond a few days. Projecting changes in climate (i.e., long-term average weather) due to changes in atmospheric composition or other factors is a very different and much more manageable issue. As an analogy, while it is impossible to predict the age at which any particular man will die, we can say with high confidence that the average age of death for men in industrialised countries is about 75.[139]

The greater the number of men that we consider, the more accurate the average is likely to be, and so the longer the time period that we consider climate predictions over, the fairer the test will be.

Things have got a lot more sophisticated in the last 40 years; the predictions have improved, and the error bounds tightened. Chapter 1 of the IPCC's AR4 provides an excellent review of the historical improvements in climate modelling. When the observed data is compared to the predictions of the first three Assessment Reports, they all fall neatly within the error bounds.[140] The report also discusses in some detail the complexities and errors involved in the process. There is no doubt that there is uncertainty in climate science and there is no end game of absolute truth – but there are also plenty of verifiable predictions. If, or when, you see something different in the media remember what we learnt about data and statistics in Chapter 7. Selectively picking data sets or model outputs can make it possible to show a much wider range of predictions, and it can be done in a way that makes them fail – this is not representative of what's happening in the atmosphere.

There will always be people willing and able to manufacture doubt when scientific results threaten their interests. And, given everything I've said about science, data and doubt, it's clear that this is not a difficult thing to do. There are two responses: the first is that once we accept utility and doubt as the lens through which we see scientific theories, it's easy to refute the claim that *the evidence isn't all in* – of course not, the evidence is never all in. That's the point of science. Or if you hear that that there's *no consensus amongst the scientists* – then we'd hope not, because that would mean the death of the scientific process.

When you come to see that the goal of science is never to reach a conclusion it becomes impossible for anyone to attack scientific output because it hasn't reached the truth yet. Instead, judge a theory by its utility, judge it by the evidence, by the predictions it makes and has made. This is going to mean getting your hands dirty and it's an understandable reaction to feel that there's just no time for all this. Don't worry, when it matters, there will be time. When it really matters there will be no shortage of motivation to sort the nonsense and the non-science from the science.

Staying Afloat

☐ *Don't be fooled by the professional sceptics trying to weaponise doubt.*

I hope that these few chapters have done justice to an immensely complex and fraught subject and provided a framework for your thinking when you next confront scientific knowledge in a situation that matters. Science is hard, and it can sometimes take a very long while to find an answer. However, more than at any other time in human history, the internet and a much more open and engaged scientific environment have made it easier to find the information. Science is still the very best way we have of understanding the world, but first we need to understand how science works.

Part 4: Staying Afloat Summary

☐ *It's important to fully understand scientific information before we rely on it.*
☐ *No one has yet successfully defined what it is that makes scientific knowledge special, but the idea of science as a powerful arbiter of truth and falsehood is still very prevalent.*
☐ *Science does not provide us with permanent truths.*
☐ *The status of scientific theories is undecided, with little understanding on either side of the argument that an alternative view exists.*
☐ *We should all judge scientific information by its utility and understand that this utility may be undermined at any moment if another, better theory comes along.*
☐ *Doubt is central to the scientific process; realising this is necessary to gaining an understanding of the information that science is telling us.*
☐ *Don't be fooled by the professional sceptics trying to*

weaponise doubt.

PART FIVE – CHANCE

Luck is everywhere, but we don't see it clearly

Those who have succeeded at anything and don't mention luck are kidding themselves.

LARRY KING

CHAPTER 12

The Fourth Gold

Max Pressure

This is a story about an extraordinary sporting performance delivered under almost unimaginable pressure – perhaps as much pressure as any single man or woman has ever faced in a sporting environment. I was writing and commentating for World Sailing's website at the 2012 London Olympics, and I watched it all unroll live. I thought back then, as I do now, that the parallels would be a decisive fifth penalty kick in a World Cup final, or Andy Murray's 2013 Wimbledon final as he fought to break a 77-year-old record of British sporting failure. This one is different from those though, because it was a performance from an individual athlete who had been completely dominant in his sporting discipline for two decades.

Ben Ainslie had already won a silver at the 1996 Olympics and gold in 2000 in the Laser class, before changing boats for the 2004 Olympics. For a period of about four years he focused on the Finn, winning the World Championship (called the Gold Cup) in 2002, 2003, 2004 and 2005, along with the Olympic gold medal at the 2004 Games. It was a period when Ainslie was untouchable; it didn't seem to matter what befell him, he'd still win. He had glandular fever in the winter ahead of the 2004 Olympics and couldn't train for ten weeks. Then at the Games he had a poor first race, was subsequently disqualified from the second in very controversial circumstances,[141] and at the end of day one was deep in the fleet. It made no difference, he went on to win comfortably, barely needing to exert himself in the final race.

After that, Ainslie started to broaden his sailing experience, joining Team New Zealand for the 2007 America's

Cup and consequently he sailed the Finn a lot less. He still won the Gold Cup in 2008 and 2012 though, the years when he was competing in the boat at the Olympic Games. When we think of people who have played the game at a different level to everyone else – Michael Jordan, Eliud Kipchoge, Tom Brady, Lionel Messi, Usain Bolt – we must include Ainslie in that list. And that's why this story is interesting, because even while Ainslie was untouchable as a single-handed Olympic sailor, chance still played a role in his story. So, if we can see the fickle hand of fate – bad luck and good – in this story, then you can be damn sure it's acting in your life. And if that's the only thing that you take away from Part 5, then it will have done its job.

When Ben Ainslie launched his 4.5-metre single-handed sailboat out on to the waters of the Olympic racecourse on 5 August 2012, the prize was an Olympic gold medal, but not just any gold medal. A win would make it his fourth gold and, when added to the silver that he won at the start of this journey in 1996, it would break the record of Paul Elvstrøm. The 'Great Dane' (as he became known) had set what was then a 52-year-old record in 1960 when he won his fourth – and final – Olympic gold medal in sailing. Another gold on this day in 2012 for Ben Ainslie would take him past Elvstrøm and make him the most successful Olympic sailor in history.

It's unlikely that there would be any second chances. The creaking and groaning from Ainslie's body was almost audible as he jumped aboard and pushed the boat out on to the sunny waters of the harbour. There were cortisone injections in both ankles. A long-term back injury had required surgery over the winter and, although it had stayed solid in the run-up to the Games, it had now flared up again. On the rest day, Ainslie had almost taken an emergency helicopter trip to a clinic in Hertfordshire for a spinal epidural. Only massage and painkillers were holding him together. He knew his body wouldn't go another four years; it was now or never.

Ben Ainslie's Olympic discipline was the heavyweight single-handed boat, called the Finn. It might have been an omen, it might not, but this was the same type of boat that Elvstrøm used to sail to three of his gold medals. And the Nothe racecourse in Weymouth, the sailing venue for the London Olympics, was not an easy place to sail. On his way out to the start, Ainslie had to watch as two of his oldest and closest friends – Iain Percy and Andrew 'Bart' Simpson – lost their gold on the final lap in the Men's Keelboat discipline. A gold medal that they had held at the final turning mark, until the unpredictable winds over the Nothe course eased it out of their anxious hands just short of the finish.

Ben Ainslie had to put this agonising vision out of his mind. He had to put everything out of his mind if he was to tune into the boat, and the elements of wind and water that would decide the fates that day. It was a task to which he was singly well adapted. Single-minded focus is what Ben Ainslie does best. It had got him through some of the toughest, most pressured racing that Olympic sailing has ever seen. It all started in 1996 when, at the age of 19, Ainslie had narrowly lost out to the Brazilian wizard Robert Scheidt on the waters off Savannah, Georgia – at the time, the South American Laser sailor was tipped to be the best ever. Most of his peers had accepted the fact – and so Scheidt had them beaten before they even launched their boats.

Gold #1

If he was going to turn silver into gold in 2000, Ainslie had to break down this psychological advantage piece by piece in the four years before the Sydney Olympics. Scheidt won the World Championships in 1997, then Ainslie beat him for the first time at the top level in the 1998 Worlds in Dubai. He repeated the feat in Melbourne the following year, before Scheidt took the title right before the Sydney Olympics in 2000. Going into the Games it was 2–2; the margins were wafer thin and no one doubted that this would be one of the contests that lit up the Sydney Games.

But by the final race, it looked as though the Brazilian had done all the hard work; the points meant that Ainslie must beat Scheidt by at least ten places to take the gold medal from him. It was unlikely that a sailor of Scheidt's class would finish that far down the fleet, and for Ainslie to rely on it was immensely risky. But the fine print of the contract, i.e. the racing rules and points-scoring system, meant that a second route was open to the top of the podium. Each sailor was allowed to discard his worst two race results. Ainslie's discarded races were much better than Scheidt's; the maths revealed that if the Brit could sail the Brazilian back past 21st place, then Ainslie would take the gold medal.

And that's exactly what he did. The resulting duel was played and replayed on television, cable and the new technology of internet streaming. It was fast and brutal, and for the uninitiated totally inexplicable. The original four-minute-mile man Sir Roger Bannister was horrified at what he regarded as Ainslie's lack of sportsmanship and said so on the record. It was rubbish; the Brit was simply ahead of his time, employing tactics that are now commonplace in Olympic sail sport. It was also brilliantly executed; Ainslie's tactics didn't just push Scheidt back the required number of places – Scheidt finished 22nd – it also suckered him into two penalty offences. The second one earned the Brazilian a disqualification and any chance of the gold medal.

Twelve Years Later

Twelve years and two more gold medals later, Ainslie's task on 5 August 2012 was relatively straightforward in comparison. Only two men could take it away from him. The man with the best chance was – ironically – a compatriot of Elvstrøm's. Denmark's Jonas Høgh-Christensen had sailed out of his skin for the first six races, beating Ainslie in all of them. By the rest day, he had a ten-point lead over the Brit, with only four races left in the regular series.

A lesser competitor might have grasped at the trip to

Hertfordshire for an epidural, but Ainslie was not about to blame the back pain. Instead, he spent the day in massage and reviewing video of the first six races. 'I remember watching Bradley Wiggins ride to gold in the Olympic time trial. The thought process that I went through was: *This guy is exceptional; he has just totally dominated the field. I am exceptional. I can and I should be dominating this fleet.* I thought harder about how I was approaching the racing. I was being too conservative, and I wasn't taking enough risk or racing to win.'[142]

Rested, revived and with a new and more aggressive attitude, Ainslie launched out of the blocks when the action recommenced in race seven and took an easy win. The pendulum had reached the top of its arc and was about to start back the other way. It was given an unlikely shove by Ainslie's two closest competitors – Høgh-Christensen and the Dutchman Pieter-Jan 'PJ' Postma. In race eight, the pair ganged up on Ainslie to force him into taking a penalty. While sailing does have umpires at the Olympic level, they don't cover the whole course at all times. If a rule is potentially broken when they aren't around, then the aggrieved party can file a protest and a hearing is held after the race when the penalty for an infraction can be disqualification.

If the alleged transgressor doesn't want to risk disqualification, they can do a penalty right there on the racecourse – usually sailing around for one or two circles to lose distance on the competition. Ainslie was adamant that he hadn't fouled, but there were no umpires around, and no cameras. It was two voices to one, and Ainslie's only realistic option was to take the penalty and sail on. It cost him two places and 50 metres, dropping him to fourth. He sailed back up to third and, more importantly passed Høgh-Christensen on the final leg.

Ben Ainslie had clawed back seven points for the day. It was huge, but there was more; Ainslie stepped ashore and said straight to a television camera, 'They've made a big mistake cos I'm angry and you don't want to make me angry.'[143] Apart from single-minded focus, this is the other thing that he does best.

Mild of manner, even shy and always polite off the water, once he's out there he never backs down and he never gives up. Ever.

The following day was the final day of the regular series with two more races, and Ainslie clawed back one more point on Høgh-Christensen to move to just two points behind. After being ten points down with the series more than half over, Ainslie had now created a winner-takes-all finale. Even if Ainslie only beat Høgh-Christensen by a single place in the last double-points scoring 'medal' race they would draw level and – since the tie-breaker would give the gold to the top performer in the medal race – that meant that Ainslie would take it.

The random factor was that PJ Postma had closed the gap on both of them; if he could win the medal race with Ainslie and Høgh-Christensen outside the top seven, then he would snatch the gold out from under both their noses.

The morning of 5 August dawned with a mix of sunshine and cloud. It was warm, the crowds on the beaches and sprawling on the grass were all in T-shirts, shorts, summer dresses. The breeze was blowing from the south-west at about 20 km/h – very pleasant conditions for sailing. The lighter conditions and inshore course favoured Ainslie, who was giving up almost 10 kilos of weight to Høgh-Christensen.

Ben Ainslie thrives on his professionalism, on perfect preparation. He knows that nerves are acceptable; in fact, nerves are inevitable, unless you simply don't care enough. The answer to those nerves comes in the knowledge of your own preparedness. It's not just about the overall picture either, it's about the detail, about washing the boat down before you race to ensure the surface is immaculate and slippery as hell. It's about doing the work on the racecourse, getting out there in time to check and find the fastest way around the track. He sailed the course with the New Zealander, Dan Slater, to compare notes and realised that – unlike almost every other time they had raced on this course – the inshore side closest to the beach was the quickest. Normally, going offshore and out into the bay paid, but not today. The knowledge would pay dividends. It would also turn out that this was not the only important intervention that Slater would make on this day of days.

The warning gun fired to begin the countdown to the start. It's the moment when the umpires begin to operate, when the boats start jockeying for position on the line, their actions now controlled by a complex set of rules. It's the moment when penalties start being given and taken, when one boat can manoeuvre against another.

Controlled Aggression

Ainslie went for the jugular from the gun. He had taken down Robert Scheidt in 2000. He had won the world championship in the one-on-one format of match racing in 2010. He knew how to get another competitor behind him, and he knew how to keep him there. But Høgh-Christensen was no fool, he knew Ainslie would be coming for him, and he had a plan. He defended well, circling the start boat like a boxer dancing around the ring. Ainslie couldn't pin him down for long enough to work any real advantage.

Finally, with thirty seconds to go, Høgh-Christensen broke for the line with Ainslie right on his tail. They sailed behind the rest of the boats – who were all lined up to start – looking for a gap that they could duck into. Ainslie wanted to push Høgh-Christensen into a small gap, into a position where he was too close to another boat. A good start requires clear water and clean wind – if anyone else is too close then one or other boat – and possibly both – will be significantly slowed. If Ainslie could push Høgh-Christensen into a tight spot the Dane would be slow off the line and give Ainslie an opportunity to sail past him and into a controlling position.

Høgh-Christensen found a gap with less than 20 seconds to go. By chance (or maybe not), on one side of that gap was PJ Postma – the only other man who could beat Ainslie for gold. Høgh-Christensen attacked, closing the gap between him and Postma so that Ainslie couldn't fit. The Brit dodged the move, accepted that he couldn't control Høgh-Christensen off the start line and bailed out to head for the space the other side of Postma. Immediately, the Dutchman sensed trouble; he had to act to defend his own position on the line. He went after Ainslie.

A flurry of manoeuvres and a handful of seconds later . . . the start gun went. Høgh-Christensen was clean off the line, while Ainslie and Postma were way too close to each other. Høgh-Christensen worked hard on his narrow advantage and quickly popped out in front. It was 1–0 to the Dane, with the three gold medal contenders side by side.

A few seconds later and Ainslie had worked out a tiny advantage over Postma, who started to slow. Soon after the Dutchman bailed out and headed the other way. He was going towards the inshore side of the course. Was it still faster? Time to find out . . . Ainslie followed Postma. Høgh-Christensen kept going; the gap and the leverage started to open. Leverage is an important word and a vital concept in sailboat racing. Leverage measures the distance between two boats at right angles to the wind direction. The greater the leverage then the greater the risk – just like finance and markets.

The closer that two boats are together, the more likely it is that they are in the same wind and water conditions. In the same conditions, it's up to the sailors to make their boat go faster than the competition – but once they start to separate, then any small difference in conditions will advantage one boat or the other. The bigger the gap between the boats, then the greater the gain will be to whoever is in the better wind conditions. This is free speed – it's as though a runner were allowed to choose a route, one of which may or may not lead to a travelator and add a couple of miles an hour to their pace with no extra effort.

One fundamental skill in sailboat racing is spotting where the better wind conditions are on the racecourse, and what the next change is going to be. No one can see the wind – no one can see the air move, but there are clues where it touches down on the land – making one flag fly more strongly than another, for instance. Or where it touches down on the water, leaving darker patches, or bigger waves. The racer who can read these clues most effectively can gain a massive advantage, if they are prepared to gamble on what they see. What they are gambling is leverage . . .

And on that sunny August morning under the gaze of thousands of spectators and millions watching on screens around the world, the leverage between Ben Ainslie and Jonas Høgh-Christensen was growing. The gold medal could be settled right there, right off the start line – but for those watching, ignorance was largely bliss. There were very few who knew the intricacies of the racecourse. Of those that did, the ones supporting Ainslie had their hearts in their mouths. *Offshore* is normally faster, it normally pays, and he's going *inshore* . . .

The gap grew and grew. Stomachs tightened. Throats constricted. Chests refused to impart a full breath. Finally, Ainslie headed back towards the middle of the racecourse, and Høgh-Christensen did the same. Both men glanced anxiously across the water at their opponent as the gap closed back up. It took a little time, but . . . Ainslie was going to come out clear ahead. The commentators knew it. The spectators on the grass with a grandstand view knew it. And soon it became clear that Høgh-Christensen knew it too. He changed direction to parallel Ainslie, to maintain the last of the leverage, hoping for a better moment, another change in conditions that would allow him to close out his position with a smaller loss.

And that's the other thing about leverage; for much of the time, either boat can choose to maintain it, and while the leverage is stable no one is winning or losing. It's only when the leverage gets closed out – like selling a stock-market position – that the gains and losses solidify and become permanent. Unfortunately for Høgh-Christensen, no one can maintain the leverage for ever. Eventually the boats must come back together at the turning marks at the end of each leg. When they got to the first mark, Ainslie had a narrow lead of about 5 metres over Postma, who was perhaps 20 metres ahead of Høgh-Christensen. It was 2–1 to the Brit.

Up To Second

The fleet turned back the way they had come, and now had the wind blowing from behind them. On to the second leg: this was a part of the race that Ainslie had always excelled in. Yes, the laser-like ability to focus was important. Yes, the ability to never blink in a confrontation was important. But we should never forget that none of this would matter without an extraordinary ability to make a sailboat go fast through the water.

By the end of the second leg, Ainslie had blown past everyone except – and only by a couple of metres – Jonathan Lobert of France. Behind Ainslie, Postma was fourth with Høgh-Christensen sixth. It was an unbelievable display of athleticism and technique, cheered all the way by the huge crowd; as the racers turned around for the second lap, it must have seemed to the cheering thousands like the job was done. They were wrong.

This time all three boats headed inshore. Ainslie's strategy was clear – he had to make sure that Høgh-Christensen was behind him. He kept his foot on the Dane's throat, covering his every move, and Høgh-Christensen took them inshore. Postma had to get past both of them though, and he was not going to do it by following them. He took a calculated risk and changed direction to go offshore – remember that this was the route that was normally advantaged.

Conditions had shifted, the streak of extra wind that had made the inshore side so profitable on the first lap had gone. Now the percentages started to reassert themselves, and the offshore side began to pay. By the next mark Postma had thrown a double six and gone past them both. And they had all dropped back – Ainslie and Høgh-Christensen were now at the back of the fleet, with Postma just in front in sixth. Luck was on the side of the Dutchman.

The situation didn't change much on the next leg, and by the end of the second lap Postma was still just ahead of Ainslie, who was just ahead of Høgh-Christensen. The gold medal was still headed for Britain and into the record books. Postma headed back towards the newly favoured offshore side. Høgh-Christensen headed inshore. Once again, Ainslie was a passenger – he had to stay with Høgh-Christensen. A bell was now ringing like a text alert in the head of PJ Postma and the message was . . . *opportunity*.

Roll The Dice

If Postma was going to win gold, he needed Ainslie and Høgh-Christensen back deeper than seventh place – and now they were. He just had to win the race, but that wasn't going to happen unless he created the leverage, took the risk necessary to try to make a big gain. So Postma bet the house on red and sailed all the way into the offshore corner of the course.

Two things now happened. Høgh-Christensen found a little extra speed and started to gain distance on Ainslie, who was forced to split away to find better conditions before the Dane simply sailed past him. Halfway up the fifth leg, Postma was all the way offshore, Høgh-Christensen all the way inshore, and Ainslie was in the middle. If you were neutral it was spectacularly exciting: they could not have got more spread out on the racecourse if they had been following instructions in a coaching exercise. If you were backing one or other of the three men, the tension was intolerable.

When they came back together at the mark it was Postma who was the big winner. This time offshore had paid out on red, and the Dutchman was now rich, very rich. He rounded the top mark in third place. Ainslie had retained control of Høgh-Christensen, but the pair were now last by a distance. If Ainslie finished ninth, and Høgh-Christensen tenth, then Postma needed to pass just one more boat to go up into gold. And the man in front of PJ was Dan Slater.

Slater and Ainslie went way back, their first serious contest coming at the 1994 Youth World Championships when the Kiwi had beaten Ainslie for the title by a single point on a tie-break. At the time, Ainslie was calm and polite despite the disappointment, and the two men began a long friendship. Now, almost twenty years later, Ainslie had done the maths, he could see the danger, but if there was one thing he was sure of after twenty years of sailing against him, it was that Dan Slater wasn't going to give that place up to Postma without a fight.

Postma had the bit between his teeth, he could smell gold now, and he closed Slater down fast. There was one final turning mark, and then a very short, straight leg to the finish line. The gap got smaller and smaller, and as they approached the final mark, Postma pushed and finally got up alongside Slater and into a passing position.

Others might have just waved the gold-medal contender by, figuring that it wasn't their fight. And a calmer, smarter, or less driven man than Postma might have settled for bronze or silver. But Slater wasn't about to wave anyone by – particularly not in front of a British home crowd – and Postma was neither calm nor smart.

They had just 50 metres to the finish after the final mark, and Postma had a medal in his hands – but he threw everything on a chance of gold. He went for an inside pass of Dan Slater at the final mark. Slater's reaction was immediate – he had the rules on his side, and he was going to use them to defend his position. He reckoned Postma had got level too late to legally take the shorter, inside track around the mark and make the pass. Dan Slater defended his position with all the force the rules gave him, and Postma's boat (the rig to be precise) touched the back of Slater's boat. It was a clear foul, the umpires pounced and while Postma was taking his penalty his medal hopes evaporated in the Weymouth sun.

All that was left for Ainslie was to sail to the finish; close out ninth place and the gold medal was his. He certainly wasn't going to screw that up. Ainslie crossed the line in ninth, with Høgh-Christensen behind him. He pumped his fist a half dozen times in celebration, but mostly he was feeling relief and as photographers, cameramen and interviewers crowded round he just wanted to hold his composure and not lose it in front of a few million people.

'Dan did the right thing and protected his position, but it would have been very easy for him, as someone out of contention for a medal, to let PJ past and turn the result. Life has a funny way of coming full circle and I guess it was also a good example of taking the time to build relationships. It is true that when times are tough you really do find out who your mates are,' he said much later.[144] It was a desperately close-run thing, but Ainslie had his fourth gold medal; he had made Olympic history. Stick a fork in it: that dream was done.

I said that I picked this story because I want to convince you of the importance of luck. If there was ever anyone that could have claimed to have lifted his performance so far above everyone else that luck didn't matter it was Ben Ainslie. He had talked to his Finn coach, David Howlett, about it when he first started sailing the Finn in 2002. 'We discussed the fact that sailing has a certain "randomness" to it at times,' he said later. 'You can't control the weather and from time to time it can put paid to the very best sailor's chances. David's view though was clear; if you want to guarantee victory in 2004 then you need to be the best beyond doubt, you need to be so good that even if you have bad luck, or equipment failure, or you are not one hundred per cent, you can still win. You need to be "exceptional". It was some of the soundest advice that I had ever heard and from then on my goal was to dominate my opposition.'[145]

And yet, right at the death, at the very end of the final race of this extraordinary Olympic career, the role of chance was clear. Ben Ainslie did everything right: immaculate tactical and strategic decision making; a demonstration of the blistering downwind speed that had been one of his trademarks. He did all the right things, all the smart things, but Postma had placed his bet and come up golden to make a huge and unpredictable jump up the fleet.

And so, Ben Ainslie had been left on the final leg of this final race needing the fates to pay that back . . . There were people racing that day who didn't particularly like Ainslie. If one of them had been in front of Pieter-Jan Postma at that final mark – and had nothing to sail for personally – then they could well have waved the Dutchman by, rather than defending second place. Instead, it was Dan Slater, who wanted and needed to hold his second place. And so it played out. Ainslie won his fourth gold, and the world rolled on.

Staying Afloat

- *Chance, randomness, lady luck, fickle fortune – call it what you like, it always plays a role in life.*

CHAPTER 13

Learning the Right Lessons

Luck Matters

There was a quote from Bruce McLaren on the glass wall of the CEO's office in the Portsmouth headquarters of Ben Ainslie's Land Rover BAR America's Cup team. 'The luck thing – really there's no such thing as good luck. It's good preparation and hard work.' I never really liked that quote, and my problem with it is that it encourages people to miss something really fundamental about knowledge. Luck plays a significant role in life and if we ignore it, then we can get fooled into believing the wrong things.

There's no shortage of sports people keen to pronounce on the nature of luck – probably because they spend their lives ruled by it one way or another. 'The harder I practice, the luckier I get' (which is often attributed to golf players Gary Player and/or Arnold Palmer) gets closer to it than the McLaren quote, with a somewhat reluctant acknowledgement that luck exists, while still telling us to work hard.

I prefer 'Luck is preparation waiting for an opportunity,' which is in Ross Brawn's book with Adam Parr, *Total Competition*, but its original author is probably Seneca the Younger, a Roman Stoic philosopher. At the other end of the scale is a saying attributed to an American baseball player from the 1930s and 1940s, Lefty Gomez: 'I'd rather be lucky than good.' Indeed, but don't forget to practise, Lefty.

Hopefully by now we can all agree on one thing: that talk is cheap, so what does the data say? There's plenty of analysis out there and the overwhelming conclusion is that luck matters . . . a lot. Eli Ben-Naim, a researcher from the Los Alamos National Laboratory, along with two colleagues from Boston University,

Sidney Redner and Federico Vazquez, took the data from five major sports leagues in England and the United States to examine, as their paper explains, 'how often a team with a worse record overcomes an apparently superior one'.[146]

Their paper churned through an immense amount of data. It analysed almost all the results from the English Premier League, the US's National Football League, National Basketball Association, Major League Baseball and the National Hockey League. It amounted to 300,000 games stretching back over a century of top-flight competition in those five sports, across two countries, and included the use of a simulation model to account for the distortions of varying season lengths.

The conclusion was a proposed 'upset likelihood' that they labelled 'q' – a measure of how often a weaker team beats a stronger one. The reasons why that happens are many and varied: the stronger team could play poorly, have a bad strategy, be missing star players to injury and so forth. It will also happen more often if the league is tight, with small performance differences between the teams. The stronger team could also be unlucky. So, it's a proxy for the competitiveness and unpredictability of the league, and the degree to which luck could be impacting the results.

In the English Premier League (at least up until 2006), the chance of a weaker team beating a stronger one was a staggering 45.2 per cent – so on almost half the occasions when a weaker team turned up to play a stronger one, they won. Amongst the US sports, Major League Baseball (44.1 per cent) and the National Hockey League (41.4 per cent) weren't much different, but basketball at 36.5 per cent and gridiron at 36.4 per cent were the most predictable of the five sports – there was only a one in three chance that the underdog would turn over the favourite. Still, however you slice it, this still leaves a significant proportion of all these sports open to chance.

There are some interesting consequences of this. If the stronger team only wins a game of football 55 per cent of the time, then what does that mean for single-game elimination tournaments like the venerable FA Cup? The favourites are always the top Premier League clubs who join in the third round proper with six (of 14) rounds left to play. The probability of the best team winning six consecutive rounds of football when they only have a 55 per cent chance of winning each match is 0.55 to the power of six,[147] which is just under 3 per cent.

So, the chances of the strongest team winning the FA Cup in any given year are a little bit under 3 per cent. Those are not great odds. And this brings us back to my first point about decision making and luck; if we ignore it, then we can get fooled into making some poor decisions. A successful season in the FA Cup can often obscure management failings at a football club – but it's mostly luck and should be ignored. The real test of competency comes in the league competitions where every club plays each other twice, once at home and once away. If your team has a poor season in the league, but the manager holds on to his job thanks to a good Cup run, don't hold out much hope for the following year.

Just as luck can impact the outcome in sport, so it can in life. The thing is not to get fooled by it. I mentioned back in Chapter 4 that it was a good idea to make a routine of revisiting choices and actions, to get better at decision making by practising it. Practice requires feedback and that only comes from analysing how a decision or action played out. It isn't just a matter of looking at the outcome though and now we can see more clearly why – luck.

We don't control all the variables in life. It's quite possible to do everything right, and still get a crappy outcome because things just didn't break your way. The important part is not just recognising this but recognising how hard it is to see it clearly. We saw in Chapter 4 that we have a strong predisposition, or cognitive bias, to look for a causal reason for any sequence of events, a story to tell about them. We already referenced Daniel Kahneman's point about this in Chapter 2; one of the consistent themes that occurs in our explanatory stories is to put too much weight on ability and intent and not enough on luck.

Luck is one of the things that we always leave out of the narratives we use to explain events. We don't like to think that luck matters in life, but it does – and while the very nature of luck is such that its impact is random, we can mitigate its effects through the choices we make. The most important of these is not to be fooled into making a bad choice because luck got missed out in the explanation of a series of events.

The fate of managers in pro sport is a very good example. If those responsible for hiring and firing them don't understand the deep role of luck in the sport they can over-react to short runs of bad results, or good ones. We can't control luck, but we can control how we react to it. Instead of firing a manager after nine or ten games, a football club chairman needs firstly to look at the manager's process, how they are doing their job. Do they have the support of the players and coaching staff, for instance? If so, then patience is valuable because luck can significantly skew the average results in such a small sample size of games.

There are two different ideas here: the first involves a thing called regression to the mean; and the second relies on the difference between assessing the outcome and the process that achieved it.

Staying Afloat

- *We should understand that luck always intervenes and often matters. Knowing this we are better able to mitigate its impact on events.*

Regression To The Mean

The argument we're making is that we must be alert to the influence of luck on the events around us. The tendency is always to write it out of the narrative, misinterpret what happened and jump to the wrong conclusion. It doesn't matter whether it's a sports star or a salesperson taking a leap in performance. We want to write a narrative that explains it: new training, new attitude, new maturity ... Sometimes it's just luck, even when the improvement lasts for weeks or months.

In the end, though, performances will even out and return to the average – this is called 'regression to the mean'. It's really important to understand the impact that ignoring it can have on judgement. Unfortunately, it's another of those topics – like Bayes' theory – that no lawyer wants to have to explain to a jury, because you are going to lose their interest, and then you're going to lose the trial. So, bear with me on this one ...

The first point is that regression is inextricably tied to correlation, which we came across in Chapter 7: a mutual relationship, interdependence or connection between two or more things. We can measure the strength of the correlation between two variables and score it as a coefficient from -1 to 1; where 0 means there is no correlation, and an absolute value of 1 means the correlation is perfect, that one variable moves precisely with another.

The value of the correlation coefficient depends on how many of the same factors contribute to the value of both variables, and by how much. An example of a poor correlation would be between people's height and the hours they spend commuting each month. There are no factors that I can think of that contribute to the value of height *and* the commute time for an individual. So, there is no correlation, the coefficient is 0.

In contrast, a good correlation would be found between people's height and the height of their parents, because there are shared genetics that will contribute to height in both cases. It was Sir Francis Galton who first noticed that this correlation is not perfect, and that it varies in a very significant way. What Galton found was that if the parents are exceptionally tall, then their children will be shorter and closer to the average, to the mean. If the parents are exceptionally short, then their children will be taller, also closer to the mean. The extremes tend to move back towards the centre. This was the first data demonstrating this phenomenon of regression to the mean.[148]

It took Galton a while to realise it was in fact ubiquitous and to come up with a general formulation: that we see regression to the mean whenever the correlation between two variables is less than perfect.

It's a revelatory notion because it explains so much of what we see around us, since many of the events that interest us – monthly sales figures, an individual's exam results or a player's results at tennis tournaments – are imperfectly correlated to each other.

In the case of the monthly sales figures, each result in the overall data set of 'all monthly sales figures' has some dependency on the quality of the product, the number of good relationships the sales person has with regular customers, the overall demand for the product and many other factors – including luck. These factors will all vary, and create the overall variability, the 'noise' in the monthly figure.

This is exactly the same as each height in the overall data set of 'height of the child relative to the parents' having some dependency on the same factors: genetics passed on by the parents, the quality of the diet, exercise, acquired illnesses and so on. These factors will all vary and create the overall variability in the height of the child relative to the parents.

Any particular month's sales figures will be linked to all the others in the data set of all monthly sales figures by an imperfect correlation. Just as the height of any child relative to its parents is linked to the heights of all the other children relative to their parents by an imperfect correlation. The key consequence of this is that the monthly sales results, like the children's heights, will always regress to the mean. Any series of exceptional results – good or bad – in children's height, monthly sales figures or sports performances will eventually be followed by ones that drag the overall data set back towards the average.

This is our experience of life: a series of exceptional events, good or bad, followed by ordinary ones. It could be an exceptional month of sales figures, a series of brilliant exam results for a student, or disastrous tournaments for a tennis player – but whatever it is, any run of exceptional events will eventually come to an end and return to the long-term average.

However, because we tend to view completed data sets like children's heights, we get into the habit of thinking that all data sets are complete. Whereas the monthly sales figures and the tournament results come in one at a time. This makes us terribly susceptible to recognising random, short-term runs of results as patterns *and then writing an explanatory story about them*. The stories are wrong and any conclusions we draw and decisions we make based on them will also be wrong.

The critical point is that there is no cause for this regression to the mean – it just happens. There is no explanation for it other than a regression to the mean. The problem is that – as we saw in Part 1 – we still want to tell a story, a causal story to explain what's happened. When we do try to explain something that's essentially inexplicable, the very real risk is that we are going to set ourselves off down a wrong path. This is where luck can have its most insidious and damaging effects – by encouraging a belief in a false narrative, a fake explanation.

I see this all the time in sailing tactics, particularly where races are sailed over several laps of the same course. On any leg there are any number of factors that can contribute to whether a boat does well or badly: variations in the wind or current, the speed of the boat, the quality of the manoeuvres and the performance of the opposition are a few of them.

At the end of each leg the crew need to review what happened and work out why gains were made, or losses taken, so that any mistakes can be avoided on the next lap. Some of the time this is obvious because there's one single dominant cause: a poor manoeuvre maybe, or a big wind shift that advantaged a particular group of boats. More often, it's not obvious at all, because there were a number of very small changes that all added up. Some were gains, and some losses, but they push the result in one direction or another. It's when the number of small changes all go in one direction to create a big effect on a particular boat – especially if it's a big loss – that people get in a tailspin.

The risk is that the urge to write a causal story to

explain what happened latches on to one of those small changes and amplifies it to explain all the losses, or the gains. This explanation – it might be that there was more wind on one side of the racecourse – then causes a change in the tactics for the next leg.

This is the wrong call, because the number of smaller effects will reshuffle in a different way on each leg, and it's very unlikely that the change in tactics will be a good one. The right thing to do would be to stick with the plan, because this one extreme outcome will soon regress to the mean and the original tactics will work again.

An awareness of the role that regression to the mean plays in any outcome can help us make better decisions. We're going to go on to look at the difference between those outcomes and the process that delivered them, but first I want to mention one other way to mitigate the impact of chance in our lives: avoid endeavours where it has a disproportionate effect.

In Chapter 7 I talked about the difference between a normal or Gaussian distribution and a power-law distribution. It's worth reiterating that point here; any activity (professional sport, music, writing books amongst them) that follows a power-law distribution is going to disproportionately reward the spoils to a few. And so, the way this handful of people are selected will inevitably involve more luck than other endeavours in which the spoils are more evenly distributed along a bell curve.

The role of luck in the careers of superstar sports people, musicians and actors is rarely mentioned because it doesn't fit the narrative they want to tell us, or the narrative that we often want to hear – which is that hard work will be rewarded. Yes, hard work will (most times) be rewarded, but only if you pick a career where the rewards are normally distributed. If you don't, then all that hard work could well be wasted.

Staying Afloat

☐ *If the correlation between two variables is less than perfect, those variables will regress to the mean – don't mistake this regression for anything else, or bad decisions will follow.*

Process And Outcome

The theme so far has been to recognise luck for what it is, acknowledge when it occurs, and accept that while we can't control luck, we can control how we react to it. This theme is recognised in the often-heard suggestion that we should focus on the process and not worry about the outcome. The advice is found in sport, life coaching, mentoring and professional and business training. The ideas behind focusing on the process are two-fold – whether it be the trained preparation and execution of a physical skill or improving a business or decision-making process. Firstly, as lots of psychologists will tell you, thinking about the outcome – the plaudits, glory or riches to be gained by success – is a distraction from the focus required to execute anything effectively.

The second and more relevant idea in the context of luck is that while we can control a great deal of the process, there are many aspects that we can't control about the outcome. The outcome is where luck intervenes. There's nothing we can do about a random gust of wind that blows a golf ball off course – if the process of taking the shot, of striking the ball, was perfect, then it was a good shot. Similarly, an intelligent decision can be made by weighting and synthesising all the right factors and considerations, but if a rare event intervenes (like a pandemic) then the outcome can still be poor.

The fact that the outcome was unexpectedly good or bad because of a random event is irrelevant and shouldn't influence our approach to the next process. It's hard to argue with this – but it's also very hard to do. We still want to blame ourselves for a poor shot. The reason that it's hard to do is a thing called 'outcome bias'.[149] This pretty much does what it says on the tin; we have a natural bias to overly weight the outcome when we are evaluating the quality of a decision or action. Instead, we should be considering the quality of the process that went into the action or decision.

We should also be careful that we don't become solely concerned with the process – the outcome still matters. After all, if the outcome is never the one that you want then maybe the process needs changing. Outcome bias overly weights the outcome, but the answer is not to discard the outcome altogether. The answer is to remember the role of luck and consider both when you are assessing any kind of performance, decision or judgement. Was luck disproportionately involved in the outcome? If so, then look to the process in any review or critique. If there wasn't any luck involved, or if a very, very long run of poor outcomes doesn't seem to be improving and does seem to be the mean, then maybe the process is wrong and needs adjusting.

Staying Afloat

- ☐ *Focus on outcomes, but if the outcome is always bad, then maybe the process needs changing.*

I hope that Part 5 will convince you to take better account of randomness when you are appraising a situation or information – but let's not fall for the opposite error of putting everything down to luck. Even when half the game is chance, there's still one half of the outcome that you can control.

Part 5: Staying Afloat Summary

- ☐ *Chance, randomness, Lady Luck, fickle fortune – call it what you like, it always plays a role in life.*
- ☐ *We should understand that luck always intervenes and often matters. Knowing this we are better able to mitigate its impact on events.*
- ☐ *If the correlation between two variables is less than perfect, those variables will regress to the mean – don't mistake this*

regression for anything else, or bad decisions will follow.
- *Focus on outcomes, but if the outcome is always bad, then maybe the process needs changing.*

PART SIX – PROBLEM SOLVING

Creativity can be created

If I had only one hour to solve a problem, I would spend up to two-thirds of that hour in attempting to define what the problem is.

ATTRIBUTED TO ALBERT EINSTEIN

CHAPTER 14

An Inspired Idea

Non-Starter Motor

There are many times when the problem is not the sifting of knowledge, not the sorting through it looking for the information we can trust – sometimes the problem is the absence of knowledge, the lack of a solution to a problem. I'm going to tell what is probably my favourite story in the book because it turns on an inspired piece of thinking, one of those answers that's completely obvious once you know it. However, it's not the brilliance of the solution that's the point (dazzling though it is): the point of Part 6 is that this kind of thinking can be learnt, can be practised and can be improved.

The story starts at Cape Horn, or close to it, although not close enough for the main protagonists. 'It's not usually like this here . . .' is one of the most-heard phrases at any sailing event. Turn up to the venue expecting strong winds and you'll get mirror-like calms, expect gentle breezes and it will blow a gale . . . It's a variation of Murphy's Law and it applies to Cape Horn just like anywhere else. So it was that on 17 February 1998, a group of racing sailboats were struggling towards Cape Horn with almost no help from the wind.

This was the Whitbread Race; beginning in 1972, it was the first crewed yacht race to circumnavigate the planet. By 1998 it was some way down the road on its journey towards a fully professional event, eventually becoming the Volvo Ocean Race that featured in Part 3. The boats were called Whitbread 60s, all built to a set of rules to determine fair and even racing and crewed by experienced and largely full-time professional sailors. I don't think we were calling them athletes at that stage and for good reason. There was still a hard-partying culture around the sport in general and that event in particular.

It was the fifth leg of the race, 6,670 nautical miles from Auckland to São Sebastião in Brazil. It wasn't the longest, but it had the most demanding mix of conditions. The boats started from New Zealand and then headed south to set up for a traverse of the Southern Ocean. The tactics were the same as those required in Chapter 6. There were no ice gates in those days though, and the skippers and crews took their chances on how far south they were prepared to push for advantage as they raced to Cape Horn. The great cape was where they could finally escape from the Southern Ocean, the moment when they could turn to the north, away from the cold and into the heat, variable weather and currents of the east coast of South America.

Fortunes had varied widely even before they got to the Horn; two boats had lost their masts and were limping towards South America. The leader had got to the famous headland two days previously, before the power supply had cut out. They had turned a narrow advantage at Cape Horn into an enormous lead, staying with the wind as they went north up the coast. They left everyone else to deal with a huge windless zone that now smothered latitudes all the way from Uruguay to Antarctica. These boats were struggling just to get to the Cape, never mind go around it. Their crews could only reflect – as they inched towards their destination on a glassy ocean at about the same speed as a baby crawling – that this was not what was in the brochure.

One of the boats was *Chessie Racing* – an exception in a largely commercially funded fleet. *Chessie* was privately financed by owner and skipper George Collins, but with a crew that included very well-known names from the pro circuits. One of those was the engineer, Rick Deppe. Rick was from Yorkshire, Bradford more specifically, where he was introduced to sailing through his local comprehensive school. Bitten by the bug, he found his way to a gravel pit and a sailing club, where he spent his weekends crewing on other people's dinghies – wooden, sometimes home-built, the kind of thing you can pick up second-hand for less than the price of an Xbox and a couple of games. When he finished school, he packed a bag, bought a ticket to Florida, and started walking the docks to look for a job.

Rick Deppe found one, and from that inauspicious start he made it on to a crew for one of the most glamorous and successful race circuits of the late 1980s and early 1990s. It was the launchpad for Deppe to finally achieve his dream of racing around the world, a goal met when he was invited to join the *Chessie* crew. And so it was that Rick and *Chessie Racing* found themselves approaching Cape Horn at the back of the fleet, in the most unseasonable of weather. The lack of wind was more than just a tiresome inconvenience though: they were fast running out of drinking water.

The generator is essential to survival aboard a modern racing boat, as they don't carry enough water to complete the voyage. Instead, they carry a small desalination plant to make seawater drinkable as they go along. These machines are run off the electrical power in the batteries, and the batteries are charged by the generator or engine. No generator or engine means no water, and since almost all the food on board is freeze-dried and needs to be rehydrated, nothing to eat either. And that's before we've got started on all the other systems that go down when there's no power on the boat – navigation, communications, lights . . . although the toilet should still work. Not that anyone would be needing it much.

The loss of these things isn't necessarily a big deal – particularly in daylight, fair weather and with the security of a harbour or marina just a short sail away – but there are times when it can be very, very serious. So, when *Chessie Racing* reported from deep in the Southern Ocean that the starter motor on the generator was dead after water had leaked into the engine compartment, it was clear that they were in trouble. Rick Deppe went through everything he had on the boat in the way of spares and tools trying to figure out a way to fix it or get it started. And just about everyone onboard had a look over his shoulder or a word of advice at some stage or other – doubtless attracting

Rick's dry and sometimes acid wit. The motor even had a hand crank – like an old 1920s automobile – which they had already used to start the engine. Unfortunately, it was also broken.

The crew of *Chessie Racing* were no slouches, and Rick is one of the most resourceful people I've sailed with. He taught himself to shoot and edit video during this race, and then converted that experience into a job as a cameraman and field producer for the multiple-Emmy-winning television documentary about Alaskan crab fishermen, *Deadliest Catch*. He then got a position as the onboard reporter in the 2008–09 edition of the Volvo Ocean Race, cleaned up the prizes for media reporting all the way around, including the overall Inmarsat Media Prize. He went on to manage the teams of onboard reporters in future races before landing a job making corporate videos for Inmarsat. Nevertheless, this problem beat him and the rest of the crew. And eventually, dry-mouthed and hungry, they sailed (very slowly) off the racecourse. They headed for Ushuaia, just north of Cape Horn, to meet some expensively freighted spares hot-footed from *Chessie*'s base in Baltimore, Maryland, USA.

Le Professeur

A couple of years later, the Vendée Globe was passing the same way. This was the race that made Ellen MacArthur famous – a solo, non-stop circumnavigation of the planet in 60-foot monohulls that's arguably the planet's toughest and biggest sailboat race. At the time, I did wonder what the non-sailing public thought of the Volvo Ocean Race requiring, by comparison, a dozen men to do the same thing as a five-foot-two-inch woman. Perhaps the near-hysterical response to Ellen's achievement was the answer. It would have been hard to believe if you'd read the headlines at the time, but Ellen didn't actually win the 2000–2001 Vendée Globe.

'It was the last day of 2000, and when I started the engine the previous day, I had heard a bad noise, but I didn't care. The day after, I wanted to start it again to charge the battery and nothing happened when I switched on the contact and pushed on the start button . . . So, my first job was to remove the starter to understand why it didn't switch on. I removed it from the engine and then I opened it, and I found out all the brushes are more or less dust, nothing repairable.'[150]

The speaker was Michel Desjoyeaux, also known as MichDesj, or Le Professeur for his analytical, intelligent approach to life. And on New Year's Eve 2000 he was leading Ellen MacArthur in the Vendée Globe, deep into the Southern Ocean and on the way to Cape Horn. 'My press officer told me, "But, you should have a spare for this, no?" And I told him, "No. If I carry a spare part for this, then I carry two boats, which is not efficient,"' he continued.

The engine had been built by YANMAR and Desjoyeaux had good contacts there, so his first act was to talk to them. 'They told me, "Oh, we are very sorry, something [like this] happen one time in one million maybe, and it's a very low occurrence issue you have now, and we are very sorry, and we can't help you because there is no solution."' The response must have seemed like the end. The rules are strict for the Vendée Globe race. Unlike the Whitbread Race, once a boat has started (and restarts are allowed within a time limit) there is absolutely no physical assistance allowed – so for Desjoyeaux, a stop anywhere to pick up spare parts would mean that he was out of the race. How could he possibly fix the starter without the parts? It would have been a harsh ending to what had been a brilliant performance to that point. However, Desjoyeaux was no ordinary sailor; there's a reason he's known as Le Professeur.

Michel Desjoyeaux grew up in his parents' shipyard in Concarneau in Brittany and sailing was his life from the very beginning. 'My home was attached to the yard, and the yard was our recreation when we were young. We didn't need to go on holidays anywhere, because . . . I mean, we didn't want to go on holidays anywhere, because we had everything we needed . . . I also did all my school lessons until I was ten with my mother, who did the teaching at home.' It's hard to imagine a better background for becoming familiar with boats and marine engineering.

He was just twenty when he competed in his first round-the-world race as crew for the legendary Éric Tabarly, and he's followed that French icon into sailing history with a series of exceptional achievements. Few would argue that he is the most successful solo racer of all time, having won the Vendée Globe not once, but twice. In 2008–09 he overcame a 40-hour deficit to win.[151] He's also won the less well known (outside France anyway) but probably more competitive Solitaire du Figaro three times, along with two major trans-Atlantic races. Desjoyeaux is also an innovator, introducing the 'swing keel' – a way of canting the keel of a yacht from one side to the other to improve efficiency and performance. It's now standard on most racing yachts whose rules will allow it, as well as more sophisticated, expensive and performance-orientated cruising boats.

The man has had a great career, and one of the most extraordinary moments came after his discovery that he couldn't start his engine in the Southern Ocean. 'I switched off all the electronics that were not useful, only the [auto-]pilot with the compass left; no displays, no computer, no satellite connection, no weather forecast, nothing. The minimum possible, no navigation lights, I was fully in the Southern Ocean and I didn't need lights because there is nobody. And I spent a lot of time at the helm to save energy, preferring to sleep during the day when there was a little of bit of sun for the solar panel to help me . . . during those days I tried to understand what I could do to try to find a good solution.

'I was a bit farther [east] than New Zealand, so it was too late to make a U-turn. This was very lucky for me, because I think that if I would have been able to get to Australia or New Zealand, then certainly I would . . . I think that maybe I would postpone, stop the race . . . put the traffic indicator light on left, and turn.' However, pulling out wasn't an option, so Desjoyeaux had to find a solution. It was a very long way to Chile without power; particularly without the desalinator, the autopilot or communications – but this was the same problem that had defeated the men aboard *Chessie Racing* two years earlier in very similar circumstances.

Reframing The Problem

The state of the starter motor and lack of spares forced Desjoyeaux to look at the problem another way. Could he start the engine without it? The boat did have a second alternator, the device that turns mechanical energy into electrical energy to charge the battery. 'There was a big additional pulley at the front of the engine, and the two alternators were horizontal, one each side. So, my first idea was to remove one belt of one alternator and drill a hole to be able to put a screw in and attach a pad-eye to the pulley.' The pad-eye would allow Desjoyeaux to attach a rope to the pulley. 'Then maybe four or five turns [of a rope] around the pulley, then find a second block on the front of the boat and go out from there to the cockpit and on to a winch.'

    The rope (it was red) that Desjoyeaux had attached to the pulley on the alternator would allow him to turn the engine over – just as a rope starts a lawnmower engine, or an outboard. Once it was led out from the interior of the boat on to the deck, he could try using the mechanical advantage of the boat's winches to help him pull. 'I turned the winch and I understood directly that the load was not necessarily very big. I had the capacity to pull this load . . . but for sure, with just a winch, I would not be able to pull long enough and hard enough to make it start. It was cold, the temperature was more or less between zero and five degrees Celsius, so it's not very easy for a diesel engine to start. And I didn't have enough battery to pre-heat the engine.'

    Still, Desjoyeaux could feel his excitement rising; back at the YANMAR offices, they had been able to start an identical engine manually. 'One of the things we asked them was to understand how much you can unscrew the injector.' Desjoyeaux's engine didn't have a decompression lever, fitted to older engines to allow them to be manually started using a hand crank. They reduce the pressure in the engine, so it's easier to turn it over. Then, once the rotation of the engine has begun and it has momentum, the pressure is reapplied and the diesel explodes.

'I unscrewed each injector . . . I remember it's a three-quarter of a turn on each screw to have the minimum pressure to make turning it over easy, but also the minimum pressure to make the explosion possible when the engine compresses the diesel. In the YANMAR factory, they were able to start the engine with three people pulling on the rope . . . I was confident,' he explained, 'because I realised that the load to turn the engine and try to start it was not very big. We didn't need tons, we just needed maybe two or three hundred kilograms, but no more . . .' And Desjoyeaux, a master problem solver, knew exactly where he could find a force that would pull a rope with 200 or 300 kilograms of load.

The sails.

'I tried to make a system to pull with the jib . . . it connected direct to the jib sheets.' The jib is the smaller sail at the front of the boat, and Desjoyeaux connected his 'starter rope' directly to the ropes that control that sail. The idea was that if he released control of the sail the wind would pull it, and the starter rope with it. 'The problem is that when you ease a sheet [release control of the sail] you get a very big load at the beginning, but when you start to ease the sheet, the sail collapses completely and you are not able to maintain power long enough to start the engine.'

Desjoyeaux realised that the jib wasn't powerful enough. 'I didn't want to use a bigger sail or a sail [like a spinnaker] that could break, because I will need to do this operation every day. So, my idea was to go to the mainsail.' Desjoyeaux sailed *PRB* on an angle to the wind that normally requires the mainsail, the biggest and best-controlled sail on the boat, to be set at about 50 or 60 degrees off the centreline of the yacht. Instead, he pulled that same sail in as hard as possible with the rope that controls it (the mainsheet) so it was as close to the centreline as possible – this is called over-sheeting.

The red rope was wrapped around the engine pulley at one end, and then run via the mainsail (attached to the boom, the spar that controls the mainsail) to a fixed point, where the other end of the rope was attached. Once everything was in place Desjoyeaux released the mainsheet. The tremendous load from the wind on the over-sheeted sail pushed it out at huge speed, transferring this force to the red rope all the way back to where it was wrapped around the pulley . . . In his own words:

'So, my red line [attached with the turns around the engine pulley] goes to a pulley at the back of the boat, up to the boom, back to the mast foot, the mast base, back to the cockpit. When I needed to start the engine, I prepare my rope in the boat and on the engine with the five turns. Then I trim in the mainsail more than needed for the performance, I pulled on the red line, pulled on the winch very strong, removed the mainsail sheet from the winch, put the contact on the engine, burn the diesel arriving at the injector with a small spark to heat it just before the injectors. And then I come to the cockpit, open the clutch of the mainsail [the device holding the mainsheet tight], and then it pushed the main out . . . the first time I tried this, the engine started. It was incredible because it means that I was able to continue the race.'

Alone in the Southern Ocean, Le Professeur had figured out a fix that had eluded Rick Deppe and the rest of the crew aboard *Chessie Racing*. It was simply breathtaking in its ingenuity. Michel Desjoyeaux was able to finish the race without stopping for spares or help and beat Ellen MacArthur to win his first Vendée Globe – rarely if ever had it been more deserved. It was an exemplary piece of problem solving that has joined the canon of MacGyver solutions, being used again by Sébastien Destremau in 2016 – and quite probably by others.

Creative Problem Solving

When I first heard the story of how Michel Desjoyeaux started his engine in the Southern Ocean, I could not help but wonder how I might have fared in the same situation – especially as I'd already seen Rick Deppe struggle with the same problem and I hadn't exactly been rushing to tell him the answer was obvious . . . The one advantage that Michel Desjoyeaux had was necessity – they say it's the mother of invention, and it may well be that Desjoyeaux was able to figure out a way to start his engine simply because he had no other options. He was forced to focus on the actual problem, the real goal – starting the engine – rather than getting distracted by the apparent problem, a broken starter motor.

Substitution bias, or attribute substitution, is a cognitive bias[152] that's usually applied to decision making. We tend to substitute an easier or more obvious question for a hard one, and there's something similar going on here. The actual question is 'How do I start the engine when the starter motor is broken' – but the easier question to try and answer is 'How do I fix the broken starter motor' because that's the thing right in front of us, broken. Perhaps the impossibility of repairing it forced Desjoyeaux to shift to the real question and look for solutions to that problem. Whether the complete absence of other options helped him or not, this was still an exemplary piece of problem solving.

Staying Afloat

☐ *The problem in front of us isn't always the one we need to fix.*

CHAPTER 15

Finding Inspiration

Learning To Solve Problems

It's easy to think that only an exceptionally creative mind could have come up with a solution like Michel Desjoyeaux's fix for his broken starter motor. However, writers like Edward de Bono, the author of *Lateral Thinking*, or Michael Michalko, who penned the much more recent *Thinkertoys*, want us to understand that there are practical methods to improve creative thinking and they can be learnt; creativity can be created by planning and knowledge of the right techniques. They have their differences over the best processes for encouraging creativity, but that doesn't undermine the central point I want to make in this chapter: that there are practical methods to improve creative thinking – to fill a knowledge gap – and they can be learnt and practised.

There is an example in *Thinkertoys* that covers exactly the ground that Desjoyeaux travelled to get to his solution. Imagine, suggests Michael Michalko, that you are in a room with two pieces of rope hanging from the roof. The challenge is to tie the loose ends of the ropes together. Unfortunately, they are sufficiently far apart that when you hold on to one, you cannot reach the dangling end of the other. The solution relies on the same thought process that Desjoyeaux used – the problem must be framed in the right way.

'Initially, you might state the problem as: "How can I get to the second string?"' wrote Michalko. This would be a mistake; it's going to lead you to expend a lot of effort trying to do something that's impossible. Instead, think of the problem differently. Michalko suggests framing it as, 'In what ways might the string and I get together?' And now a new and different range of solutions opens up, like tying a weighty object to the loose end of one rope and setting it off in a pendulum motion that will swing it towards you, while you are still holding the other rope.[153]

We saw that what led Desjoyeaux right up to the moment of inspiration was the way he framed the problem. Edward de Bono makes an interesting point in this respect in *Lateral Thinking*. We tend to think of milk bottles that are half filled as half empty, but when they are half filled with water they become more readily described as half full. And the reason is that we start with a bottle full of milk and it becomes half empty, whereas an empty milk bottle becomes half full of water. As de Bono says, 'The history of a situation has much effect on the way it is looked at.'[154]

In many cases, the way a situation develops defines what de Bono calls the dominant idea. The difficulty is escaping the dominant idea to a space where alternatives will spring up. De Bono again: 'Unless one can pick out the dominant idea one is going to be dominated by it.'[155] A great way to start solving a problem is to work out what idea is going to dominate the range of solutions. Only when you have recognised it can you work around it, go off at a tangent to it, or otherwise avoid becoming trapped by it.

A great deal of de Bono's *Lateral Thinking* process is about reframing things, or at least escaping the obvious framing, because that's often the route to an answer. 'Lateral thinking is concerned not with development but with restructuring.'[156] When the problem is structured in the right way, the answer will come. After talking it through with him, I don't think Michael Desjoyeaux knows how he arrived at his solution. It's trite to say that it just came to him, but that is the way it works sometimes. What de Bono and Michalko want us to understand is that this moment of it 'just coming to us' can be made more likely with the right techniques. I want to show the power of this by looking at a couple of techniques that might have – should he have employed them – pushed Desjoyeaux towards the same answer.

The first is a technique called 'Slice and Dice' which comes from *Thinkertoys*, 'identify and list the various attributes of a problem and work on one attribute at a time,' says Michalko.[157] The attributes are just the components of the problem; they may be simply descriptive, they may explain any process involved, the function of a device, a social context, financial or environmental considerations.

One example that Michalko provides is of a frozen-fish processor whose product tastes bland. He tries to fix it by keeping the fish in tanks until the very last moment, but they aren't interested in cooperating, and 'remained listless'. When the attributes of the fish were listed, one of them was 'Constantly moves to escape from predators' and this led to the solution. They put a small shark in the tank and that kept the fish on the move, and that extra movement gave them a much fresher flavour.[158]

If we take this approach with the diesel engine, what attributes might we list?

- Metal
- Precision engineering
- Burns diesel fuel to create mechanical energy
- Efficient method of conversion of fuel to energy
- Diesel ignites through mixing with highly compressed hot air
- Delivers power when an exploding gas expands and moves a piston to rotate an axle
- Starts when required pressure and temperature is achieved in pre-combustion chamber so that the diesel will burn
- One of many ways of creating mechanical energy by burning carbon fuel
- Exhausts carbon monoxide and hydrocarbons with ecological consequences

Everyone's list will be different, but there's a good chance that something in there will spark the right line of thought. In this case, it's probably the notion that the starter motor isn't doing anything that clever. All that's required is sufficient force to compress the air and some warmth applied to the fuel. The problem then becomes one of applying the necessary force. And there's sufficient force on a sailboat to move it through the ocean, so why can't that be applied to starting the engine?

Another technique is called SCAMPER,[159] and this relies on the idea that 'Manipulation is the brother of creativity' as Michalko puts it. When you're stuck, manipulate something that already exists to find a solution. SCAMPER is a set of prompts that will help with that process, originating with Alex Osborn, the 'O' in the American BDO advertising agency (he's also credited with coming up with the idea of brainstorming). The mnemonic came about in 1971 with Bob Eberle's book, *SCAMPER: Games for Imagination Development*, and these are the driving ideas (they can also be framed as questions):

- Substitute
- Combine
- Adapt
- Modify
- Put to another use
- Eliminate
- Reverse or rearrange

In the case of Desjoyeaux's engine, *substitute* immediately suggests a line of thinking – what else could provide the functionality of the starter motor, particularly when combined, adapted or modified? I'm not suggesting that this was Desjoyeaux's process; as I said, I think the idea just came to him, as it sometimes does to the most creative of people. I'm just trying to demonstrate that for those of us not blessed with this superpower, there are well-established techniques that can help get to a solution, and these are just a couple of examples of those creative pathways.[160]

Staying Afloat

☐ ***Problem solving is a skill that can be learnt.***

Randomness

If there's one simple thing that can inspire creativity – something that we can all carry around with us – it's randomness. In Part 5 we saw how chance changes outcomes; now it's time to *harness* chance to change outcomes. Randomness helps to solve problems because it can provide the nudge that reframes a problem. There are lots of stories of chance events spurring significant discoveries – like the apple that fell on Sir Isaac Newton and inspired his thinking on gravity. Or Archimedes 'Eureka' moment – when a bath in an overfull tub inspired his discovery of the principle that now bears his name (that a body in a liquid experiences an upthrust (buoyancy) equal to the weight of the water displaced). While these stories are probably apocryphal, this is one of those times when the truth of the story doesn't lie in its facts – random experiences do generate insights that solve problems.

So how do we harness chance to help us solve problems? The time-honoured method is to take a walk or do something completely unrelated to the problem. Open the space up so chance can take hold; a chance encounter with something or someone in the world, or a chance encounter with a thought that will drift into your head once you stop hammering at a problem.

If that's not your thing – and I'm spectacularly bad at walking away from any kind of problem – then there are some well-regarded tools. One of them is Oblique Strategies, a set of cards developed back in 1975 by the musician and producer Brain Eno and painter Peter Schmidt.[161] It's a simple box of cards with a few words or sentences that're intended to jolt people out of a rut, to ease the stuckness by providing a link to a new direction, a reframing of the problem. They are now available (and much more cheaply than the cards) as an app for iPhone and Android – well worth the money next time you're facing a problem that resists solution, or even before that. Understanding techniques like this can really help when you most need it and taking time to do the groundwork now and tune up problem-solving skills will – at some point – pay a high rate of return on the investment.

Staying Afloat

- ☐ *Learn problem-solving techniques because you never know when or where you're going to get stuck next.*

Part 6: Staying Afloat Summary

- ☐ *The problem in front of us isn't always the one we need to fix.*
- ☐ *Problem solving is a skill that can be learnt.*
- ☐ *Learn problem-solving techniques because you never know when or where you're going to get stuck next.*

PART SEVEN – COPING WITH COVID

Knowledge 2.0 at work

It's going to disappear. One day, it's like a miracle, it will disappear.

DONALD TRUMP

CHAPTER 16

Knowledge in a Pandemic

A Novel Coronavirus

On 31 December 2019 a new virus – a novel coronavirus that would soon come to be called Covid-19 – was reported to the World Health Organisation. It was first seen in the city of Wuhan, in Hubei Province, China. Over the next 24 months it would cause almost a million excess deaths in the United States, and over 135,000 excess deaths in the UK.[162] The Covid-19 pandemic was the most extraordinary personal, national and international challenge that I've seen in my lifetime, and all of the topics of Knowledge 2.0 were at the heart of dealing with the threat.

The chances of coming through the Covid-19 pandemic with family, health and wealth intact were improved for anyone who could see-through the fake *narratives*, like the ones about injecting bleach, breathing steam or the pandemic being a global conspiracy. The national leaders who understood the threat clearly and weren't pumped up by an irrational over-*confidence* would protect their people better. Those who could understand the *predictions* for the development of the disease would be properly prepared. Those who could understand the *science* and pick the right advice to act on would significantly raise their chances of survival. Understanding that *chance* would play a role in whether they caught it, and how their body might react to it if they did, allowed people to correctly calibrate their behaviour to the threat. And, finally, it was *problem solving* that provided the escape route from the crashing wave of chaos – from vaccine development to 3D-printing masks at home – and allowed humanity to overcome this immense challenge. Let's look at some of the ways that this played out.

Narrative

Politicians and their tribes fought tooth and nail to control the narrative around Covid-19. Do you remember the stories about nurses relating how dying patients would gasp with their final breath, 'This can't be happening, the pandemic isn't real!'? There was a frenzy of media attention in November 2020 around tweets from a South Dakota ER nurse that reported this event. *Wired* journalist David Zweig followed up on the story. He called other hospitals in South Dakota but couldn't find any other nurses who'd had the same experience. Zweig's *Wired* story reported, 'None said they'd interacted with Covid patients who denied having the disease.'[163]

It's possible that one nurse did hear this from a patient or two, but it was nothing like the widespread phenomenon that subsequent media coverage would have had us all think. Maybe there was a kernel of truth to it, but the story had the power to replicate and spread because it was useful; it played to the expectations of a proportion of the audience. The virus had become highly politicised in the US. This evidence of someone's sad, hopeless denial of the existence of Covid-19 was tailor-made for Democrats wishing to hit Republicans over the head with the consequences of misinformation about the disease. So, they did, without bothering to check the depth and veracity of the story any further. Knowing or unknowingly, they were fighting misinformation with more misinformation. Don't be seduced by a good story.

Confidence

It should not have required a growing death toll to get British Prime Minister Boris Johnson to attend his first Covid-19 crisis meeting – he skipped the first five.[164] He was a long way from being the only one to be over-confident about the pandemic though, as documented by researchers at the Federal Reserve Bank of New York. They showed that 'there is a significant gap between the perceived public and personal risks, especially in the near term. For the three-month horizon, the expected personal exposure is lower than the public exposure by 17.5 percentage points.'[165] No one's judgement is perfect, so be prepared.

Prediction

One of the most controversial aspects of the British Government's response to the early stages of the crisis was its initial reliance on computer modelling to predict the spread of the virus. And there was clear doubt about the output of these models. An Oxford University study in the spring of 2020 created headlines reporting half of the population could have been exposed to the virus.[166] If half the population had already been exposed and so few were sick what was there to worry about? It turned out there was a lot to worry about as this result was generated by an extreme set of initial assumptions.

Until the Government finally intervened with social distancing restrictions on 23 March 2020, every individual had to make their own choice on how to respond to all this information – essentially, to stay at home, or to carry on as normal. The modelling data and news reports from other countries that had got the disease first were all part of that decision process. So, let's look at how the early Covid-19 models fared when we examine them in the light of our tips for 'staying afloat' that relate to prediction with data and modelling. The idea is that this process will help us work out how to treat predictions when we have no personal expertise in that area.

I wrote the responses to these questions in the spring of 2020 after an hour or so of internet research – I've subsequently changed the tense and added the footnotes (which aren't the original sources in all cases) but not much else.

> *Consider whether a prediction includes the influence of everything that might affect the outcome.*

No one was sure whether there was a seasonal element to transmission of the virus at that stage.[167]

Always ask if the science behind a prediction is well developed and effective.
Both virology and epidemiology appear to be well resourced and mature disciplines – however, the need for assumptions about human behaviour will always mean there is room for doubt, and some people appear to even question the status of epidemiology as a science.[168]

Check if the data used in a prediction is accurate and comprehensive enough to make it useful.
In the early stages little was known about the virus and even the data on who was ill was highly questionable. For one thing the amount of testing was massively variable from country to country, which completely undermined the data on the number of confirmed cases, while the number of deaths was prone to errors from uneven reporting and different standards for what constituted a death due to Covid-19.[169]

Consider if the science behind a prediction allows for a completely accurate answer or is the system unstable?
Chaos theory is a consideration in epidemiology, and there is evidence that some systems are susceptible to chaotic outcomes making completely accurate answers impossible.[170]

If there is no measure of the confidence or potential error in data or a prediction, treat it with suspicion.
There was in the original academic studies. However, I could never find an example in the mainstream media on which much of the individual decision making was based (this doesn't mean that examples never existed).

Be more wary of predictions based on correlations than those based on causation.
The relationship between the wave of illness sweeping across

the world, and the virus that had been genetically identified by the Chinese was causal.[171]

After researching these answers, I decided that I shouldn't put too much weight on the modelling, not least because there was a far better data source: the news bulletins out of China, Italy, Germany and Spain. It was very clear which public health strategies were working and which weren't – the best data was the real-time experiments being run in the countries that got it before the UK.

It seemed that the British Government's strategy was wrong, and that minimum social contact was the best individual response. A week later, the Government finally agreed. I don't think my reaction was unique by any means. The British public's private and commercial responses led the political leadership right up to the big change of strategy on 23 March when the UK's lockdown began. A pattern that continued throughout the pandemic, with tragic results.

It's important to note I'm not saying that the Covid-19 modelling was useless – far from it. If we ask the same questions of weather forecasting the answers are just as bad – and yet as a race-boat navigator I had to put significant weight on the weather forecast when developing a race strategy. And this is one of the most important points about models; if you are familiar with them and understand the limitations and assumptions, then even poor models can be helpful. The problems start when people don't understand how they work, or their limitations. In the hands of professionals who understood what they were dealing with the pandemic modelling undoubtedly helped some countries and hospitals prepare. It was one of the tragedies of that period of time in the UK that Boris Johnson and his leadership team weren't among those people. No one can see the future perfectly, but some can see it better than others.

Science

Fast-moving scientific research left many people confused and exposed during the Covid-19 pandemic. The early advice that wearing a mask was unnecessary for the general public was a perfect example.[172] It turned out that this advice was wrong, and it was changed.[173] But this U-turn was unsettling – didn't these people know what they were doing? – and it made it less likely that further advice would be followed, particularly in the US, once positions on health policy had become tribal political dogma.

At the same time, things were made worse by a tidal wave of information and misinformation on every aspect of the disease, and it was incredibly difficult to sift through all this and understand what was really going on. There was even research into the impact of all this confusion. A paper published by the Royal Society looked into the susceptibility of people – in five different countries – to misinformation about Covid-19. The research concluded: 'Across all countries surveyed, we find that higher trust in scientists and having higher numeracy skills were associated with lower susceptibility to coronavirus-related misinformation.' It went on to say, 'Taken together, these results demonstrate a clear link between susceptibility to misinformation and both vaccine hesitancy and a reduced likelihood to comply with health guidance measures, and suggest that interventions which aim to improve critical thinking and trust in science may be a promising avenue for future research.'[174] An understanding of how science works and the meaning of 'scientific knowledge' gave people a better chance of reacting correctly to the rapidly changing and dangerous environment created by the virus.

It was vital to understand that the U-turn on masks was just science doing what it does: probing, testing and evaluating, with theories changing to reflect the results and the new evidence. Armed with an appreciation of this, changes in advice were more understandable and acceptable – it was simply a response to better data and more information about the transmission mechanisms of the disease. That's how science works and, as John Maynard Keynes may or, actually, may not have said, 'When facts change, I change my mind.'

Unfortunately, for those who lacked any real understanding of how scientific knowledge is generated and what it means, there was often muddle, confusion and bad outcomes as people fell back on either blind acceptance, or extreme scepticism. Understanding science means understanding the role of doubt.

Chance

The novel Coronavirus finally arrived in my own home a little over two years after it was first identified, in January 2022. It arrived with one of my children, who got it from a friend at school as the British Government peeled back the protections that had previously kept them safe. My youngest son gave it to the eldest and isolating them became difficult given that we had to care for them. Both my wife and I had already had our three vaccine shots, each of them within a few weeks of each other. She got sick, and I didn't.

I'm sure that there is an explanation for that, buried deep in virology, genetics and vaccine efficacy, but at its core I was just lucky that I stayed well. And that role of chance was there in everyone's individual experience of the illness – there was a lot of luck involved in who got it, and who got really sick from it. And yet our behaviour often ignored this, as the research on people's overconfidence about whether they would get the disease demonstrated.[175]

We were rolling dice with the virus when we left our homes and exposed ourselves to other people, all potential carriers. Some of that exposure was necessary, and some of it wasn't. There was evidence that the British Government's scheme to encourage people back into restaurants (by offering a £10 discount three days a week for the month of August in 2020) drove infections and fuelled a second wave of the disease in the UK. The research used a link between rainfall, eating out and infection.[176] While there are confounding factors – different ways in which rain could impact infection, other than just keeping people from going out to lunch or dinner – the research did point to the way in which the choices that people made increased exposure, and increased infection. Did all of them understand that they weren't just getting an (almost) free lunch? Did they understand that it was only luck that was protecting them? Did they understand what the odds were? Did they understand that this was a game of Russian Roulette? Luck is everywhere, but we don't see it clearly.

Problem Solving

The search for an effective vaccine against Covid-19 began as soon as the virus had been identified and sequenced in January 2020. The development, testing and eventual licensing of a new vaccine is normally measured in years or even decades, but by December of the same year a Pfizer-BioNTech vaccine had been licensed, the first to be approved in the UK. It was the beginning of a massive roll-out of billions of doses of this and other vaccines that gained regulatory approval from the winter of 2020–21 onwards.

A lot of the preparatory work for this overnight success was done years in advance. There was a significant body of research into similar or related viruses after the previous outbreaks of severe acute respiratory syndrome (SARS) and Middle East respiratory syndrome (MERS). This knowledge was combined with new vaccine technology that had been in development for decades and was finally focused on the successful efforts by Pfizer-BioNTech and Moderna. They both use a different mechanism to traditional vaccines, utilising the messenger ribonucleic acid (mRNA) molecule to carry a code to the cells. The code instructs the cell to produce a protein that will provide an immune response to the virus.

It was probably the most remarkable piece of problem

solving the world has ever seen, but it didn't happen overnight, and it's worth noting the role of **chance**. If this virus had turned up five years earlier, if it had been Covid-14 and not Covid-19, then the mRNA vaccine would not have been ready. Instead of which, an incredible new technology with immense potential in countering many different illnesses has been proven to work in spectacular fashion – years ahead of when this event might otherwise have happened.

Increasing our understanding and knowledge of the world can come about in many ways, but one of the most important is through problem solving. History shows how the ability of humanity to solve the problems that it has been faced with has been its saviour over and over again. Malthus first predicted in 1798 that population growth would eventually overwhelm food production,[177] but he was proved wrong by scientific developments in agriculture.[178] I'm confident that Malthus won't be the last to be proved wrong about an existential threat – at least, let's hope not – but it won't just be the remarkable insight of a gifted few that will do it. It will take the application and inspiration of many, many more people to make the solutions to our modern clutch of problems a reality.

In contrast, the **narratives** we tell about the development of these solutions is often that of a lone genius and a single moment of inspiration. The origin story of vaccines is typical: it focuses on Frenchman Louis Pasteur. Pasteur realised that milder forms of a virus might protect against the full disease after an assistant injected chickens with an ageing, weakened culture of chicken cholera. The chickens only got mildly sick, and that gave Pasteur a theory to test. He dosed the same chickens with a fresh batch of bacteria. It should have killed them, but they showed no symptoms – and vaccines were born.

It's a great story, but there are many steps to be taken from that moment of inspiration and insight to get to the point where vaccine production can be scaled up to supply hundreds of millions of people. There were many more problems that needed to be solved and many more people were needed to solve them.

Problem solving is not just for those with a creative superpower, it's for everyone.

Similarly, the narrative around Moderna and BioNTech[179] and the development of mRNA vaccines often headlines moments of insight by a handful of individuals – Derrick Rossi at Moderna, and Özlem Türeci and Uğur Şahin at BioNTech, both drawing on the work of Katalin Karikó and Drew Weissman – but the reality is that it was founded on research done by many, many others over decades. 'In reality, the path to mRNA vaccines drew on the work of hundreds of researchers over more than 30 years,' explained Elie Dolgin in *Nature*.[180]

And this is just the work done before the focus became a Covid-19 mRNA vaccine. After that point there must have been many more obstacles and problems, any one of which might have stopped this great idea becoming a scalable, manufactured reality. All those problems were solved by someone – maybe the answer just came to them, maybe they worked at it, maybe they even used a technique like SCAMPER to get there. Problems big and small, some worthy of Nobel Prizes and some just worthy of a pat on the back from the supervisor, all contributed to getting this extraordinary new vaccine into the arms of the world's population.

In the introduction to this book I framed the 'Knowledge 2.0' problem as one of being overwhelmed with our access to new information, which moves and changes at a speed that's almost impossible to keep up with. But every challenge is also an opportunity and now I want to finish on a positive note about this extraordinary new world of knowledge.

The business of knowledge, be it pure science or technical problem solving, has never been so democratic. It is no longer the prerogative of a handful of curious, wealthy white males. It may well be that your path in life doesn't lead to a lifetime of research in academia, but that doesn't mean that you cannot contribute – more people than ever before have the opportunity to contribute to the solutions, and the world has plenty of problems to solve. Science and technology have improved the lives of billions of people,[181] but they have also had unintended consequences that could snatch it all away. Science and technology created many of the messes that we find ourselves in, but only science will lead us out of them.

Maybe someone reading this will have the idea that leads to a fully recyclable plastic, or maybe they will figure out something simpler. Perhaps they work in a factory where the injector is overfilling random bottles on a production line and wasting product. Maybe they will solve that problem. The world has too much plastic and not enough of important resources like fresh water and carbon-free energy (plenty of which is used to make new plastic). Big and small, all ideas are important contributions to a world where the only way to stop people fighting over limited and fast-disappearing resources is to find ways to make less go further. The planet needs more than just a handful of geniuses to hold the line and maintain the progress. Everyone can solve problems; everyone is capable of innovating. Creativity can be created.

Part 7: Staying Afloat

☐ *Get out there and be a part of the Knowledge 2.0 world.*

FURTHER READING

Part 1 – Narrative

Thinking, Fast and Slow by Daniel Kahneman, Penguin Books
Freakonomics: A Rogue Economist Explores the Hidden Side of Everything by Steven Levitt and Stephen J. Dubner, Penguin Books
Narrative Economics: How Stories Go Viral and Drive Major Economic Events by Robert Shiller, Princeton University Press
The Black Swan by Nassim Nicholas Taleb, Penguin Books
The Hidden Brain: How Our Unconscious Minds Elect Presidents, Control Markets, Wage Wars, and Save Our Lives by Shankar Vedantam, Random House
The Writer's Journey: Mythic Structure for Writers by Christopher Vogler, Pan Books

Part 2 – Confidence

The Wave: In Pursuit of the Rogues, Freaks, and Giants of the Ocean by Susan Casey, Doubleday
Thinking in Bets: Making Smarter Decisions When You Don't Have All the Facts by Annie Duke, Portfolio
The Big Short: Inside the Doomsday Machine by Michael Lewis, W. W. Norton & Company
Perfectly Confident: How to Calibrate your Decisions Wisely by Don Moore, Harper Business
Sydney Hobart Yacht Race: The story of a sporting icon by Rob Mundle, ABC Books
The Last Grain Race by Eric Newby, HarperCollins
Across Three Oceans by Conor O'Brien, Grafton
Once is Enough by Miles Smeeton, HarperCollins
The Last Time Around Cape Horn: The Historic 1949 Voyage of the Windjammer Pamir by William F Stark, Basic Books

Part 3 – Prediction

Algorithms to Live By: The Computer Science of Human Decisions by Brian Christian and Tom Griffiths, William Collins

Risk Savvy: How to Make Good Decisions by Gerd Gigerenzer, Penguin Books
Measurements and Their Uncertainties: A Practical Guide to Modern Error Analysis by Ifan Hughes, Oxford University Press
The Dice Man by Luke Rhinehart, HarperCollins
The Signal and the Noise: The Art and Science of Prediction by Nate Silver
Trick or Treatment: Alternative Medicine on Trial by Simon Singh and Edzard Ernst, Bantam Press
Expert Political Judgment: How Good Is It? How Can We Know? by Philip Tetlock, Princeton University Press
Superforecasting: The Art and Science of Prediction by Philip Tetlock and Dan Gardner, Random House
Lies, Damn Lies, and Statistics: The Manipulation of Public Opinion in America by Michael Wheeler

Part 4 – Science

Science in a Free Society by Paul Feyerabend, Verso
Bad Science by Ben Goldacre, Fourth Estate
How To Make the World Add Up: Ten Rules for Thinking Differently About Numbers by Tim Harford, The Bridge Street Press
The Structure of Scientific Revolutions by Thomas S. Kuhn, University of Chicago Press
The Scientific Attitude: Defending Science from Denial, Fraud and Pseudoscience, Lee McIntyre, MIT Press
Knowledge: A Very Short Introduction by Jennifer Nagel, Oxford University Press
Merchants of Doubt: How a Handful of Scientists Obscured the Truth on Issues from Tobacco Smoke to Global Warming by Naomi Oreskes and Erik M. Conway, Bloomsbury Paperbacks
Science Fictions: How Fraud, Bias, Negligence, and Hype Undermine the Search for Truth by Stuart Ritchie, Metropolitan Books
Reality Is Not What It Seems by Carlo Rovelli, Penguin Books
What We Cannot Know: Explorations at the Edge of Knowledge by Marcus du Sautoy, Fourth Estate

Part 5 – Chance

Close to the Wind by Ben Ainslie, Yellow Jersey Press
Total Competition by Ross Brawn and Adam Parr, Simon & Schuster

Part 6 – Problem Solving

Lateral Thinking: A Textbook of Creativity by Edward de Bono, Penguin Books
Thinkertoys: A Handbook of Creative-Thinking Techniques by Michael Michalko, Ten Speed Press

Part 7 – Coping With Covid

Factfulness: Ten Reasons We're Wrong About the World - and Why Things Are Better Than You Think by Hans Rosling, Ola Rosling and Anna Rosling Rönnlund, Sceptre
Covid By Numbers: Making Sense of the Pandemic with Data by David Spiegelhalter and Anthony Masters, Pelican Books

APPENDIX

Expected Value

The theory of expected value assesses the value of all the possible outcomes for each decision and multiplies them by the likelihood (the probability) of those outcomes. The results of each of these multiplications (Value (V) x Probability (P)) are then added together to give the expected value (E) for that decision: E = (V1 x P1) + (V2 x P2), etc.

Once all the expected values have been calculated, then the decision with the highest expected value is the one to go for . . . and while it's not always that simple, as we will see, the concept of expected value is very useful in all sorts of situations. For instance, we can use probabilities to calculate expected values and assess the strategic choices for *Team AkzoNobel* and *Team Brunel* as the storm approached. The value for the outcome will be the points available for each position in the leg. These were scored in reverse, and this leg was worth double points, so the winner got 14 points, second place 12 points and so on down to last place which was worth two points.

We're going to make some assumptions to keep the analysis relatively simple. So, we'll assume that the rest of the fleet made the same choices that they actually did in the race and finished the leg successfully. So, two boats went north, both of whom *Team Brunel* and *Team AkzoNobel* will beat if they don't suffer damage, while three boats went south, none of whom they will beat, damage or no damage.

On the southern route the pair's best possible result was a fourth, and that would have been worth eight points. A second potential outcome was a seventh and two points (if they suffered sufficient damage to stop them racing competitively, but not to stop them racing altogether). The final possibility was that they suffered more serious damage and were unable to finish the leg, and also unable to start the next one. In this case they would have lost all the points from this leg, plus the next one. I'm going to give this outcome a score of minus four points, equating to zero points for leg 3 and a loss of a potential fourth-place finish in the following leg (the next leg was not double points, so fourth scored four points).

I'm assessing the probability of them racing hard all the way to the finish (and scoring a fourth) as 60 per cent, suffering moderate damage and coming last as 30 per cent, and suffering more serious damage as 10 per cent. So now we can prepare a table:

Southern Route

Outcome	Probability	Points Scored
Fourth	60%	8 points
Seventh	30%	2 points
Not finishing	10%	-4 points

We could build a much more complex table listing more outcomes and their probabilities, but I think the method is clearer with just these three options. The expected value (E) is the sum of the gains from each of these outcomes:

E = (0.6 x 8) + (0.3 x 2) + (0.1 x -4) = 5.0

So much for the south . . . On the northern route the best possible score was a fifth, and that would have netted them six points, with the outcome for moderate damage again a seventh and two points. The outcome for serious damage was also minus four points.

While it wasn't guaranteed that they would successfully complete the leg on the northern route, the chances were a lot higher, and I'm going to call it 90 per cent, with a 9 per cent chance of moderate damage and a 1 per cent chance of serious damage. The table for the northern route looks like this:

Northern Route

Outcome	Probability	Points Scored
Fifth	90%	6 points
Seventh	9%	2 points
Not finishing	1%	-4 points

And the expected value will be:
E = (0.9 x 6) + (0.09 x 2) + (0.01 x -4) = 5.54

This analysis produces an expected value on the northern route of 5.54 points compared to 5.0 points on the southern route. Any decision based on expected value would be in favour of the northern route, supporting the earlier conclusion. Now, maybe others would score the probabilities of damage differently – and it's fun to play around with the numbers to see how the outcome changes – but there's no doubt that the analysis helps to clarify the choices.

An expected-value analysis can also help with some of the issues of over-confidence and planning that we came across in Part 2. Sailing is a very complex sport and one of the big problems facing any race-boat campaign – be it an America's Cup team or a small keelboat shooting for a top ten at the national championship – is that there are more ways to improve performance than there is time or money to pursue.

This problem can also be approached using expected value, calculating an expected cost for each unit of performance gain. The process starts by creating a list of the performance projects that are under consideration – let's say that they are practising for a weekend, buying new sails or hiring a coach for the season. First, we need to assess the value of the outcome of these projects. I'm going to measure these gains as speed improvements in miles per hour (mph),[182] and I'm going to assess the gains for each of three possible outcomes: the best case, worst case and the most likely. Finally, I'm also going to assign these outcomes a probability so I can calculate an expected value for this performance-enhancement project. I should add that I got these numbers by sticking a finger in the air, they mean nothing other than providing an example.

Practising For Two Days

Outcome	Probability	Gain in mph
Best case	30%	0.25
Worst case	10%	0
Most likely	60%	0.1

Two days' practice could go really well and realise significant gains. However, good quality practice is hard to achieve and there's also a chance of very poor conditions, so no sailing and no gains being made at all. So, the expected value of practise will be:

$$E = (0.3 \times 0.25) + (0.1 \times 0) + (0.6 \times 0.1) = 0.135$$

Buying New Sails

Outcome	Probability	Gain in mph
Best case	10%	0.2
Worst case	10%	0.05
Most likely	80%	0.1

The new sails will come from a highly respected supplier and so the gains will be much more likely, but smaller. The expected value of new sails will be:

$$E = (0.1 \times 0.2) + (0.1 \times 0.05) + (0.8 \times 0.1) = 0.105$$

Hiring A New Coach

Outcome	Probability	Gain in mph
Best case	20%	0.3
Worst case	30%	0.05
Most likely	50%	0.15

The coach is well known and should provide a significant improvement, although they have a reputation for being temperamental so there's always the possibility that they won't get along with the crew. The expected value of a hiring a coach will be:

E = (0.2 x 0.3) + (0.3 x 0.05) + (0.5 x 0.15) = 0.15

These expected values capture the performance gain that will be the outcome for each of our proposed performance-improving projects. And the greatest gain should come from the coach. Now we just need to include the costs of that gain and we can compare them directly for bang for the buck. So, our next estimate is the cost to realise this gain. This needs to take account of all the costs, so we must include everything – in the case of practising this might include travelling to the venue, accommodation, lost earnings and so on.

Costs
Practising = $4,000
Buying new sails = $6,000
Hiring a coach = $10,000

We now have everything we need to calculate a cost-effectiveness ratio (CER) for each performance gain[183] – this is the cost divided by the expected value (E).

Cost-Effectiveness Ratio
Practising = $4,000 / 0.135 = 29,630 $/mph
Buying new sails = $6,000 / 0.105 = 57,143 $/mph
Hiring a coach = $10,000 / 0.15 = 66,667 $/mph

On this analysis the team would be better off, by some margin, if they practised, and the new sails are now better value than the coach.

The expected-value approach tackles the issue of balancing resources in a parallel way to balancing risks and expected value can be just as useful in revealing the trade-offs. It's a great way of tackling the problem of how resources are utilised, as the whole team can be brought into the discussion on the performance gains to be made, their cost and the likelihood of them being fulfilled.

Now, this is not the whole story – there's no allowance for how these gains will degrade with time. For instance, the benefits from the new sails and the coach may well last longer than the practise.[184] High-risk, cheap options with big potential gains also test this analysis since the risk element isn't fully captured. There might be a new keel shape available at low cost with great potential performance gains, but it also might not be faster at all – if there was an 80 per cent risk of failure, but a similar cost-effectiveness ratio to practise, which would you choose?

We can reveal more about this weakness in expected value by slotting some numbers into the problem of house insurance. What we're looking at is the expected value of taking insurance over a year and to keep it simple I'm just going to look at the one most serious risk – fire. Let's assume for the sake of the example that the average cost of household insurance in the UK is £150 and there are two possible outcomes: either there's a fire or there's not. I'm also going to assume that there were 35,000 household fires and a total of 24 million homes in the UK in 2020 – these figures aren't too far off.

This gives us a probability of a house fire each year of: (35,000 / 24,000,000) x 100 = 0.146%.

If we assume that the average cost of repair for a fire is £20,000, we can now prepare our two tables and work out the two expected values of the losses.

Insurance

Outcome	Probability	Cost	Premium
No fire	99.854%	£0	£150
Fire	0.146%	£0	£150

The expected loss is the sum of these outcomes minus the premium:

E = (0.99854 x 0) + (0.00146 x 0) - 150 = -£150

So that's an expected-value loss of £150 for the house that buys insurance.

What happens if there's no insurance? This is what our table looks like:

No Insurance

Outcome	Probability	Cost	Premium
No fire	99.854%	£0	£0
Fire	0.146%	£20,0000	£0

In this case there is no premium paid so the expected loss is:

E = (0.99854 x 0) + (0.00146 x ⁻20,000) = ⁻£29.20

And that's a lot less than the expected loss when buying insurance. A fire is not the only risk covered by the policy, but the point would remain the same even if we added the risks for burglary, flood and so on. Expected value tells us that it makes no sense to buy insurance – we're throwing money down the drain. And of course, it couldn't really be any other way; insurance companies have to make a profit to stay in business.

What's not being captured here is the subjectiveness of the risk to the individual. The probability of a fire is 0.146% but that includes a lot of quite small fires that don't cost much to repair. This isn't really why we buy house insurance; the concern is losing the whole house and while that is much, much less likely it's this fear of a highly unlikely but very big loss that makes us buy insurance and keeps insurance companies in business.

Take another example: let's say I've helped a crazy billionaire yacht owner win a few big races and she offers me one of her two $100-million yachts. I can accept the offer and walk away with the keys. Or I can take a gamble, she will flip a coin and if it comes up heads then she'll give me both $100-million yachts. If we work out the expected value of this, then in the first case it's a $100 million since the probability is 100 per cent:

E = $100m x 1 = £100m

In the second case, the probability of winning both yachts is 50 per cent so the E is also $100 million:

E = $200m x 0.5 = £100m

The expected value is the same, and so theoretically I could take either offer and it would make no difference. However, most of us would prefer to take the guaranteed $100-million yacht rather than risk walking away with nothing. It's the risk that's not being captured in all these examples – the new keel, the house insurance and the $100-million yacht.

The theory of expected utility seeks to take this into account by substituting utility for value, where utility is a measure of the subjective preference of the outcome – and that will vary with the individual's circumstances. Someone with $20 billion in the bank may well prefer to take the coin toss with a chance to win $200 billion or nothing. The utility of $100 million will feel very different to them, compared to someone who has little or nothing. The problem is putting a number on this subjective utility – risk can be an emotional subject.

There are going to be difficulties using either expected value or expected utility to help with our decision making. In the first case there's the difficulty of deriving realistic probabilities for the expected outcomes (no surprise, since we are trying to predict the future), and the problem of not fully capturing the risk in the decision process. And in the second case there's the difficulty of making good judgements about the subjective utility of an outcome. These issues are discussed in Chapters 7 and 8.

ENDNOTES

Introduction

[1] 'Segment View: Scientific, Technical & Medical – 2021' by Tatiana Khayrullina, Outsell,(26 May 2021), 7, https://outsellinc.com/product/segment-view-scientific-technical-medical-2021/

[2] The evidence for this is compellingly presented in *Factfulness: Ten Reasons We're Wrong About the World – and Why Things Are Better Than You Think* by Hans Rosling, Ola Rosling and Anna Rosling Rönnlund (Sceptre, 2018).

Chapter 1

[3] A knot is one nautical mile per hour, equivalent to about 1.15 miles per hour.

[4] There were more casualties amongst non-competitors.

[5] The Beaufort Scale by RMetS Editor, https://www.rmets.org/resource/beaufort-scale.

[6] 'The spread of true and false news online' by Soroush Vosoughi, Deb Roy and Sinan Aral, *Science*, 359: 6380 (9 Mar. 2018), 1146–51, https://www.science.org/doi/10.1126/science.aap9559.

Chapter 2

[7] 'The Man Behind the Myth: Should We Question the Hero's Journey?' by Sarah E. Bond and Joel Christensen, *Los Angeles Review of Books* (12 Aug. 2021), https://www.lareviewofbooks.org/article/the-man-behind-the-myth-should-we-question-the-heros-journey/.

[8] 'Mythic Discovery Within the Inner Reaches of Outer Space: Joseph Campbell meets George Lucas – Part 1' by Lucas Seastrom, StarWars.com (22 Oct. 2015), https://www.starwars.com/news/mythic-discovery-within-the-inner-reaches-of-outer-space-joseph-campbell-meets-george-lucas-part-i.

[9] *The Writer's Journey: Mythic Structure for Writers* by Christopher Vogler (Pan Books, 2nd edn, 1998), preface.

[10] *The Black Swan: The Impact of the Highly Improbable* by Nassim

Nicholas Taleb (Penguin Books, revised edn, 2010), 62-84.

[11] Try *Freakonomics: A Rogue Economist Explores the Hidden Side of Everything* by Steven Levitt and Stephen J. Dubner, (Penguin Books, 2006), or *The Hidden Brain: How Our Unconscious Minds Elect Presidents, Control Markets, Wage Wars, and Save Our Lives* by Shankar Vedantam, (Random House, 2010). Both have expanded into very successful podcasts.

[12] *Thinking, Fast and Slow* by Daniel Kahneman (Penguin Books, 2012), 199.

[13] *Thinking*, Kahneman, 85.

[14] Recent research shows that the higher cadences favoured by Armstrong, i.e. 100 rpm and above, may actually be less efficient, except on climbs where a higher cadence (although less efficient) can reduce the build-up of lactate in the muscles: 'Effects of Cadence on Aerobic Capacity Following a Prolonged, Varied Intensity Cycling Trial' by Charles L. Stebbins, Jesse L. Moore and Gretchen A. Casazza, *Journal of Sports Science and Medicine*, 13: 1 (Jan. 2014), 114–19, https://www.ncbi.nlm.nih.gov/pmc/articles/PMC3918546/.

[15] *Thinking*, Kahneman, 162.

Chapter 3

[16] *Sydney Hobart Yacht Race: The Story of a Sporting Icon* by Rob Mundle (ABC Books, 2019).

[17] This is a hydrofoil-shaped structure that's fixed underneath the boat. The weight stops the yacht from tipping over, and its shape helps the boat to go in a straight line, rather than crab sideways through the water.

[18] 'He was waving and screaming' by Ted Howes and Vic Levi, *Sydney Morning Herald* (2 Jan. 1994). All subsequent quotes from Shaw are from this article.

[19] This and subsequent quotes are from my interview with Tom Braidwood (Apr. 2021).

[20] This and subsequent quotes are from my interview with John Quinn (June 2021).

Chapter 4

[21] This and subsequent quotes are from my interview with John Quinn (June 2021).

[22] 'The better-than-average effect in comparative self-evaluation: A comprehensive review and meta-analysis' by Ethan Zell, Jason E. Strickhouser, Constantine Sedikides, Mark D. Alicke, *Psychological Bulletin*, 14: 2 (Feb. 2020), 118–49, https://pubmed.ncbi.nlm.nih.gov/31789535/.

[23] 'Divorces in England and Wales: 2021' by the Office for National Statistics (2 Nov. 2022), https://www.ons.gov.uk/peoplepopulationandcommunity/birthsdeathsandmarriages/divorce/bulletins/divorcesinenglandandwales/2021.

[24] 'Why Restaurants Fail' by H. G. Parsa, John T. Self, David Njite and Tiffany King, Cornell *Hotel and Restaurant Administration Quarterly*, 46: 3 (1 Aug. 2005), 304–22, https://doi.org/10.1177/0010880405275598.

[25] Are We All Less Risky and More Skillful than Our Fellow Drivers?' by Ola Svenson, Acta *Psychologica*, 47: 2 (Feb. 1981), 142–8.

[26] 'Sinking of Tall Ship Bounty', National Transportation Safety Board, Marine Accident Brief ID DCA1 3 LM0 0303.

[27] 'Daniel Kahneman wants you to doubt yourself. Here's why', Daniel Kahneman interviewed by Chris Anderson, TED Interview (11 Dec. 2018), https://www.ted.com/talks/the_ted_interview_daniel_kahneman_wants_you_to_doubt_yourself_here_s_why/transcript?language=en.

[28] *Thinking, Fast and Slow* by Daniel Kahneman (Penguin Books, 2012), 13.

[29] *Thinking*, Kahneman, 417.

[30] Darwin Online, notes on the back of a letter dating to 1838, http://darwin-online.org.uk/content/frameset?viewtype=side&itemID=CUL-DAR210.8.1&pageseq=1.

[31] Darwin Online, conjecturally dated to July 1838, http://darwin-online.org.uk/content/frameset?keywords=d%20e%20q%20marry&pageseq=1&itemID=CUL-DAR210.8.2&viewtype=text.

[32] 'I knew it would happen: Remembered probabilities of once–future things' by Baruch Fischhoff and Ruth Beyth,

Organizational Behavior and Human Performance, 13: 1 (Feb. 1975), 1–16, https://www.sciencedirect.com/science/article/abs/pii/0030507375900021?via%3Dihub.

[33] At the top of my search was 'How to Build Self-Confidence' on mindtools.com, https://www.mindtools.com/selfconf.html and 'How to Be More Confident: 9 Tips That Work' on Verywell Mind, https://www.verywellmind.com/how-to-boost-your-self-confidence-4163098.

[34] 'Performing a Project Premortem' by Gary Klein, *Harvard Business Review* (Sept. 2007), https://hbr.org/2007/09/performing-a-project-premortem.

[35] 'Back to the future: Temporal perspective in the explanation of events' by Deborah J. Mitchell, J. Edward Russo and Nancy Pennington, *Journal of Behavioral Decision Making* (Jan./Mar. 1989), https://onlinelibrary.wiley.com/doi/abs/10.1002/bdm.3960020103.

[36] 'Design by Deception: The Politics of Megaproject Approval' by Bent Flyvbjerg, *Harvard Design Magazine*, 22 (June 2005), 50–59.

[37] *Thinking*, Kahneman, 249.

[38] 'Over budget, over time, over and over again: Managing major projects,' by Bent Flyvbjerg in *The Oxford Handbook of Project Management*, P.W.G. Morris, J.K. Pinto and J. Soderlund (eds.) (Oxford University Press), 95-121

[39] 'Betting to Improve the Odds' by Steve Lohr, *New York Times* (9 Apr. 2008).

[40] 'The social transmission of overconfidence' by Joey T. Cheng, Cameron Anderson, Elizabeth R. Tenney, Sebastien Brion, Don A. Moore and Jennifer M. Logg, *Journal of Experimental Psychology*, 150: 1 (Jan. 2021), 157–86, https://doi.apa.org/doiLanding?doi=10.1037%2Fxge0000787.

[41] *Report, Findings and Recommendations of the 1998 Sydney to Hobart Race Review Committee*, Cruising Yacht Club of Australia, 1999.

Chapter 5

[42] *The Last Time around Cape Horn: The Historic 1949 Voyage of the Windjammer Pamir* by William F. Stark (Basic Books, reprint

edn, 2004).

[43] *Once is Enough* by Miles Smeeton (1st edn, 1959; republished by HarperCollins, 2014). My account of their voyage is taken from Smeeton's book; I can recommend the original.

[44] *Once is Enough*, Smeeton, 199.

[45] *Once is Enough*, Smeeton, 163.

[46] There's even a Wikipedia page that lists them: https://en.wikipedia.org/wiki/List_of_rogue_waves.

[47] The photo can be found online at the European Space Agency, https://www.esa.int/ESA_Multimedia/Images/2004/06/Rare_photo_of_a_rogue_wave.

[48] 'The Draupner wave: A fresh look and the emerging view' by Luigi Cavaleri, Francesco Barbariol, Alvise Benetazzo, Luciana Bertotti, Jean-Raymond Bidlot, Peter Janssen, and Nils Wedi, *Journal of Geophysical Research: Oceans*, 121: 8 (Aug. 2016), 6061-6075, https://doi.org/10.1002/2016JC011649.

[49] 'Were extreme waves in the Rockall Trough the largest ever recorded?' by Naomi P. Holliday, Margaret J. Yelland, Robin W. Pascal, Val R. Swail, Peter K. Taylor, Colin R. Griffiths, and Elizabeth Kent, *Geophysical Research Letters*, 33: 5 (11 Mar. 2006).

[50] 'Rogue Waves: Results of the MaxWave Project' by Wolfgang Rosenthal and Susanne Lerner, *Journal of Offshore Mechanics and Arctic Engineering*, 130: 2 (May 2008), 21006–13.

[51] *The Wave: In Pursuit of the Rogues, Freaks, and Giants of the Ocean* by Susan Casey (Doubleday, 2011), is well worth reading for more on this topic.

[52] A CNN clip of Rumsfeld from the press conference on 12 Feb. 2002 can be seen online at https://youtu.be/REWeBzGuzCc.

[53] *The Big Short: Inside the Doomsday Machine* by Michael Lewis (W. W. Norton, 2010).

Chapter 6

[54] 'Nokia and David Witt takes on the big Breeze in Auckland', available on YouTube, https://youtu.be/9LTRO8n_tqg.

[55] Interview with Jules Salter, Jan. 2020.

[56] There is more detail on this in the Appendix.

[57] 'Pascal and the Invention of Probability Theory' by Oystein Ore, *American Mathematical Monthly*, 67: 5 (May 1960), 409–19, https://www.jstor.org/stable/2309286?origin=crossref.

[58] See Appendix 1 for a fuller explanation of expected value with worked examples.

[59] See Appendix 1 for the full worked example.

[60] See Appendix 1 for the full worked example.

[61] There are ways of dealing with this, but they are beyond the scope of this analysis.

[62] There is more detail on this in the Appendix.

Chapter 7

[63] 'Should I take a statin?' by Dr Mike Knapton, *Heart Matters*, https://www.bhf.org.uk/informationsupport/heart-matters-magazine/medical/ask-the-experts/statin-uncertainty.

[64] There is a difference between uncertainty and risk. Risk can be calculated, while uncertainty is, in the words of Nate Silver; "risk that is hard to measure". *The Signal and the Noise: The Art and Science of Prediction* by Nate Silver (Penguin Books, 2013), p29.

[65] *Trick or Treatment: Alternative Medicine on Trial* by Simon Singh and Edzard Ernst (Bantam Press, 2008), 63 ff. describes clinical trials in more detail.

[66] 'Deterministic Nonperiodic Flow' by Edward N. Lorenz, *Journal of the Atmospheric Sciences*, 20: 2 (1 Mar. 1963), 130–41, https://journals.ametsoc.org/view/journals/atsc/20/2/1520-0469_1963_020_0130_dnf_2_0_co_2.xml.

[67] This is the difference between uncertainty and risk – a risk can be calculated precisely, or imprecisely. To put it another way, it's vital to know the amount of uncertainty in the prediction of the risk.

[68] I'm not going to outline how physicists do error analysis since that would take another book and I'm not qualified to write it, but if it interests you, try *Measurements and Their Uncertainties: A Practical Guide to Modern Error Analysis* by Ifan Hughes (Oxford University Press, 2009).

[69] The standard deviation measures how far numbers in the

data set are spread out from the mean; a low number indicates that the data set is close to the mean, while a high number indicates that it is spread out.

[70] The confidence interval is the probability that a number lies in a given range, so a statement using the confidence interval might say something like 'there is a 95 per cent chance that the total weight of the boat lies between 1425 kg and 1445 kg' – this provides a lot more information about the accuracy of the weighing process than the statement 'the boat weighs 1435.0 kg'.

[71] 'Owning a dog could extend your life' by Natalie Rahhal, *Daily Mail* (8 October 2019), https://www.dailymail.co.uk/health/article-7547871/Owning-dog-cut-risk-death-65-studies-suggest.html.

[72] 'Dog Ownership and Survival: A Systematic Review and Meta-Analysis' by Caroline K. Kramer, Sadia Mehmood and Renée S. Suen, *Circulation: Cardiovascular Quality and Outcomes*, 12: 10 (8 Oct. 2019), https://pubmed.ncbi.nlm.nih.gov/31592726/.

[73] The mean is calculated by adding all the variables together and then dividing by the number of variables; the median is the middle value when they are all listed from low to high; and the mode is the most frequently occurring value.

[74] 'Trump Is the Worst Kind of Socialist' by Bernie Sanders, *Wall Street Journal* (26 June 2019), https://www.wsj.com/articles/trump-is-the-worst-kind-of-socialist-11561589372.

[75] 'Bernie Sanders on target saying 3 richest have as much wealth as bottom half of all Americans' by Tom Kertscher, PolitiFact (3 July 2019), https://www.politifact.com/factchecks/2019/jul/03/bernie-sanders/bernie-sanders-target-saying-3-richest-have-much-w/.

[76] *The Black Swan* by Nassim Nicholas Taleb (Penguin Books, revised edn, 2010), 218.

[77] 'Earnings soar for UK's bestselling authors as wealth gap widens in books industry' by Richard Lea, *The Guardian* (15th Jan. 2016), https://www.theguardian.com/books/2016/jan/15/earnings-soar-for-uks-bestselling-authors-as-wealth-gap-widens-in-books-industry.

[78] 'EC study puts average author earnings at £12,500' by

Katherine Cowdrey, *Bookseller* (18 Oct. 2016), https://www.thebookseller.com/news/average-author-earnings-12500-reveals-ec-study-414566.

[79] 'The 2010 RCVS Survey of the UK Veterinary and Veterinary Nursing Professions' by Gemma Robertson-Smith, Dilys Robinson, Ben Hicks, Priya Khambhaita and Sue Hayday, Institute for Employment Studies (2011), https://www.rcvs.org.uk/news-and-views/publications/rcvs-survey-of-the-professions-2010/surveyprofessions2010.pdf.

[80] 'Breast cancer risk from using HRT is "twice what was thought"' by Sarah Boseley, *The Guardian* (29 Aug. 2019), https://www.theguardian.com/science/2019/aug/29/breast-cancer-risk-from-using-hrt-is-twice-what-was-thought.

[81] 'Type and timing of menopausal hormone therapy and breast cancer risk: individual participant meta-analysis of the worldwide epidemiological evidence' by Valerie Beral, Richard Peto, Kirstin Pirie, and Gillian Reeves, *The Lancet*, 394: 10204 (28 Sept–4 Oct. 2019), 1159–68, https://www.thelancet.com/journals/lancet/article/PIIS0140-6736(19)31709-X/fulltext.

[82] There's a good analysis of this in ch. 7 of *Risk Savvy: How to Make Good Decisions* by Gerd Gigerenzer (Penguin Books, 2014).

[83] 'False-Positive Psychology: Undisclosed Flexibility in Data Collection and Analysis Allows Presenting Anything as Significant' by Joseph P. Simmons, Leif D. Nelson and Uri Simonsohn, Psychological Science, 22: 11 (17 Oct. 2011), 1359–66, https://doi.org/10.1177/0956797611417632. For a more readable introduction to p-hacking: 'Science Isn't Broken' by Christie Aschwanden, FiveThirtyEight (19 Aug. 2015), https://fivethirtyeight.com/features/science-isnt-broken/#part1.

[84] This finding was explored in Tetlock's 2005 book, *Expert Political Judgment: How Good Is It? How Can We Know?* from Princeton University Press.

[85] 'Forecasting Tournaments: Tools for Increasing Transparency and Improving the Quality of Debate' by Philip E. Tetlock, Barbara A. Mellers, Nick Rohrbaugh and Eva Chen, *Current Directions in Psychological Science*, 23: 4 (4 Aug. 2014), 290–95, https://journals.sagepub.com/doi/10.1177/0963721414534257.

[86] *Superforecasting: The Art and Science of Prediction* by Philip

Tetlock and Dan Gardner (Random House, 2015), 228.

[87] *The Hedgehog and the Fox: An Essay on Tolstoy's View of History* by Isaiah Berlin (Weidenfeld & Nicolson, 1953).

[88] *The Dice Man* by Luke Rhinehart (1st edn, 1971 William Morrow, republished by HarperCollins, 50th Anniversary edition, 1999) achieved cult status.

[89] 'Heads or Tails: The Impact of a Coin Toss on Major Life Decisions and Subsequent Happiness' by Steven D. Levitt, *National Bureau of Economic Research Working Paper No. W22487 (Aug. 2016)*, https://www.nber.org/papers/w22487.

[90] 'Catalyzing decisions: How a coin flip strengthens affective reactions', by Mariela E. Jaffé, Leonie Reutner and Rainer Greifeneder, *PLoS One*, 14: 8 (14 Aug. 2019), https://www.ncbi.nlm.nih.gov/pmc/articles/PMC6693849/.

[91] 'A Psychological Tip' by Piet Hein, https://piethein.dk/gruk-database1/.

Chapter 8

[92] *Algorithms to Live By: The Computer Science of Human Decisions* by Brian Christian and Tom Griffiths (William Collins, 2016), 146 ff., but the whole of ch. 6 will be of interest on this topic.

[93] *The Signal and the Noise: The Art and Science of Prediction* by Nate Silver (Penguin Books, 2013), 240 ff., but most of the book is relevant to this topic.

[94] 'Interpretation of statistical evidence in criminal trials: The prosecutor's fallacy and the defense attorney's fallacy' by William Thompson and Edward Schumann, *Law and Human Behavior*, 11: 3 (1987), 167–87, https://doi.org/10.1007/BF01044641.

[95] 'Bayes and the Law' by Norman Fenton, Martin Neil and Daniel Berger, *Annual Review of Statistics and Its Application*, 3: 1 (June 2016), 51–77, https://www.annualreviews.org/doi/abs/10.1146/annurev-statistics-041715-033428.

[96] There's an excellent analysis of the use of the base rate in prediction in *Superforecasting: The Art and Science of Prediction* by Philip Tetlock and Dan Gardner (Random House, 2015), 116 ff. *Thinking, Fast and Slow* by Daniel Kahneman (Penguin Books, 2012), ch. 14, also deals with this and what Kahneman calls the

'outside' and 'inside' view.

[97] 'Perception of Risk Posed by Extreme Events' by Paul Slovic and Elke U. Weber, prepared for the conference *Risk Management Strategies in an Uncertain World* (Jan. 2002), https://www.researchgate.net/publication/209805350_Perception_of_Risk_Posed_by_Extreme_Events.

[98] 'Driving Fatalities After 9/11: A Hidden Cost of Terrorism' by Garrick Blalock, Vrinda Kadiyali and Daniel H. Simon, *Applied Economics*, 41: 14 (1 June 2009), 1717–29, https://www.researchgate.net/publication/46528808_Driving_Fatalities_After_911_A_Hidden_Cost_of_Terrorism.

[99] 'Radiation: 5G mobile networks and health', World Health Organisation (27 Feb. 2020), https://www.who.int/news-room/q-a-detail/radiation-5g-mobile-networks-and-health.

Chapter 9

[100] *The Black Swan* by Nassim Nicholas Taleb (Penguin Books, revised edn 2010), 160.

[101] Despite this early failure, I stayed with the team and became a navigator.

Chapter 10

[102] *The Scientific Attitude: Defending Science from Denial, Fraud and Pseudoscience* by Lee McIntyre (MIT Press, 2019), introduction.

[103] *Knowledge: A Very Short Introduction* by Jennifer Nagel (Oxford University Press, 2014).

[104] Paul Feyerabend attacked the idea of science as objective truth in *Science in a Free Society* (Verso, 1978) specifically to undermine the status of scientific knowledge way back in 1978.

[105] *Reality Is Not What It Seems* by Carlo Rovelli (Penguin Books, Kindle edn), 121.

[106] 'The Correspondence Theory of Truth' by Marian David, *The Stanford Encyclopedia of Philosophy* (Summer 2022 edn), ed. by Edward N. Zalta, https://plato.stanford.edu/archives/sum2022/

entries/truth-correspondence/.

[107] A review of the various GCSE syllabuses for the UK can easily be done at the BBC's Bitesize website: https://www.bbc.co.uk/bitesize/subjects/zpm6fg8.

[108] *A Philosophical Essay on Probabilities* by Pierre-Simon, Marquis de Laplace, now in the public domain. It proposed that a demon with knowledge of the position, the velocity and the force on all the particles in the universe at any one time could predict the future for all time. There are many problems with the idea, not the least of which is Heisenberg's uncertainty principle, which states that you cannot know precisely the position and velocity of a particle at the same time.

[109] The CERN website has a clear and simple description of what the standard model is and does: https://home.cern/science/physics/standard-model.

[110] Appropriately there is a clear and much more in-depth explanation of the Higgs field and the Higgs boson on the CERN website, https://home.cern/science/physics/higgs-boson.

[111] *Reality*, Rovelli, 125.

[112] *The Structure of Scientific Revolutions* by Thomas S. Kuhn (University of Chicago Press, 1962).

[113] The name comes from Marcus du Sautoy's 2016 book, *What We Cannot Know: Explorations at the Edge of Knowledge* (Fourth Estate) in which he investigates many of these edges.

[114] 'On Formally Undecidable Propositions of Principia Mathematica and Related Systems' by Kurt Gödel, *Monatshefte für Mathematik* (1931).

Chapter 11

[115] 'Healthcare Global Market Opportunities and Strategies to 2022', report on ResearchAndMarkets.com, no longer available, but referenced by businesswire.com, https://www.businesswire.com/news/home/20190625005862/en/The-11.9-Trillion-Global-Healthcare-Market-Key-Opportunities-Strategies-2014-2022---ResearchAndMarkets.com.

[116] Anyone who has read Ben Goldacre's *Bad Science* (Fourth Estate, 2008) will know this, and anyone who has not, should

read it.

[117] The medical community defines an allergy as a misguided reaction by the immune system against something that the body has come into contact with, whereas intolerances appear to be bodily reactions by something other than the immune system.

[118] https://sciencebasedmedicine.org/gluten-update/.

[119] https://www.nhs.uk/conditions/food-intolerance/.

[120] 'Non-coeliac gluten sensitivity?' by A. Ellis and B. D. Linaker, *The Lancet*, 311: 8078 (24 June 1978), 1358–9, https://www.thelancet.com/journals/lancet/article/PIIS0140-6736(78)92427-3/fulltext.

[121] This was called the 3rd International Expert Meeting on Gluten Related Disorders and it should be noted that it was supported by the Dr. Schär Institute, which is linked to the brands Glutafin and Schär, both of which make gluten-free foods. The criteria can be found in the paper 'Diagnosis of Non-Celiac Gluten Sensitivity (NCGS): The Salerno Experts' Criteria' by Carlo Catassi, Luca Elli, Bruno Bonaz et al., *Nutrients*, 7: 6 (18 June 2015), 4966–77, https://pubmed.ncbi.nlm.nih.gov/26096570/.

[122] A 2020 paper reviewed all the research to date and was less dismissive of NCGS than previous similar studies. See 'Nonceliac Gluten and Wheat Sensitivity' by Anam Khan, Milena Gould Suarez and Joseph A Murray, *Clinical Gastroenterology and Hepatology*, 18: 9 (Aug. 2020), 1913–22, https://pubmed.ncbi.nlm.nih.gov/30978535/.

[123] 'Between Celiac Disease and Irritable Bowel Syndrome: The "No Man's Land" of Gluten Sensitivity' by Elena F. Verdu, David Armstrong, and Joseph A. Murray, *American Journal of Gastroenterology*, 104: 6 (June 2009), 1587–94, https://www.ncbi.nlm.nih.gov/pmc/articles/PMC3480312/.

[124] *Causality and Chance in Modern Physics* by David Bohm (Routledge, 2nd edn, 2016), foreword.

[125] 'Fructan, Rather Than Gluten, Induces Symptoms in Patients with Self-Reported Non-Celiac Gluten Sensitivity' by Gry I. Skodje, Vikas K. Sarna, Ingunn H. Minelle, Kjersti L. Rolfsen, Jane G. Muir, Peter R. Gibson, Marit B. Veierød, Christine Henriksen and Knut E. A, Lundin, *Gastroenterology*, 154: 3 (Feb.

2018), 529–39, https://pubmed.ncbi.nlm.nih.gov/29102613/.

[126] *Bad Science*, Goldacre, 225.

[127] We saw some examples of this in ch. 7 when we were looking at data manipulation; Ben Goldacre provides a full list in ch. 13 of *Bad Science*.

[128] *How to Make the World Add Up: Ten Rules for Thinking Differently About Numbers* by Tim Harford (The Bridge Street Press, 2021), 110 ff.

[129] https://www.cochrane.org/

[130] *The Lancet* published the paper that started the MMR scare, see *Bad Science*, Goldacre, 294.

[131] *Thinking, Fast and Slow* by Daniel Kahneman (Penguin Books, 2012), 310.

[132] *Merchants of Doubt: How a Handful of Scientists Obscured the Truth on Issues from Tobacco Smoke to Global Warming* by Naomi Oreskes and Erik M. Conway (Bloomsbury Paperbacks, 2012).

[133] *Bad Science*, Goldacre, 324.

[134] 'Carbon Dioxide and Climate: A Scientific Assessment', Report of an Ad Hoc Study Group on Carbon Dioxide and Climate, Woods Hole, Massachusetts, for the Climate Research Board, Assembly of Mathematical and Physical Sciences, National Research Council and the National Academy of Sciences, July 23–7, 1979.

[135] 'Man-made Carbon Dioxide and the "Greenhouse" Effect' by J. S. Sawyer, *Nature*, 239 (1 Sept. 1972), 23–6, https://www.nature.com/articles/239023a0#citeas.

[136] 'Climate: Sawyer predicted rate of warming in 1972' by Neville Nicholls, *Nature*, 448 (29 Aug. 2007), 992, https://www.nature.com/articles/448992c#citeas.

[137] Accessed via the Environmental Protection Agency (EPA) website, https://www.epa.gov/climate-indicators/climate-change-indicators-atmospheric-concentrations-greenhouse-gases.

[138] The data is accessible and downloadable at https://data.giss.nasa.gov/gistemp/graphs_v4/.

[139] 'Historical Overview of Climate Change' by H. Le Treut, R. Somerville, U. Cubasch, Y. Ding, C. Mauritzen, A. Mokssit, T.

Peterson and M. Prather in *Climate Change 2007: The Physical Science Basis. Contribution of Working Group I to the Fourth Assessment Report of the Intergovernmental Panel on Climate Change*, ed. by S. Solomon, D. Qin, M. Manning, Z. Chen, M. Marquis, K.B. Averyt, M. Tignor and H. L. Miller (Cambridge University Press, 2007), 104.

[140] 'Historical Overview', Le Treut, Somerville, Cubasch, Ding, Mauritzen, Mokssit, Peterson and Prather in *Climate Change 2007*, 98, fig. 1.1

Chapter 12

[141] *Close to the Wind* by Ben Ainslie, Yellow Jersey Press (2009), 133. This chapter relies on a combination of the book, television coverage of the Olympic racing, a keynote speech at a dinner for Sunseeker International and my conversations with Ben Ainslie.

[142] Ben Ainslie, keynote speech to Sunseeker International, 2015.

[143] *Close to the Wind*, Ainslie, 255 details the incident, although the quote in the text is slightly different to what was said.

[144] Ainslie, Sunseeker speech.

[145] Ainslie, Sunseeker speech.

Chapter 13

[146] 'Parity and Predictability of Competitions' by Eli Ben-Naim, Sidney Redner and Federico Vazquez, *Journal of Quantitative Analysis in Sports*, 4: 2 (Jan. 2006), 1–1, https://www.researchgate.net/publication/46554914_Parity_and_Predictability_of_Competitions.

[147] $0.55^6 = (0.55 \times 0.55 \times 0.55 \times 0.55 \times 0.55 \times 0.55) = 0.0277$

[148] 'Regression towards Mediocrity in Hereditary Stature' by Sir Francis Galton, *The Journal of the Anthropological Institute of Great Britain and Ireland*, 15 (1886), 246–63, https://www.jstor.org/stable/2841583.

[149] *Thinking, Fast and Slow* by Daniel Kahneman (Penguin Books, 2012), 203.

Chapter 14

[150] All the quotes in this chapter are from an interview with Michel Desjoyeaux, June 2020.

[151] After an early breakdown Desjoyeaux returned to the start in Les Sables-d'Olonne and repaired the boat, eventually restarting 40 hours after the rest of the fleet.

[152] *Thinking, Fast and Slow* by Daniel Kahneman (Penguin Books 2012), 243.

Chapter 15

[153] *Thinkertoys: A Handbook of Creative-Thinking Techniques* by Michael Michalko (Ten Speed Press, 2nd edn, 2006), 29.

[154] *Lateral Thinking: A Textbook of Creativity* by Edward de Bono (Penguin Books, 1990), 80.

[155] *Lateral Thinking*, de Bono, 123.

[156] *Lateral Thinking*, de Bono, 106.

[157] *Thinkertoys*, Michalko, 53.

[158] *Thinkertoys*, Michalko, 58.

[159] *Thinkertoys*, Michalko, 72 ff.

[160] *The Creative Act: A Way of Being* by Rick Rubin (Canongate Books, 2023) is also deeply thoughtful and interesting on the topic of creativity.

[161] There is a website introducing the idea at: http://www.rtqe.net/ObliqueStrategies/OSintro.html.

Chapter 16

[162] Statistic sourced from Our World in Data, https://ourworldindata.org/excess-mortality-covid.

[163] 'Are Covid Patients Gasping "It Isn't Real" As They Die?' by David Zweig, *Wired* (19 Nov. 2020), https://www.wired.com/story/are-covid-patients-gasping-it-isnt-real-as-they-die/.

[164] 'Coronavirus: 38 days when Britain sleepwalked into disaster' by Jonathan Calvert, George Arbuthnott and Jonathan Leake, *Sunday Times* (19 Apr. 2020), https://www.thetimes.co.uk/article/coronavirus-38-days-when-britain-sleepwalked-into-disaster-hq3b9tlgh.

[165] 'Are People Overconfident About Avoiding COVID-19?' by Rawley Heimer, Haoyang Liu and Xiaohan Zhang, *Federal Reserve Bank of New York Liberty Street Economics* (7 Oct. 2020), https://libertystreeteconomics.newyorkfed.org/2020/10/are-people-overconfident-about-avoiding-covid-19.html.

[166] 'Coronavirus may have infected half of UK population – Oxford study' by Clive Cookson, *Financial Times* (24 Mar. 2020), https://www.ft.com/content/5ff6469a-6dd8-11ea-89df-41bea055720b – note that the online version is now a more measured piece to reflect the pushback from other scientists.

[167] 'Seasonality of SARS-CoV-2: Will COVID-19 go away on its own in warmer weather?' by Marc Lipsitch, Harvard School of Public Health, Center for Communicable Disease Dynamics, https://ccdd.hsph.harvard.edu/will-covid-19-go-away-on-its-own-in-warmer-weather/.

[168] 'Epidemiology is a science of high importance', *Nature Communications*, 9: 1703 (7 May 2018), https://www.nature.com/articles/s41467-018-04243-3.

[169] 'Special report: The simulations driving the world's response to COVID-19' by David Adam, *Nature* (2 Apr. 2020), https://www.nature.com/articles/d41586-020-01003-6.

[170] 'Chaos, population biology, and epidemiology: some research implications' by P. Philippe, *Human Biology*, 65: 4 (Aug. 1993), 525–46, https://pubmed.ncbi.nlm.nih.gov/8406405/.

[171] 'Chinese researchers reveal draft genome of virus implicated in Wuhan pneumonia outbreak' by Jon Cohen, *Science* (11 Jan. 2020), https://www.science.org/content/article/chinese-researchers-reveal-draft-genome-virus-implicated-wuhan-pneumonia-outbreak.

[172] 'Should you wear a face mask? WHO officials weigh in at today's COVID-19 briefing' by Linda Lacina, World Economic Forum (30 Mar. 2020), https://www.weforum.org/agenda/2020/03/who-should-wear-a-face-mask-30-march-who-briefing/.

[173] 'Mask use in the context of COVID-19', World Health Organisation (1 Dec. 2020), https://www.who.int/publications/i/item/advice-on-the-use-of-masks-in-the-community-during-

home-care-and-in-healthcare-settings-in-the-context-of-the-novel-coronavirus-(2019-ncov)-outbreak.

[174] 'Susceptibility to misinformation about COVID-19 around the world' by Jon Roozenbeek, Claudia R. Schneider, Sarah Dryhurst, John Kerr, Alexandra L. J. Freeman, Gabriel Recchia, Anne Marthe van der Bles and Sander van der Linden, *Royal Society Open Science* (14 Oct. 2020), https://royalsocietypublishing.org/doi/10.1098/rsos.201199.

[175] 'Are People Overconfident?', Heimer, Liu and Zhang.

[176] 'Subsidizing the spread of COVID19: Evidence from the UK's Eat-Out-to-Help-Out scheme' by Dr Thiemo Fetzer, CAGE Research Centre, University of Warwick, https://warwick.ac.uk/fac/soc/economics/research/centres/cage/manage/publications/wp.517.2020.pdf.

[177] An Essay on the Principle of Population by Thomas Robert Malthus (1798).

[178] The discovery in 1909 by Fritz Haber that nitrogen and hydrogen could be combined to produce ammonia, and the subsequent industrialisation of that process by Carl Bosch in 1909 (now called the Haber–Bosch process), allowed the large-scale production of ammonia. This is the central ingredient in the nitrogen-based fertilisers that have increased the efficiency of food production many times over.

[179] 'The story of mRNA: How a once-dismissed idea became a leading technology in the Covid vaccine race' by Damian Garde and Jonathan Saltzman, *STAT* (10 Nov. 2020), https://www.statnews.com/2020/11/10/the-story-of-mrna-how-a-once-dismissed-idea-became-a-leading-technology-in-the-covid-vaccine-race/.

[180] 'The tangled history of mRNA vaccines by Elie Dolgin', *Nature*, 597 (14 Sept. 2021), 318–24, https://www.nature.com/articles/d41586-021-02483-w.

[181] *Factfulness: Ten Reasons We're Wrong About the World – and Why Things Are Better Than You Think* by Hans Rosling, Ola Rosling and Anna Rosling Rönnlund (Sceptre, 2018).

Appendix

[182] To be technically accurate this should be Velocity Made Good

in the Direction of the Course (VMC) and measured in knots, but mph is clearer to anyone not steeped in nautical jargon and lore. It's also worth noting that while practising may create specific gains at points in the racecourse like the start and mark rounding, these can then be averaged over a whole race and converted to a speed gain.

[183] I've used the idea of a cost-effectiveness ratio rather than a cost–benefit analysis because it avoids having to have costs and benefits in the same units, the idea has been borrowed from health economics.

[184] There are ways of dealing with this, but they are beyond the scope of this analysis.

ACKNOWLEDGEMENT

The origins of this book date all the way back to my school days, so any attempt at a comprehensive thank you for the people that have influenced the work will inevitably have serious omissions. Fortunately, some of those people are already in the text, the others that my shaky memory can pick out include: Paul Mitchell for (almost) a lifetime of friendship, conversation and the occasional reckless adventure; the teachers at Kirkley High School including John Pawsey, Barry Pearson, Tony Philpin, Mike Sarsons and Jim Stather; and at University, Dieter Peetz, Rob Black and Greg McCulloch. Susie Aikin-Sneath was my first agent and the first person to believe I could write a publishable novel, other people that have provided support in the publishing industry include Jeremy Atkins, Daniela Bernardelle, Stephanie Cabot, Mel Cain, Peter Coles, Tim Davison, Lorain Day, Anne Farmer, Oliver Johnson, Sylvia May, Janet Murphy, Michael Ridpath, Timothy Sonderhüsken, Lorraine Steele and Jeppe Wikstrom. Many, many thanks to everyone, both mentioned and missed.

The people that were important to the final book that I would like to thank include all those people that agreed to be interviewed and let me tell their stories; David Luxton and Liz Multon for their help trying to find a publisher; Rob Andrews, Roger Badham, Paul Boyce, Damian Byrne, Adrienne Cahalan, Fiona Caulfield, Paul Dickinson, Marina Johnson, Will King, Jeremy Robinson, Gordon Smith and Graeme Winn for reading various drafts, talking through problems, or helping with the research; Richenda Todd for her extraordinary attention to detail in making the final text presentable; David Reed of Sailing World who was kind enough to publish some shortened versions of these chapters in his magazine to give them their first public airing; and Andrew Mays for his fantastic cover design.

Mark Chisnell
2023

ABOUT THE AUTHOR

Mark Chisnell

Mark Chisnell has spent over thirty years working across diverse areas and topics. He's written five novels and eleven non-fiction books, been translated into five languages and topped sales and download charts in the USA, UK, Germany, Italy and Spain. He's sold a movie option to Working Title for one of the novels and won a non-fiction book award from Sportel. He has written on technology, travel and sport for Esquire, The Guardian, The Daily Telegraph and many others.

Mark has also developed technical solutions to complex problems in marine electronics, hosted a broadcast event that won the Royal Television Society's Best Live Event award and won three sailing world championships. He's sailed and worked with seven teams in yacht racing's America's Cup. While completing this book, he worked as Rules Adviser for the British team for the 2024 America's Cup, a partnership between four-time Olympic gold medallist Ben Ainslie's sailing team, and the Mercedes F1 team.

PRAISE FOR AUTHOR

The Defector

'An excellent drug-smuggling thriller.'

— THE BOOKSELLER

The Defector

'This is a remarkable thriller – chillingly violent, full of tension and with a very original ending.'

— PUBLISHING NEWS

Spanish Castle to White Night

'I doubt I'll ever circle the globe in a racing boat, and I'm not sure I even want to, but Mark Chisnell has made the experience real. This is a marvellous book about a great adventure, and anyone fascinated by sailing should have it on their shelf.'

— BERNARD CORNWELL, NOVELIST

Spanish Castle to White Night

'Racing around the world looks as though it has progressed significantly since I had a go on Drum in '86; certainly on a technical level. The boats are lighter, faster and sailing more on the edge than ever before. But the experience of the men who sail them remains the same. It's muscle and nerve and the will to win, to get you across a big, big ocean. There's a whole lot of seawater out there to drive you crazy as you go around.'

- SIMON LE BON, MUSICIAN (DURAN DURAN) AND SAILOR (DRUM, WHITBREAD 1985-86)

Spanish Castle to White Night

'Emotions, tactics and conditions are brought to life for the reader throughout and, whether you are a sailor or not, you will find yourself carried around the world on a captivating journey.'

- DEE CAFFARI, FIRST WOMAN TO SAIL SINGLE-HANDED AROUND THE WORLD IN BOTH DIRECTIONS

Risk to Gain

'There are many accounts of man against the sea, and man against man at sea, but seldom has there been such a panoramic portrayal of life at its cramped, frenetic and frightening worst as this examination of the latest winning Whitbread Round the World Race campaign.'

- STUART ALEXANDER, INDEPENDENT, 'SPORTS BOOK OF THE WEEK'

Risk to Gain

'What it does brilliantly is get under the skin of what it is like to live and breathe a Whitbread Race.'

> \- TIM JEFFERY, THE DAILY TELEGRAPH

Risk to Gain

'It's the best book yet on this race. Great writing.'

> \- YACHTS AND YACHTING

BOOKS BY THIS AUTHOR

The Defector

What will you do, when it's you or them?

This is the dilemma at the heart of this breathtaking psychological thriller - can Martin Cormac turn his back on his ruthless past as a dealer, a major city player, and do the right thing? Not when he's looking for answers in a succession of sleazy dives...

One night, Cormac gets caught trying to chat up the bar owner's girlfriend and soon needs rescuing. Unfortunately, his white knight is anything but - Janac's a big-time drug baron with a psychotic urge to test people to the limit, and if possible... over it.

And soon Cormac is running from more than his past, he's running from the most dangerous game he will ever play.

The Wrecking Crew

What will you do, when it's them... or the woman you love?

Drug baron Janac has turned to piracy to fund his battle for control of the Australian narcotics trade. When he attacks the MV Shawould on an evil night in the South China Sea, it seems he has also found the perfect victim for his terrifying psychological games.

Phil Hamnet and his wife Anna are sharing a last voyage on the Shawould before the arrival of their twins. Hamnet escapes Janac's attack, but Anna is taken and held hostage to ensure first his silence and then his cooperation. But when Janac's rogue ex-Special Forces crew attack more ships and men start dying, Hamnet has to decide if he can continue to sacrifice the lives of unknown sailors to save the woman he loves.

It's an awful decision for anyone to have to make, but for a man who's already had the same dilemma - in a lifeboat, adrift in the vastness of the Pacific Ocean - it's a living nightmare.

The Sniper

The Sniper is a short story featuring the central character from Mark Chisnell's 'Janac's Games' thrillers; The Defector and The Wrecking Crew.

An empty clearing in the Vietnamese jungle in 1969. An explosive, complex and compromised war rages to the north and south, to the east and the west. Two men come to the clearing with a simple task in mind – to kill a man. A man who wants to visit his girl.

A simple task made dangerous and ultimately deadly by a startling intervention. Soon, US Marine Corps sniper, Paul Robert Janac has to look deep inside to survive a pulse-pounding jungle manhunt that will leave him with a life-or-death choice.

So what will he do, when...

The Fulcrum Files

The young Ben Clayton was one of Britain's brightest boxing prospects, until the day he slammed a left hook into a fragile chin. Sickened by the consequences he turned away from the ring, found solace in the arms of the beautiful Lucy Kirk and looked for new challenges.

On the 7th March 1936, after almost two decades of peace in Europe, Hitler ordered the German Army back into the

Rhineland. It was a direct challenge to Britain and France. Still unnerved by the toll of the Great War, the politicians dithered. The French Army stayed in its barracks, while the aristocratic British elite looked on from their country retreats.

History teetered on a knife edge, but the spymasters were busy.

Just one man could make the difference between war and peace, victory or defeat. And that man was Ben Clayton. Thrown into the maelstrom of plot and counter-plot, into a world of murder, spies and traitors, Ben must battle not just to survive, but to protect all that he loves and holds most dear.

Powder Burn

Sam had given up her Manhattan job, and her cute apartment in Brooklyn. She'd abandoned her astonished boyfriend to the charms of ESPN, and flown off into a new dawn to chase her dream of becoming an investigative journalist.

Three months later, alone in a soulless internet café, she's facing some cold, hard facts; she's unpublished, unhappy and broke. And right then, the gorgeous Pete Halland blows into her life – headed for the mythical Powder Burn mountain to write history and blast into legend.

If she throws in her lot with Pete and reports the story for National Geographic magazine it could rescue her ambitions, but he's holding back some crucial information – the question for Sam is… what?

Soon, Sam is up to her neck in snow and the weather is the least of her problems; lost in a secretive Himalayan kingdom with – what could be – a magic sword and a simmering and potentially bloody revolution.

But the father she lost to the war in Iraq was a marine, and he taught her a few tricks in the Vermont backcountry that might just get her out alive – and with a story to tell that could make the front page of the New York Times.

Chinese Burn

Sam Blackett has moved on from her adventures in the Himalayas, and moved on from her relationship with Pete. Fortunately, things are going a little better with her journalism, and she's in Shanghai working on a commission for the Boston Globe.

If only she hadn't treated herself to dinner at the five star Peninsula Hotel she might even have got it finished and published - but she did, and so Roger Ravert died in her arms. Now Sam was on the run from the Detroit police, the FBI, the CIA and China's security service. And she had no idea why.

Risk To Gain

Have you ever dreamed of sailing around the world?

Stomach-churning storms, frustrating calms, broken gear, shattered hopes and stunning victories - Risk to Gain is the story of the men and women aboard two boats sailing around the world in the classic Whitbread Race. Travel with them on their voyage and gain a unique insight into their inspirational journey.

Spanish Castle To White Night

So, you think you'd like to sail around the world?

Imagine sunsets across calm oceans, cocktails at cosy anchorages, landfalls in amazing new places.... and then imagine something else.

Imagine taking part in one of the planet's last great adventures. Imagine the story of an incredible race, ripping and roaring through the seven seas. Imagine a tale of endurance, deprivation, fear and courage, a story of winners and losers, those who made it and those who did not. Imagine 'Spanish Castle to White Night – the Race Around the World'.

The Volvo Ocean Race 2008-09 ran for 37,000 miles through 10 stages across the world's seas and oceans. It was raced in the planet's fastest and most demanding monohull, the Volvo Open 70, capable of sustaining speeds of well over 30 knots. The boat and the course made this the most exacting of all crewed sailboat races, a microscopic examination of the sailing skill, seamanship, stamina and strategy of the 11 men aboard each boat.

This book charts the story of some of the 88 men who left Alicante in October 2008 to win that race. It followed them through the next nine months as they endured and enjoyed every possible emotion, their human story intertwined with the raw elements of nature and the extraordinary technology on which their success and sometimes even their survival depended.

Mastering Data To Win

The modern racing yacht is awash with onboard instruments and electronics giving enormous amounts of data. But few people fully understand how to get the most out of all the information at their fingertips, let alone make it useful for the team to enable them to win races. But ace navigators, Mark Chisnell and Gilberto Pastorella, do – both have worked with professional sailing programmes all over the world – from America's Cup to Maxi, ORC / IRC and one-design fleets.

In Mastering Data to Win they take the reader through the

process: from understanding the concepts, ensuring accuracy, using the data to win races and then post-race analysis to find performance gains. By mastering your instruments you can make the right calls every time and know for certain when to tack, which shift to look out for and how the tide can work with or against you. With colour diagrams and photographs throughout, this instructional guide turns information into excellence. Accessible to those new to racing, it also has a depth of information that will transform the performance of even professional sailors.

Sails For Cruising

Limp and wrinkly or smooth and billowing? If your sails are set right your boat will be faster, safer and look better Mark Chisnell, one of the best sailors in the world, here demystifies the black art of sail trim. He shows how to set the sails and use them properly in all wind strengths.

The Secrets Of Sailboat Racing

A "little book of" racing. Hot tips from two experienced racers on how to win! Neal McDonald and Mark Chisnell have been racing with and against each other for longer than either cares to remember. They have progressed from International 420 dinghies in the RYA's Youth Squad, to a combined total of twenty five years as professional racing sailors, competing in every major event (and winning several). They have competed in dinghies - the Olympics, World Championships in 18 foot Skiffs, International 14s, Tornados, International 470s; and in yachts - the Whitbread Race, America's Cup, and the Admiral's Cup.

These are the lessons they have learnt - 180 rules that will cut down the simple expensive mistakes in preparation and racing, and immediately improve your fleet position. Everyone makes mistakes but the winner makes the least. This book is the answer - follow the rules and win!

Dinghy Systems

A comprehensive analysis of the sailing systems that can be fitted to dinghies. Every aspect of the design and layout of a functional, race-winning system, is covered. The mast and rig, mechanical advantages, mainsail, headsail and spinnaker controls plus hull and mast fittings are all covered.

A Sailor's Guide To Regatta Preparation

Providing a blueprint for a successful approach to improve sailing performance, A Sailor's Guide to Regatta Preparation informs the reader how they can achieve better results at a regatta. The book covers every aspect of race preparation including; goal setting, mental skills, physical fitness, crew, practice and coaching.

Sailing Gold

This gorgeous photographic coffee table book reflects the entire history of Olympic sailing, with spectacular photographs celebrating heroes such as Paul Elvstrom and Ben Ainslie, fabulous locations, legendary classes - and the never-ending struggle of an Olympic sailor to make his mark.

Shooting H2o

"This is Rick Tomlinson's thoughtful and exciting account of his day to day life as a photographer, told through his wonderfully dramatic photography.

"Rick Tomlinson is probably the best known name in marine photography and his action photos of all manner of sailing scenes are in evidence all over the world. This new edition, with many new photographs, tells the story of Rick's journey - from raw Whitbread crewman to National Geographic photographer.

"It is the most comprehensive collection yet gathered of his photographs, across all spheres of his work. Sailboat racing inshore and offshore, from the Caribbean to the high latitudes of the Southern Ocean and North Atlantic; monohulls and multihulls, dinghies, Maxis, lifeboats and superyachts plus America's Cup photos too.

"Alongside the stunning photographs are many great stories, written with the help of long-time collaborator, Mark Chisnell. 'His eye for the nature of the sea is what brings a sense of life to all Tomlinson's work."
Classic Boat

Printed in Great Britain
by Amazon